D1403359

THE THIRD SOURCE

A Message of Hope for Education

DUSTIN HULL HEUSTON
with JAMES W. PARKINSON

DEDICATION

This book is dedicated to the finest woman who has lived on this earth: my wife Nancy. She is so remarkable that even I, without calling on my professional tools such as the speed of light, transistors, computers, lasers, the Internet, or Moore's Law, understand she is goodness incarnate. She is also a superb administrator, educator, mother, wife, and daughter of God.

ACKNOWLEDGMENTS

I Would Like to Express Thanks to:

My parents who sheltered, loved, and guided me in the Bronx during the lean depression years and made certain that I received a sound education while sacrificing what few worldly goods they had on my behalf; My children, grandchildren, and great grandchildren who have taught me (a typical obtuse male) about the importance of family; Charles Whitaker Turner, a Naval Officer and colleague who provided inspiration and guidance that changed the trajectory of my life; Jim Parkinson and Wilbur Colom who love the important things; Marilyn Adams who brilliantly tended the light of literacy for decades and showed us how we could help children and honor our mentors while she remained a lady at all times; Clayton Christensen who decoded the laws of disruptive technology that will govern our future and applied them to different delivery systems to help us understand their relevance; and to all the quiet scholars and teachers who have toiled in obscurity to help children achieve their divine potential. There are few words as important as "teacher." Finally, my thanks to all of my colleagues, friends, and professionals who helped in the publication of this book.

FOREWORD

Dr. Heuston and the Waterford Institute, with its technology-delivered instruction, are the face of what is coming in education in the 21st Century. Unfortunately, this new "educational delivery system" is one of the best-kept secrets in America. Hopefully, this book will serve to awaken the government, education, and corporate leaders to the potential of technology and save the next generation from the pedagogical inefficiencies of the current reforms.

Waterford Institute celebrates 35 years of providing high-quality early educational models, programs, and software. Since 1996 its partner, Pearson®, has generated over $½ billion in sales, placing product in over 50,000 U.S. classrooms. I have personally been involved in 3 separate pilot programs: Dakar, Senegal; Columbus, Mississippi; and La Quinta, California. The data from these pilot programs—and other Waterford Institute programs, e.g., UPSTART—are astounding; children who use the program excel when they enter kindergarten and are ready to learn.

Waterford Institute programs have been developed to incorporate the advances in technology to make the educational delivery system more efficient and affordable. Each program is designed to supplement the classroom experience by providing a unique individualized education, focusing on developing children's cognitive skills.

The story of Waterford Institute is told in this book by its founder and chairman, Dr. Heuston. His vision of the use of technology in classrooms will change the world of education, impacting the lives of millions of children. When and how this vision is embraced and implemented is a function of our government, education, and corporate leaders. The American children can no longer afford the inefficiencies and costs of a manual delivery system. It's time to put the children first.

JAMES W. PARKINSON
February, 2011

CONTENTS

ILLUSTRATION CONTENTS

A PREFACE OF HOPE:
ENHANCED INSTRUCTION AND THE THIRD SOURCE

The purpose of this book is to acquaint the reader with absolutely spectacular and wonderful news: After centuries of thrashing about trying to improve our schools, educators are finally moving into position to introduce new technologies working at the speed of light that are capable of providing educational excellence and equity to all children on the globe almost overnight. This has not traditionally been the case in our educational systems where limited resources have long favored those with capital who can afford private schools or those who are naturally talented and capable of winning admissions and scholarships to the finest schools.

Traditionally, there have been 2 sources of instruction for children: their families and their schools. Now technology is offering a "third source" of instruction. As this book will describe, the family appears to have a much greater influence than we thought in establishing the trajectory of student learning, but ultimately the family's role is limited because most parents lack educational expertise, and the time, and patience to teach their children academic subjects such as reading, science, mathematics, and foreign languages. Similarly, the school has the expertise and physical plant, but offers limited access to the child because, unfortunately, it is usually understaffed and open less than half the days in the year for only 6 to 7 hours and requires the child to commute to access its resources.

Thus, there is a bit of a standoff where the family has the time and access to the child, but lacks the needed expertise, and the school with expertise can only offer limited access. Fortunately, there is a new method of educating children emerging which bridges this standoff by using technology to deliver formal, individualized, interactive curriculum in support of both the family's and school's efforts. This third source of instruction uses microcomputers in laptops, tablets, traditional desktops, and a broad range of new devices which are connected via telephones and the Internet to a support group which then provides human contact to reinforce, complement or stand in place of the parents' or teachers' efforts.

This human interface is invaluable as it monitors, motivates, and measures the activities of the users as a third source of instruction and guiding intelligence for both the family's and the school's efforts. In addition to supporting the other 2 traditional sources of instruction in homes or schools, this third source can also act as an independent entity capable of providing outstanding instruction to students in a variety of settings from community centers, churches, tiny home-based preschools, kitchen tables, libraries, cars, trains, buses, airplanes, and even bedrooms.

For example, in its UPSTART project, the Waterford Institute is providing the Utah state legislature a formal online preschool academic program for 4 year old children independent of the school system or the formal preschool community. The goal has been to insure that children starting public school in kindergarten have received enough preliteracy training so they are prepared to learn to read, calculate and have a basic understanding of science and the scientific method. The UPSTART organization is under the direction of an independent committee and the state legislature. Children are expected to work on computers that are connected to the Waterford UPSTART support group where their usage and progress are tracked daily over the Internet. Reports are provided to the families weekly over the Internet and, when necessary, over the phone. The families are dealing with a formal organization that is providing guiding intelligence. The communications between the families and the UPSTART group are brisk. After the first 1,500 students were registered and brought online, there were about 17,000 telephone calls logged during the first 5 months of the project, half of which were initiated by the families and half by the support group. The preliminary data are stunning and discussed at length later in this book.

And the news will just keep getting better. The instructional capabilities of these new technologies will be buttressed by a new wave of "enhanced instructional software" that will offer individualized interactive instruction with precision and artistic beauty for all children, not just children with access to excellent schools. Furthermore, the cost of providing these capabilities will continue to plummet as the technologies assume an increasing proportion of academic instruction and at less than 5% of the cost of traditional methods of education. Clearly, the democratization of educational excellence is underway.

The Waterford Institute has not only pioneered this third source, but has invested 35 years and more than $135 million during the past 20 years in developing a package of enhanced instructional software designed to empower student learning both at home and at school for young children of all social classes and locations. The enhanced Waterford software can begin educating young children in their homes during the preschool years and take them up through the 2nd or 3rd grade in their elementary schools. This rigorous curriculum enables the students to keep up with their peers at an acceptable rate. This staying up with peers, when the children are young, is much more important than generally understood. Contrary to the belief of many people, from a statistical standpoint, children rarely have the luxury of recovering from a slow educational start unless significant resources in a highly structured and expensive environment can be brought to bear on their behalf under the guidance of trained and motivated professionals—something that recent research has identified as absolutely crucial to a child's motivation and ability to progress.

As the reader will gradually understand, the preschool and kindergarten years appear to set a learning trajectory that is difficult to change. The National Institutes of Health (NIH) has noted that slow starters are often very sensitive to their relative lack of skills. For example, if they discover in preschool that most of their peers already know their letters and are starting to decode successfully, they begin to develop a "sense of shame" about their own shortcomings. This sense of shame is not a minor irritant; it is a serious and debilitating problem. Over time, the sense of shame leads students into "print flight" where they will start avoiding any attempts at mastering reading. They want nothing to do with a process that makes them feel ashamed and vulnerable.

Of course the educational future of any given child can be changed via structured and intensive intervention, but such intervention is both economically and emotionally expensive and often comes too late to help children overcome the effects of a linguistically impoverished home or poor preschool environment. Recognizing this, our society is working on improving access to early educational training for disadvantaged children to compensate for the poor learning environments that they face—something Waterford has already accomplished.

Without noticing it, America seems to have initiated an "education race" or "knowledge race" which is similar to an "arms race." Countries are being pulled into an educational competition which is fueled by twin realities:

(1) Many mothers are fighting to give their children an excellent early start which has started to ignite a competitive global frenzy that is becoming difficult to ignore. When the news of the comparative scores of 34 nations in reading, math, and science were released in December of 2010, the United States displayed mediocre results in reading (14th), science (17th), and math (25th) placing America 23rd, overall, of 34 nations.

There was an international outcry when, for the first time, China allowed testing in one of its large cities, Shanghai, with a population of over 20 million; and their scores topped every other nation's by a considerable degree. Breathless press interviews quickly established that students in China (and other committed nations) have no time for athletics or any other activity except studying, which often begins before 7:00 AM and continues after school and on into the weekend and summers. Interviews have also reported that some of the parents are spending more money on kindergarten than college tuitions to insure the proper start for their children.

(2) Unfortunately, we are also pressured by scholarly data that reinforce the importance of the early years because there appears to be a biological advantage for young learners. The PACE study (Policy Analysis for California Education) conducted by scholars from Stanford, Berkeley, and UCLA (2007) studied the data from an excellent government analysis of over 21,000 students during their preschool years and concluded that the optimal time for children's learning is between the age of 2 and 3. James Heckman, a Nobel Laureate in economics from the University of Chicago, has offered similar data recommending that society invest

heavily in its youngest children for a maximum return on investment. He concludes that the closer the intervention is to childbirth, the higher the return on investment. As soon as a country or society begins to accelerate the instruction of its young, other nations are forced to begin to take the preschool years seriously lest their students fall behind.

As the reader will learn in this book, instructional technology and software can play an important role for even our youngest children in their homes. At first blush, the thought of adding another technology to the busy life of these children seems to be an anathema considering many young children are already watching TV for over 5–6 hours a day. As popular education books like *Brain Rules for Baby* and *The Shallows* have pointed out, too much time in front of technology, from television to the Internet, interferes with the development of both academic learning and social skills.

Fortunately our research indicates we can have a strong impact on the young child's learning with only 15 minutes a day spent on the software. This software instruction can be a pleasurable experience for children because the instructional materials are laced with graphics, animation, stories, music and games. Fifteen minutes a day requires only 1 percent of a child's day to be focused on the Waterford materials.

In order to make certain that parents of 4 year old children were not upset because of this time commitment, Waterford hired an outside consulting firm to sample parental opinion after the first year of the UPSTART (2009–2010) project in Utah. UPSTART provided home-based instructional software in reading, math, and science to four year olds and their families. Student usage was monitored by Waterford personnel over the Internet. In answer to the question as to whether the parents thought this daily commitment of 15 minutes cut into the children's play time, 88% reported that it did not.

According to brain research, the short, intense, daily, instructional periods provided during the 15-minute sessions are optimal. This modest recommended usage could also free up some time in the child's life by replacing less efficient educational activities the child may be involved in. By implementing the steady usage of the materials for short bursts of time, the child's mother will be able to sponsor more play or other desirable activities in the remaining time. In this case, rather paradoxically, the child may end up with more play time through committing to a rigorous technology schedule for just 15 minutes a day. Just as freedom is cemented through discipline, so a balanced and creative life can be buttressed and enhanced by short periods of intensive software instruction.

ENHANCED SOFTWARE:

The difference between standard educational software and enhanced software is that the former simply mimics the sequence of instruction followed by a teacher's lesson plan or the class textbook. Enhanced software, on the other hand, is interactive, intelligent, and full of engaging graphics, animation, music, and photography. It is also organized by an artificial intelligence "software kernel" that individualizes the path of instruction for each child depending on what he or she needs to master next. The work of a software sequencer starts after a child answers a question when it analyses the child's response and branches to a new topic that is precisely what the child should be studying next.

Thus enhanced software offers four key enhancements: (1) it is designed to make learning a pleasant experience through harnessing the power of the arts with stories, plots, music, 2D and 3D graphics, animation, and photography; (2) It is interactive and forces the student to become an active learner and to respond to the materials; (3) It uses artificial intelligence to provide an individualized path through the curriculum; and (4) is carefully designed to teach the student using the latest science of instruction available. Because the instructional materials can be updated overnight, they never grow obsolete as Waterford continually modifies its instructional materials over the Internet. This insures each child is receiving the latest instruction in fields that are changing rapidly (particularly in areas such as the sciences).

THE PROBLEMS INVOLVED IN DEVELOPING ENHANCED SOFTWARE:

The gating-factor that has limited the development of enhanced software is its expense. Developing each module involves the equivalent of combining the cost of writing and publishing many books, making a Hollywood animated movie, developing a new musical, and writing computer software that has billions of bytes of storage. The Institute has spent over $135 million and taken 20 years just in developing its initial round of enhanced software for the preschool and early elementary years in reading, math, and science.

Thus, a secondary consideration of this book is to suggest to the reader that the hardware will develop on its own because of the size of the market that uses computer chips in every area of our civilization. The sheer potential volume of the new chips will have many outstanding corporations backing strong research and development efforts to capture new market segments through innovative changes in their chips for everything from digital cameras, to cell phones, iPads, and traditional computers. Thus, for education the critical need for the next couple of decades will be to find appropriate funding sources to develop the educational software for these emerging technologies. The hardware advances are being taken care of by the broad international market that is spending hundreds of billions of dollars a year on hardware R & D.

MY EDUCATIONAL QUEST:

This book tells the story of what I have learned about education. I have spent over 50 years involved in educational activities such as teaching (Brigham Young, Vassar, Pine Manor, Spence, and Waterford); chairing a college English Department (Pine Manor); becoming a headmaster of a world-class K-12 girls school in New York City (Spence); helping found a school (The Waterford School); opening a commercial corporation to develop educational software (WICAT Systems); and finally founding the nonprofit Waterford Institute some 35 years ago. As the reader will learn, my saga documents my growing awareness of the extraordinary potential that educational technology offers as a humane solution capable of providing all children with both equity and excellence, a condition that has never existed before in history. The reason I have personalized my quest is my hope that in following my story the reader will gradually assimilate the counterintuitive lessons that I had to master in order to develop a new set of educational metaphors that will help guide us into the use of the new technologies that will humanize affordable education for all children.

Notice how counterintuitive my message is: my desire is to change the reader's educational metaphors to clarify what is the best affordable approach to give children the optimal education for the 21st century. I want the reader to reach the same position that I have, which is the conviction that, for the first time in recorded human history, educational technology will ultimately insure access to an excellent education for every child. And paradoxically, only in harnessing technology can we provide children with the most humane education possible. I also want to influence those readers with means to understand that this potential will only become available after large pools of capital become available for software development.

This is quite a mélange of strange concepts to assimilate: metaphors, humanity, technology, and enhanced software offered through a third source. But I know of no better way to help the reader understand the promising new metaphors that will guide the future of education than to invite you to follow my quest. Naturally, since I have a PhD in English, I will smuggle in bits of plots and stories to enhance the message.

The story begins long before I became obsessed the dream of developing a technology strategy to provide an outstanding and affordable education for all children. My younger brother and I grew up in the Bronx during the Depression, raised by 2 wonderful working-class parents. My first schools were PS 81 and PS 7. After I graduated from PS 7 in January 1946, I spent a semester at the Bronx High School of Science before moving first to Mount Hermon, a New England Boarding school, and then to Hamilton College in upstate New York. While at Hamilton I changed my pre-medical major to a major in English and a minor in History. After graduation in 1954, I briefly pursued a Wall Street Banking career and then spent more than 3 years as a Naval Air Intelligence officer briefing pilots during 2 cruises in the Pacific as the Korean War wound down.

By then I had decided I wanted to be a college English teacher, and I enrolled in a master's program in American Literature at Stanford just before my 26th birthday in 1958. After receiving my master's degree in 1959, I paused for 3 years to teach at Brigham Young University before earning a PhD from New York University in American literature a few years later. During my college teaching years, I also taught at 2 women's colleges: Vassar and Pine Manor, where I was chairman of the English Department. In 1969, I became the Headmaster of the Spence School, a prominent K-12 girl's school in New York City. My 8 years at Spence taught me invaluable lessons about educating children from age 5–18 to complement the lessons I had assimilated in my university years.

In 1976, approaching the age of 45, I founded the nonprofit Waterford Institute which is dedicated to furthering the progress of educational hardware and software. After 4 years of pursuing funding from foundations, individuals, corporations, and the government, I raised $100 million to found WICAT Systems, a for profit educational technology company. I maintained my role as chairman of the nonprofit institute while working at WICAT. In 1989, shortly before WICAT was sold to Jostens for about $115 million, I once again turned my full attentions to the Waterford Institute. As of the winter of 2011, I continue to serve as its chairman and CEO.

CHANGING THE EDUCATIONAL METAPHORS:

Although the preliminary outline for understanding the importance of educational technology is becoming clear, the full potential will languish and drift until our educational leaders adjust to the new educational metaphors which will guide them in how they will be able to dramatically increase the impact they can have on education. As we shall see, the phrase "metaphor," while traditionally associated with literary analysis, ultimately has a very serious influence on our thinking and decision making that is far from poetic. In fact, metaphors frequently determine our biases, thinking, judgment, conduct, and decision-making. Metaphors filter what we notice and often control our decisions. From a historical perspective, I am asking the reader to shed the metaphor of the pony express in exchange for the metaphor of the telegraph.

I am hoping that this book will help prepare a climate for the acceptance of these new metaphors and, conversely, a letting go of the traditional ones that have trapped our educators and leaders in an endless and futile attempt to improve schools by using traditional reform approaches. The quest for improving school performance has reached a natural mature limit using the current workers and traditions and needs to be modified. The more money we spend in trying to prop up the current delivery system, the more we waste.

As will become clear in the succeeding chapters, research is telling us that we will save money and lives if we concentrate initially on working with our youngest citizens in the preschool and early elementary years. First we need to stop the hemorrhaging and provide a fair start to all of our children, rather than spending billions trying to resuscitate our failures with questionable, but expensive, remediation programs. The cost for eternal remediation (during the elementary grades, again in junior high, again in high school, again entering college, and again when hired by corporations) is unacceptably high.

In a knowledge-based society, we are blocking the productivity and potential for success for too many of our citizens who will then have to be subsidized for much of their lives while they drift through careers in a restless search for fulfilling work opportunities that they are barred from because of their lack of education.

My audience is anyone that loves education or is involved in education, such as parents, legislators, foundation officers, businessmen, teachers, and interested members of the general public. The adoption of the new metaphors will encourage the development of a new generation of enhanced educational software that will be capable of activating the new delivery systems and will herald a new day of equality and excellence for children. Only great software supported by the help of a third source can enlist the stunning hardware and networking potential that is emerging independently of the education market but will provide the solution we all desire for our children.

Chapter One: The Fundamentals of Hope

Almost unnoticed, the fundamentals surrounding the educational delivery system are beginning to shift. We have reached the end of a spending binge on education that has left us (1) in debt, (2) without improved educational outcomes, and (3) seemingly bereft of new ideas to alleviate our educational problems. One of our thoughtful educational commentators, Frederick M. Hess, has just published a book on the status of educational reform in America, and his title sums up the current mood: *The Same Thing Over and Over: How School Reformers Get Stuck in Yesterday's Ideas* (2010).

At the same time, our nation's scores, reported in December of 2010, suggest we have to do something. The latest international survey of educational effectiveness reported that the United States is rated 23rd overall in education out of 34 nations in a competitive world despite our enormous investment. And in this our winter of discontent, we, along with much of the world, have been stunned to discover that China's scores have soared in Shanghai well past any other nation.

Despite this educational malaise, there are hopeful signs that a new and exciting educational opportunity is stirring:

(1) We have tried everything over and over, renamed the same reforms, and then tried them again. We are finally ready for something truly new. No matter how we have tried or how much we have spent on each new reform, the gains have been disappointingly small and frustratingly local and temporary. Still worse, our educational budgets have

1

become too rich for us to afford: economically, we are being forced to pare these budgets back even when, educationally, it is so obvious that far more is needed. Some school districts realize they may be approaching bankruptcy. The positive element in this situation is the cooling down of the reform frenzy and a forced willingness to assess other options.

(2) Educational technology is the one area where the economics and potential are improving at a stunning rate. Here the fundamentals are quite exciting because we are improving the capacity of computer-based technologies at about 1% a week, doubling their capabilities every 2 years, without any additional cost to the user. Whenever doubling occurs over a sustained period of time, the forces involved in the doubling begin to exponentiate the capabilities of the system where the doubling is taking place. No other reform will be a fraction as effective, and as the doubling continues, it mathematically compounds its impact and will continue to distance itself from any alternative.

(3) The educational field is starting to develop new metaphors which will focus the reformers efforts on using technologies that can dramatically improve the effectiveness of our educational delivery system.

THE NEW METAPHORS: UNDERSTANDING THE CONCEPT OF A DELIVERY SYSTEM:

When I started my educational saga over 5 decades ago as a college English teacher, I had no idea that, as humans, we organize in delivery systems to offer goods and services to others; that I myself was working in the educational delivery system; and that the greatest determinant of my potential would be the energy sources I could harness to help me deliver my goods and services to others. At that time I had no idea of the importance of (1) the speed of light as an energy provider or of (2) transistors.

In 1946, as I trundled off to my freshman year of boarding school at age 14, I did not realize that something called the ENIAC computer was being turned on for the first time a few hundred miles southwest at the University of Pennsylvania. Nor did I suspect the computer relied on 18,000 vacuum tubes to amplify electrical current traveling at the speed of light (although I *did* know that vacuum tubes had been invented decades before by an alumnus of my school, Lee De Forest).

I likewise passed my sophomore year in blissful ignorance that another device called the transistor was being invented in 1947 at Bell Labs also only a few hundred miles to the south, and was destined to replace vacuum tubes, not to mention that it was also destined to impact my future career. Now, as I look back, I am amazed by the way these 2 inventions—the harnessing of the speed of light for the wireless telegraph, radio, TV, telephone, and the Internet; and the introduction of transistors as the key working element in computers—would change my life as well as impact the educational history of generations not yet born because these inventions would change the educational delivery system.

The implications of the new educational metaphors about delivery systems, the speed of light, and the importance of enhanced software will become clear to the reader in this book. My hope is that as you read it and become comfortable with its new metaphors, that you will discover the extraordinary sense of hope that these metaphors offer us, particularly since we have run out of feasible reform options as each reform has exhausted itself and run aground in our current static and manually driven educational delivery system.

We are about to experience an abundance of new energies flooding our homes and formal educational institutions. Just as the steam engine launched the Industrial Revolution and added undreamed of amounts of energy to support the workers in their tasks, so will the new technologies, programmed with exquisitely written software, flood education with new life and vigor as it provides undreamed of support to teachers and administrators.

The advantages of technological innovation quickly became apparent 200 years ago when the Industrial Revolution offered the working classes of Western Europe liberation from a grim cycle of famine and starvation as well as access to consumer goods previously available only to the wealthy. The advantage of the new technological revolution in education will be to offer all children liberation from an equally grim sentence of educational mediocrity and instead give access to true educational excellence. The children will gain access to computers from their personal devices as well as from homes, schools, and transportation which will connect them through the Internet and other telecommunication networks.

Thus, we are now evolving into position to offer a quality education as the norm instead of the exception. Traditionally only the wealthy, who could pay for the finest education, or the academically talented, who could obtain scholarships, were assured access to solid educational opportunities. Fortunately, we are now about to democratize educational excellence. What a wonderful thought! Strange bedfellows will thrive as both equity and excellence come together. Elitism in education, paradoxically, will become commonplace.

One caveat we have to worry about is whether or not our children will want to take advantage of the new educational opportunities. Prosperity traditionally warps motivation by providing a plethora of opportunities for entertainment and pleasure that can drain the focus of the young.

Another caveat is that we need to start exposing children in their preschool and kindergarten years to certain cognitive skills, particularly children of the poor with single parents. Starting serious instruction when they are younger might keep some of them involved in schooling; whereas, the more traditional leisurely approach might never train them to a level of competence before their adolescent hormones begin to rage and their attention falters under the distraction of technological games and the lure of the plentiful attractions available on the Internet.

WHY HAS TECHNOLOGY NOT BEEN ADOPTED?
THE SEMMELWEIS LESSON:

Mere exposure to something that is important or true does not guarantee its acceptance. Imagine the reaction of Semmelweis, a Hungarian obstetrician, when he discovered in 1847 that the women who were dying in hospitals from childbed fever were actually being infected by germs introduced on the unwashed hands of their doctors. Even more terrible, however, was the fact that his colleagues paid no attention to his horrifying discovery, even after he proved that they could avoid infecting their patients by simply rinsing the doctor's hands in a chlorine solution.

Although Semmelweis quickly demonstrated his ability to halt the spread of the terrible fever, he had difficulty holding a job. The problem was that he could not find a way to describe his theory to his colleagues in a way they could accept. His suggestion that doctors who worked on cadavers must be infecting the women with bits of dead flesh they carried on their hands and instruments seemed to his colleagues to be nothing more than a superstitious old wives' tale. Without a helpful metaphor, which is to say without a way of describing his discovery in terms that were meaningful to his audience, Semmelweis was doomed to failure.

In 1865, after 18 long years of trying and failing to convince the medical establishment of his discovery, Semmelweis was overwhelmed by frustration. He could no longer think or do anything besides talk compulsively about childbed fever. With the knowledge of Semmelweis's wife, an associate tricked him into visiting a Viennese insane asylum where he was bound in a straitjacket, brutally beaten by the guards, and locked in a dark isolation cell. He died 2 weeks later. The autopsy revealed that the beating had left him with extensive internal injuries which became infected and led to blood poisoning, the very process which he had been trying to eradicate in his war against childbed fever.

To add to the bitter irony, Semmelweis died just as 2 other scientists were publishing findings similar to his. While his work made him a target of scorn, theirs would lay the foundation for 2 of the most celebrated and successful medical careers of the 19th century, that of Louis Pasteur and Joseph Lister. The difference between Semmelweis's tragedy and their triumph? Louis Pasteur and Joseph Lister described the process of infection with the help of metaphors that the profession could accept.

In 1861, 4 years prior to Semmelweis's death, the French chemist Louis Pasteur published a paper explaining something he called "germ theory." That was a metaphor the scientific community could accept. Six years later, the great English physician Joseph Lister published his version of the same findings. Like Semmelweis, Lister demonstrated that if the doctors' hands and surgical instruments were washed before working with patients, the transmission of infection was halted through some hidden means (now understood to be germs, not pieces of a diseased cadaver). About the only difference between them, besides Lister's use of the germ metaphor, was the compound Lister proposed to combat infection. He advocated a solution of carbolic acid (trade name: Listerine), while Semmelweis had preferred a solution of chloride (trade name: Clorox).

THE IMPORTANCE OF METAPHORS:

In my view, the Semmelweis tragedy resulted, in large part, from a failure of metaphors. Metaphors are simply comparisons people use to help explain or emphasize a quality that 2 items share. For example, an individual might liken big government metaphorically to evil, and then vote for those who agree with him or her on this.

In the 1840s the German states perceived themselves to be emerging from centuries of superstition, alchemy and magic. They prided themselves on thinking rationally and scientifically, and eschewed anything that smacked of folklore. They found Semmelweis's announcement highly offensive because it suggested the doctors themselves were to blame for spreading childbed fever, and also quite silly because he suggested they were carrying pieces of diseased cadaver on their person and instruments, and that the whole problem could be avoided if they simply washed their hands in a simple chemical solution. His metaphors suggested that he was calling them dirty. Had he been able to convey the same idea to them using language that seemed more enlightened and scientific, they would have been much more likely to pay attention.

Metaphors are important to us because we use them to filter out confusion and guide us in our decisions. They pre-bias our conclusions and frequently are subconscious arbiters of our conduct. In their book *Metaphors We Live By*, Lakoff and Johnson note in a summary of their findings after decades of research, "We live our lives on the basis of inferences we derive via metaphor."

In lacking a clear cause/effect metaphor, Semmelweis's approach offended the doctors when he suggested that the problem was their personal lack of hygiene. The idea that washing their hands would cure the problem suggested superstition somewhat akin to magic charms or fictional tasks assigned by a genie in a folk tale.

But once Pasteur proved, through his germ experiments in 1861, that microorganisms could breed infections, the doctors were provided with a simple metaphorical view that they could understand. Then when Pasteur further clarified his experiments with more data telling them how to block the progress of these microbes using 1 of 3 methods, they were ready to believe his scientific data and test his theses. Pasteur's 3 ways to stop the progress of these unseen microbes were: (1) filtration, (2) exposure to heat, or (3) exposure to chemical solutions. (Lister recommended chemical solutions because he felt that filtration and exposure to heat were impractical for most doctors.) By describing a world where dangerous microbes could be easily transmitted and suggesting that he had learned 3 ways to protect humans against them, Pasteur set the stage for future coherent research.

Oddly enough, Semmelweis had been extremely scientific and precise in his analysis of different hospitals and their rates of infection. His notes and diagrams were developed with careful Germanic precision and enabled him to uncover the cause, which at the time was quite counter-intuitive. He finally realized that in one hospital the outbreaks of childbed fever had started after doctors began to dissect cadavers before working with the female patients. He carefully recorded how he could lower these rates by using a chemical solution that sterilized the doctors' hands and instruments, but even though he quantified the reality of the diseases under different settings with extraordinary details, he had no acceptable metaphors that provided a clear cause/effect relationship because he lacked an understanding of microbes. As a result, his solution appeared silly and worthy of contempt to his contemporaries because it reminded them of the metaphors of alchemists and magicians that they were trying, as scientists, to put behind them. Notice how the failure of Semmelweis's metaphors trumped even the brilliance of his scientific analysis and data.

THE NEED FOR NEW EDUCATIONAL METAPHORS:

I have belabored the Semmelweis saga because it contains a poignant parallel with the status of American education where the current practitioners are unable to accept a new technological approach because they are offended by the inhumane metaphors associated with technology and are more comfortable following the traditional metaphors of the delivery system they were raised in. Most of our current educational leaders are unable to see the solution because they are enmeshed in a set of traditional educational metaphors that act as blocking metaphors, preventing them from comprehending that there is a new solution emerging that has a whole new set of metaphors waiting to be assimilated. They need to transition from the old educational metaphors to the new ones.

If we accept only the traditional metaphors that guide our current educational delivery system, we are unwittingly assuming the reality of a fixed educational delivery system with its standard schools, classrooms, teachers, students, books, school buses and calendar which we have all experienced, just as our parents and their parents have as well. In the traditional approach, the only way to improve this delivery system is through tweaking the various components and making them more efficient. At some point, however, almost every tweak possible has been experimented with, and the delivery system has becomes mature and has very few options left. This is where our current educational delivery system is now, and instead of renaming and retrying variants of the same manual system where the teacher does most of the work, we need to turn to designing a new delivery system which is guided by new metaphors, not revisions of the old ones.

What we are missing are the larger metaphors that subsume the traditional ones and suggest the direction our reforms should take, much as Pasteur and Lister did in their work on minimizing dangerous microbes and organizing ways to use them.

BUILDING THE HIGHEST CAPACITY METAPHORS:
DELIVERY SYSTEMS AND ENERGY SOURCES:

First, we need to understand that there is a hierarchy of metaphors if we are going to invest wisely in improving education. The highest capacity metaphors (the ones that are the most powerful because they set the ultimate bounds of what can be accomplished by a group of humans working together) require us to go up one level from the traditional educational metaphors (Level I) and introduce the concept of delivery system technologies (Level II). Society organizes workers around delivery systems to deliver goods and services to other people. Education is one of many delivery systems such as agriculture, transportation, communications, construction, medicine, the military, entertainment and a host of other delivery systems.

The reason delivery systems need to be identified is that their effectiveness is ultimately determined by their capacity to introduce and successfully use new technologies. This means that humans must understand that if they are interested in improving the delivery system (such as education) they are working in, then they must first analyze whether or not they are using the available technologies to exponentiate the amount of work the average educational worker is able to accomplish (such as the teacher, parent, or student).

Failing to understand this insures that a great deal of money and effort will be spent trying to improve the effectiveness of a delivery system that has matured and reached the natural limits of the human workers in the system. Education is an excellent example of this problem. Because we realize how important it is, we keep trying new reforms and pouring more capital into the system hoping that we will find a magic bullet; but so far, even though we have tripled our per pupil expenditure in constant dollars, our scores remain essentially the same.

It is imperative that we come to terms with the understanding that all delivery systems are dependent primarily upon: (1) The efforts of the workers in the system coupled with (2) The additional work that can be harnessed from using available technologies to help increase the workers output. The history of mankind is the history of people developing inventions to lessen the burden of manual labor and transfer some of the work the delivery system requires to appropriate technologies. As we will see in this book, education is ripe for the introduction of new technologies to help support the traditional workers in the system, i.e. the teachers, parents, and students.

There is, however, another level (Level III) we need to understand. This resides above delivery system technologies (Level II) and controls the technologies that determine the theoretical limit of how powerful a delivery system can become. This Level III represents the source of energy that fuels the technologies of the delivery systems being harnessed to accomplish the work of the delivery system in Level II. Technologies are intermediaries that help translate the power available from the energy source (such as coal, oil, or electricity) into a useful format to support the efforts of the workers. Thus at the top of the metaphorical hierarchy, even above delivery systems, is the source of energy that is available and adopted by humans and organized to accomplish the work of their delivery systems.

Although we tend not to notice it, humans organize their work around delivery systems which are in turn organized around sources of energy that provide the useful work required for the delivery system to become more efficient and affordable. For example, in the transportation delivery system people have a long history of using technology to help them transport themselves and their goods. To accomplish these goals, they have invented technologies (Level II) such as ships, animals (controlled by the technology of reins, bits, saddles, and yokes), trains, cars, buses, trucks, airplanes, and rockets. The introduction of each new technology improves the ability of the transportation delivery system and its workers to become more effective and efficient at a lesser cost. But behind each of these technologies is an energy source (Level III), such as coal, gas, oil, wood or electricity which sets the ultimate capacity of the delivery system the energy source is serving.

The diagram on the following page provides a visual example of the 3 levels depicting the ever-ascending leverage associated with the higher levels. Most of us work at Level I and are occasionally interrupted when a new technology is introduced at Level II, which exponentially increases the amount of work as productive workers that we can accomplish for our delivery system. We rarely pay any attention to the Level III sources of energy unless they grow scarce.

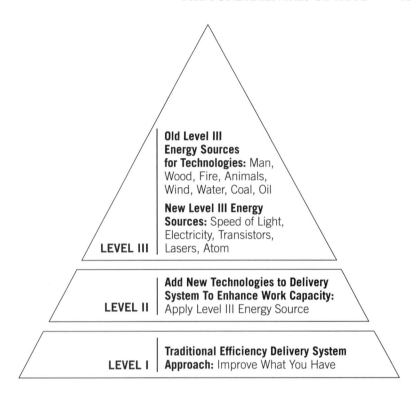

The greatest news of all about the new technologies coming on stream in support of the educational delivery system is that, unlike any previous time in history, the Level II energy sources are doubling in potential every 2 years, and as they double, they harness more of the speed of light in addition to doubling the number of transistors. As we will see in chapter two, this doubling of potential has unbelievably positive implications because, mathematically, a doubling over time introduces an exponential sequence (*multiplying* the variables) rather than a linear sequence (*adding* the variables). In other words, one approach brings multiplication into play while the other approach is limited to addition. Remember as children how we learned how much more powerful multiplication was than addition? The graph on the following page shows what happens when we introduce a doubling improvement sequence compared to a linear improvement.

Discussing this phenomenon in his book *The Singularity is Near,* Ray Kurzweil offers the following diagram:

LINEAR VS. EXPONENTIAL GROWTH

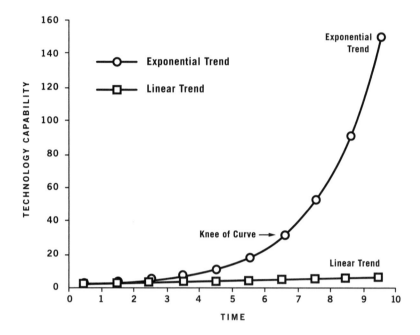

Linear vs. Exponential: Linear growth is steady; exponential growth becomes explosive

This description of the doubling phenomenon explains why the Level III energy source in the new technologies will have such an extraordinary impact on education and increasingly minimize any alternative reforms. Most of the standard energy sources such as coal, gasoline, or oil have a clearly defined limit in terms of the energy they can unleash. Research scientists have worked hard to yield a more efficient combustion to preserve more of the energy potential, but their efficiency improvements at best increase only a few percentage points at a time. Their progress is best illustrated above by the linear line which is slowly rising. Notice, however, in the linear trajectory there is nothing close to even a single doubling, much less the 2 year doubling that is taking place in the chip industry. Also notice how the doubling produces a compounding impact, with each doubling building on the cumulative total of what has gone before.

The doubling potential in chips is a byproduct of the invention of the transistor in 1947 which allowed scientists to replace vacuum tubes with a transistor on a silicon chip. Then as they experimented with these, they found ways to fabricate a chip the size of a fingernail able to hold many transistors. Here is where the story gets exciting.

In 1965 Gordon Moore, an electrical engineer who would soon cofound a chip company (Intel in 1968), noticed that as his group of scientists improved their processes, they were able to double the number of transistors they could put on a chip every 2 years. This phenomenon is now known as Moore's Law. Six years later, in 1971, Intel was able to build the first microcomputer on a chip which contained 2,300 transistors and was only an eighth of an inch by a sixth of an inch in size. To help you understand the extraordinary implications of this discovery, I would note that this first microcomputer was the same power as the first mainframe computer, the ENIAC, which had been built 25 years earlier at the University of Pennsylvania in 1946 and weighed 30 tons and was powered with 18,000 vacuum tubes.

But, as this doubling has advanced to the present, it has produced chips that have started to have billions of transistors on them, and each doubling adds billions of additional transistors, someday to be trillions. In other words, as the graph on the previous page illustrates, when you incorporate doubling and its multiplicative capabilities compared to the linear growth of other traditional energy sources, such as coal and oil, then you are presented with a Level II situation where the energy source continues to improve at a breathtaking rate. This is the first time that the Level II energy source has had the capability to double in power and storage every 2 years without additional cost or space requirements.

The fact that the educational delivery system can convert this Level III energy source into interactive artistically compelling individualized instruction is compelling. But even more compelling is the recognition that its potential is not fixed. Instead it is doubling without adding cost to the products every 2 years. For the first time in recorded history, we will be doubling the potential of a priceless commodity every 2 years without inflating its cost. Furthermore, unlike most other sources of energy, there is no danger we will run out of silicon and face price inflation as we have in other natural resources such as oil or coal. Almost all kinds of sand, clay, or rock contain silicon. In fact, over time, not only will the transistor capacity continue to grow, but also the cost will continue to decline. I find it difficult to imagine a more favorable set of circumstances for education that is facing devastating cost issues in the future as its per pupil cost will continue to soar. Here is an exemplary opportunity: a new solution is evolving that can offer superior interactive individualized instruction for only a fraction of the cost of the standard approach.

Our educational workers (the teachers, parents, and students) deserve the support of as many of these tireless transistor workers as we can muster. They will work for us 24 hours a day without becoming exhausted or complaining. Throw in the speed of light (the fastest known entity in the universe) to connect us to them, and the reader can get a glimmer of why this third source triggers such a message of splendid hope.

The only limiting factor will be the cost of developing quality software worthy of the emerging hardware. The hardware's potential cannot be unlocked unless enhanced software is available. Gaining financial support for enhanced educational software development has been very difficult, but as the financial gatekeepers to nonprofit, corporate, and government funding become aware of these new metaphors and the data that support their claims, this should provide a strong case for our leaders to start to fund the development of educational software. Educational software is the missing component required to activate the potential of the hardware.

What an extraordinary state of affairs! Experts, such as Kurzweil, who study these trends suggest that the doubling trend will continue which means that before long the educational delivery system will have a source of almost infinite Level III energy available to educate people. The key hardware issue is not just the status of the transistor, but the status of the computer because it is the computer which is performing the educational work!

Happily lurking quietly in the wings there is a new type of computer being developed called the quantum computer which will continue to extend the future generations of doubling after the fabrication techniques for transistor chips slow down. In fact, some computer scientists argue that the quantum computer will automatically increase the capabilities of the traditional computer a billion times, and that is just for starters!

Currently the energy source for most of education is human teachers, and although they can draw upon the stored work of technologies such as books and movies, most of the work has to be supplied by them. Because of the unique contribution of the transistor, the Level III energy sources (the speed of light and the transistor) will increasingly be utilized by the Level II evolutions of technologies that will effectively continue to double the potential of the Level II technologies, with each doubling increment growing larger.

Remember that there is another favorable element at play on Level III: the Speed of Light. The circuits with transistors on the chips will always offer some resistance and generate heat, so it will never be possible to utilize the full speed of light at which electricity travels in circuits or over wires, and yet their capabilities will continue to double because of another phenomenon. As the transistors become smaller, more of them can work in concert to generate useful work. What is doubling, then, is the number of elements doing the work in this emerging micro world.

Furthermore, the jumps become enormous because each doubling starts with a cumulatively larger base amount of potential.

Given the discussions of the dazzling new technological breakthroughs and abstract comparisons of arithmetic vs. geometric growth, I believe it might help to review the principles behind delivery systems to maintain a simple focus on the new basics to help maintain this bewildering new world of technology in perspective.

REVIEWING FOUR LAWS OF DELIVERY SYSTEMS:

(1) As workers, we organize ourselves into delivery systems which help us deliver goods and services to others. Education is another delivery system that is subject to the same rules as all other delivery systems.

(2) The introduction of new technologies into delivery systems has provided the most significant cultural changes and opportunities throughout human history. Successful new delivery systems have been the greatest civilization enhancers and have enabled mankind to move beyond survival mode. Thus those interested in improving a delivery system always benefit beyond expectation when they are able to introduce a new technology to improve the productivity of the workers, particularly when the delivery system is staffed with manual workers as school systems are. Thus, it pays whenever possible to invest heavily in technology to help the current workers become more productive and efficient.

Prior to the technological breakthrough of the industrial revolution, Malthus noted that humans were breeding at a geometric rate while the food supply was only growing at an arithmetic rate (sound familiar), and he predicted that this would force mass starvation as the population grew too rapidly. In fact, the history of civilization seemed to confirm this. But quite unexpectedly the new steam technologies were invented and helped humans improve farming, produce excess calories, improve their nutrition, grow a foot in height, and live longer as the delivery systems harnessed, improved, and implemented new technologies. These technologies, in turn, helped the mining, steel, textile, agriculture and transportation delivery systems flourish. My thesis is that we will soon see the educational delivery system expand and flourish as the new technologies come on stream.

(3) The speed of light is currently the fastest entity in the universe, so any technology that uses the speed of light will capture the greatest advantage. Think of the impact of the telegraph on the communications delivery system. It used the speed of light compared to its competition (the Pony Express) which used the speed of the horse. One averages 10 miles per hour using the technologies associated with the horse (saddle, reins, bit, and horseshoes) to maximize the energy available from its energy source.

The other harnesses the speed of light which travels at 670,616,629 miles per hour, or roughly 67 million times faster (less the friction in the telegraph lines). No wonder the Pony Express folded in 2 days in 1862 after the final link of the cross country telegraph line was hooked up.

The implications of this third rule are that if we are interested in improving the educational delivery system we need to start by harnessing the speed of light to support our efforts and not invest in a plethora of traditional reforms that try to improve the efficiency of the current workers saddled with Level I metaphors in the delivery system (teachers, parents, students, classrooms, 180-day years, teacher training, merit pay, accountability, Teach for America, Charter Schools, vouchers, Universal Preschool, etc.). We are not facing an efficiency problem; we are facing a delivery system problem where the current energy source being harnessed is primarily the manual labor of the teacher. Manual labor, no matter how sophisticated, is in the end just manual labor. Our goal should be to support the manual labor of the teacher, parent and student with the best technology available both at home and in school.

Notice in the past 2 decades the cell phone networks and the Internet have suddenly permeated most of the planet as far out as many of the poorest villages. This provides us with a worldwide network operating at the speed of light in the very air we breathe. Developing financial models for the use of these networks will take time, but there is no question that the rudiments of the new educational delivery system for our planet have been worked out.

(4) The fourth rule is that software is the single most important component of the new educational delivery system. This software is the intelligence that imitates the teachers' tasks and focuses the work bonus on providing an ideal instructional sequence for each child depending on the child's current needs.

Unfortunately, the hardware is what excites most people, and as projects are being financed there is an assumption that the acquisition of the hardware is the critical element and that the teachers will be able to develop excellent uses for these new tools the children find so attractive. In the current technological frenzy, there are new exciting hardware devices appearing every month, from iPads to intelligent whiteboards, and schools and teachers are quick to try to find applications for them because they are attractive to the children.

While the use of new technologies generates excellent press and photo opportunities, the actual instructional impact is negligible unless the software is well-designed and used daily for a brief period of explicit, intense, carefully sequenced and sustained activity for each child.

Good educational software is very expensive to develop and update; therefore, this is where the large investments should go, at least for the foreseeable future.

THE HERITAGE OF THE CURRENT EDUCATIONAL METAPHORS:

We have a problem unless we realize that the current educational metaphors are inappropriate for our time. They belong to the last century. They assume a fixed delivery system that is hundreds of years old involving the traditional elements that we all grew up with such as students, parents, school year, classrooms, teachers, books, taxes, libraries, curriculum, special education, tutoring, testing, grades, a 180-day school year, vacations, and school boards. The underlying assumption is that most of the work is accomplished by 3 sets of workers: (1) the teachers, (2) the parents, and (3) the students themselves. There is only a modicum of technology available in the form of books (that represent stored work), blackboards, chalk, and paper, and even occasionally overhead projectors and TV sets.

The danger of restricting our thinking to these metaphors is that people who want to improve the schools continue to focus on spending more and more money on what is now a mature delivery system (one with a fixed capacity) hoping that they will be able to increase instructional effectiveness through a reform that interests them. The data show the futility of this approach as we have tripled our per pupil expenditure over the past few decades without producing significant results. Once a delivery system is mature, then it is very difficult to generate improvements.

In any case, the advent of a new technology, such as the telegraph, makes a mockery of trying to wrest additional efficiency from old workers, such as the horse and rider. Even if by spending years on the project, we could improve the efficiency of the horse and rider by

50%—a very unlikely event—we would then average only 15 miles an hour leaving the telegraph still about 45 million times faster.

THE IMPORTANCE OF DEVELOPING NEW TECHNOLOGY METAPHORS FOR EDUCATIONAL REFORM: ENERGY, TECHNOLOGY, AND DELIVERY SYSTEMS:

Unfortunately, even though we have developed new educational metaphors involving energy, technology and delivery systems that would serve us well in offering new educational solutions, we find the educational culture still trapped in the old metaphors which are blocking successful educational reforms. Just like the problem that Semmelweis faced where he failed to find the proper metaphors to help him convince the doctors they were killing their patients because they failed to wash their hands and instruments in a chlorinated solution, so have the technologists failed to halt the educational destruction of up to a third or more of our students, who are failing to succeed academically and thereby disqualifying themselves for financial security in the knowledge-based culture of the future. Although there is more to life than financial security, there is very little chance of enjoying our existence when all of our efforts are required for survival—struggling with a minimum wage or a low paying job.

The prognosis is not good for those who fail to finish high school and do not go on to college. Tom Friedman in his New York Times column of November 23, 2010 notes that in an interview with Arne Duncan, the Secretary of Education, Duncan pointed out that 50 years ago you could drop out of high school and get a job in a steel mill or a stockyard and "still own your own home and support your family," but this is no longer possible because there are no longer good jobs for high school dropouts. "They're gone…That's what we haven't adjusted to." As a result, "they're condemned to poverty and social failure."

According to Friedman, technology can be a 2 edged sword. "Just as the world was getting flattened by globalization, technology went on a rampage—destroying more low-end jobs and creating more high-end jobs faster than ever. What computers, hand-held devices, wireless technology and robots do in aggregate is empower better-educated and higher-skilled workers to be more productive—so they can raise their incomes—while eliminating many lower-skilled service and factory jobs altogether."

My Quest: In this first chapter I have outlined the framework of hope I see emerging. The concepts are abstract and at times may seem in-humane, so now I will take the reader on a review of the very human tales that I have experienced in my journey of learning over the past 53 years. I hope that in explaining the source of my insights, through recapitulating my actual experiences, the reader will have a richer un-derstanding of the exciting potential of the future of education not only for America, but also for the world's children and their countries. What is about to happen as the educational delivery system begins to shift only happens rarely in human history.

Boy, is it going to be fun!

Chapter Two: The Quest

The "Quest" began in 1961 with a lecture I gave on "who" and "whom" to my English class at Brigham Young University in Provo, Utah. I was in my late twenties and teaching freshman English to over 100 students composed of 4 sections of 25–27 students, each of whom wrote a theme a week which I had to grade. Considering the mundane nature of the experience, I naturally did not realize for many years the importance of what had happened and what I had learned there. I say "mundane" because it is difficult to make a college freshman English class lecture on "who" and "whom" sound significant.

I was working earnestly to help the students clarify when to use the proper form of "who" and "whom" in their writing and speech in order to free them from a constant sense of uncertainty and potential embarrassment in their usage. For many years I had smarted under corrections from my parents and teachers concerning my own usage of "who" and "whom," and I was determined to make the material come alive for my students so as to enable them to master this curse once and for all. I was in my third year of teaching and still young enough to pour endless energy and enthusiasm into my material, and since I was teaching freshman English to over 100 students, I was having a great deal of practice.

I taught them that to avoid improper usage they would have to discover whether the pronoun who or whom was a subject of a sentence (who) or an object of a verb or preposition (whom or whomever). In order to accomplish this they would have to find the verbs first and establish whether or not the pronoun was a subject or object of the verb. And they also had to be careful to make sure that, if there was a preposition in the sentence which was using the pronoun as an object, they would have to use the objective whom or whomever form.

On this particular day, after spending hours in preparation, I rose to new heights of excellence as the examples flowed smoothly. The class was lively and awake, and my attempts at humor brought roars of appreciation from the students. I had researched the material carefully and wedded it skillfully to a chapter in their English book. Just before the bell I assigned some review problems to give the students practice in the lesson's larger points. As the class filed out of the room, I was filled with a quiet sense of contentment. I loved teaching and felt I was starting to achieve some competency. Then my brightest and hardest working student lingered after class to ask me to clarify "just one small point" and changed my life forever. I quickly answered the question. Only the slightest suggestion of an unresolved conflict flickered across the student's face as she thanked me and turned to go. For a moment I was not certain I had even seen it, but after a slight hesitation I called the student back. This time her question was less guarded and clearly indicated that the substance of the lesson had been lost on her. In fact it became clear that the student had neither understood nor retained any of the material.

I was surprised that the lesson I thought I had so skillfully taught her was totally missed, particularly since the student was so bright, and I knew the materials had been taught with considerable precision and clarity. But I attributed the lapse to some compelling trivial personal problem that had interfered with her attention or comprehension, and I put the incident out of my mind. For some reason, however, I thought to check, at the start of the next class, to see how many other students might have been daydreaming through the lesson, and I asked a series of quick, precise questions of all the students (in the spirit of a social scientist,) to see what percentage had not learned from my lecture. I suspected that 2 or 3 of the students might have missed the whole lesson, 5 would be shaky, 10 would be reasonably conversant with the material, and the remaining 7 or so would know the material very well.

To my shock and horror, however, I found that none of the students comprehended the material, or came even close to mastering it. Naturally this was upsetting to a young teacher, but after a great deal of thought, I managed a shaky resolution. The problem was that if the teaching process was not working in my class, then the fault had to lie with 1 of 3 variables:

(1) Myself as a poor teacher

(2) The students and their motivation

(3) The teaching process itself

Of course, I was not fully coming to grips with the true emerging issue. I recognized that I might be partially at fault, but I also believed that, in relation to other teachers, I was at least average and could therefore expect at least an average response from my students, and probably a good deal more from this particular lecture which I had labored on for many hours and that had created such a positive response from the students during the class itself. Similarly, I knew my students were at least average, and obviously the system being used (a teacher instructing a class of students) was about as good as mankind had been able to devise over a number of centuries. Furthermore, the classroom facilities were brand-new and air-conditioned, so they could not be faulted.

What I did not want to face was the conclusion that the results of an average teacher instructing an average class using the standard instructional process was an unequivocal waste of time. Flickering in and out of my consciousness was the frightening thought that perhaps all of us—that is the teachers and students as well as the parents funding the exercise—were all living a surrealistic lie as we played the educational game. Ultimately I denied this conclusion for both sentimental and practical reasons: sentimentally because I loved every aspect of the educational process and had chosen it as my profession, and practically because I realized that I had learned a great deal in my own education, inefficient as it may have been. Still, in order to gain this knowledge I had spent 20 years going to schools plus an additional year spent in naval schools. The naval schools involved intense daylong lectures as I was trained to be an air intelligence officer who briefed and debriefed pilots on an attack aircraft carrier, with a sub-specialty in atomic weapons carried by aircraft. I was also sent to legal school for a few months in order to become a squadron legal officer.

But now, I felt uneasy and sensed that, with my musings, I had inadvertently opened Pandora's Box. I had to acknowledge that there were certain questionable inefficiencies lurking in my educational experiences:

(1) I had spent 21 years in school, but most of it was spent sitting in a relatively passive mode. This left me often bored and restless.

(2) Unless the teacher ran drills after presenting the instruction (as in the case of learning letters for reading or times-tables for mathematics), I tended to delay any conscious learning effort on my part until "later." In fact, "later" was the norm. If I understood what the teacher was saying, I was pleased and delayed the dull memorization of the mere details until "later"; and if I did not understand after a brief attempt to do so, I also delayed trying to work out the solution to my confusion until "later."

(3) "Later" rarely came. I had notebooks filled with notes I never memorized and hundreds of pages of books that I used pens and magic markers on as I underlined in an orgy of notation in a panoply of gorgeous colors. Unfortunately, when I later scanned my notes, I rarely recognized the material. Only when forced by the teachers to become involved with drills, or threatened with being called upon in class or of being tested, did I become an active learner.[1]

---

[1]For readers interested in exploring what scholars have to say about this, I would recommend the work of Robert Bjork of UCLA who runs the Bjork Learning & Forgetting Lab and has published extensively and brilliantly on it.

(4) I appreciated interesting teachers because they made time pass more pleasantly. If they were good, they often helped me by breaking new and complex concepts into discrete units that I could follow. But, in fact, they could rarely teach me. I also found that good teachers helped give me an overview of the importance and depth of the materials that we were studying, even though my knowledge was, at best, of the surface variety. Clearly I knew Plato from Pluto, but then after that it got shaky. I had to learn by myself by actively trying to master the material "later."

(5) Ironically, I never learned the proper use of "who" or "whom" with any certainty until I taught students. Thus I learned that the major learner in a school setting was the teacher, who was also the most active agent in the process.

As the term progressed and I monitored my students more carefully to see when they were learning, I found that their experiences seemed to parallel mine. The announcement of a quiz, test, or midterm usually produced a flurry of learning activity. As an experiment, I stopped teaching one week early at term's end and devoted 3 class periods to administering previous final exams full of examples of tricky usage in areas such as "who" and "whom." These drills produced an astronomical leap in the student learning curve. From this I concluded that if I gave them a number of trials in any area, they would respond by actively learning.

Just asking them to answer questions and examples with immediate feedback on how they were doing stimulated them to try "then" instead of "later," and engaged them in active learning without the need for extensive planning and discipline. For a time I was tempted to restructure my class in order to avoid the passive lecture syndrome, but I decided against this for a number of reasons:

(1) In the Navy I had taken courses in which we were asked to memorize examples of rules without ever pausing to understand the rules themselves. I found this process very painful and frustrating.

(2) There was something in the lecture ritual itself that apparently gave the students a necessary perspective about their materials so they could then begin the work of mastering them. Once they understood the parameters of the teacher's points, then they felt free to settle down and either do the work or relax, but they apparently viewed class time as "scouting time" in order to take in an overview of the terrain. They seemed to need to understand what would be required of them before they began work.

However, lecturing encouraged a great deal of overview and very little work. This was fine for the highly motivated student who went home daily and conscientiously did that work, and even for the brightest students who could learn the materials with very little effort, but it was not an optimum process for most students. The teacher really could not afford to pause and drill the students because it would slow the course pace.

(3) In addition, I realized that there might very well be other important processes taking place during the lecture that I was not noticing, and I was afraid that if I made radical changes in my approach I might inadvertently destroy the efficacy of these hidden processes. I had to respect the Darwinian conclusion that men and women had tried every possible model of teacher-student instruction and probably ended up with the most useful approach, even though it might be riddled with shortcomings. In other words, almost every civilized nation had ended up with a standard educational model which involved classrooms, a curriculum, students, a teacher, blackboards and whiteboards, books and writing supplies.

I thought about trying to modify my course in a less dramatic fashion by instituting more frequent drill and practice sessions during the class; however, this meant I would have to either teach less material or simply not cover large segments of the assigned materials. Since I was already grading over 100 themes a week, I knew that this was out of the question. What I needed was an extension of myself that could encourage individual learning trials for my students that would be appropriate to their current individual needs and would take place in a setting of their choice. This inkling was a forerunner of my future interests in technology.

I sensed that unless I could provide mastery for the individual members of the class through encouraging individual efforts on their part after the class lectures, that the practical consequences of my teaching efforts would be either nonexistent or extremely limited. If, in fact, my job was to teach the students certain patterns of English usage and writing, and they failed to learn them, then I was failing. I rationalized that I was laying a foundation that could be built upon later if they ever decided to master the materials. But I also realized that I was not producing a very effective educational setting because most of my students were not very successful learners. Therefore, both the system and I were failing. Except for the bright and motivated exceptions, I was leaving my students marginally educated and probably with a strong sense of guilt for their shaky performance in trying to learn how to write very skillfully or assimilate the prescribed subject matter of the course. No matter how I twisted and turned at night, I could not rationalize my contribution to the students as representing much of a meaningful heritage.

My solution was to redouble my efforts. I tried to become a more successful teacher through organizing my time as skillfully as possible. I resolved to add on many hours of additional effort and analysis; however, I was surprised to discover how full my schedule was, and that I already averaged over 80 hours a week working on school assignments. This included: teaching 4 sections of English composition; grading over 100 themes a week; preparing lectures for both the compositional components of the course as well as materials on supplementary reading from literary anthologies; holding individual theme conferences; offering general office hours; attending department meetings; working on department committee assignments; attending school faculty meetings; and scheduling personal writing time for my own research articles.

The only free time that I could find was on Saturday, so I extended my office hours to include Saturday mornings through the early afternoon. Then, like Benjamin Franklin, I started a careful record of how I used my time to see if I might discover some additional efficiencies that I could employ. After a few months of concerted effort, I realized that I was having a negligible additional impact on my students. In fact, despite my best efforts, the students were learning about the same amount as before. This finding led to some additional analysis on my part in order to identify the specific shortcomings common to my students as they began to write. The sequence that most of them followed is quite predictable. Initially, they scrambled together a lot of pronouns and would begin a paper with phrases such as "everybody," "I", or "people" which quickly transitioned into "we," "they," "you," or "one," and led to such memorable sentences such as "One does their best because you should, I think, since it is important for people and everybody around one to encourage world peace for us and their society."

Having unscrambled the pronouns, the teacher's next task is to teach basic punctuation so that students are helped to understand exactly what constitutes a sentence. This starts with teaching them that a typical sentence begins with a capital letter and ends with a period. Major problems soon surface. For example a student may open with a crisp phrase that he or she takes to be a sentence, such as, "Having registered for English!" (sentence fragment) or perhaps they might clarify their view of English with, "I have Heuston, I hate English!" (comma splice) or perhaps complete the famous trio of sentence errors with, "I go to school I study English I find it difficult I do not like you you take me for granite!" (Fused or run-on sentences with an interesting insight about granite and their minds).

Faced with these problems, teachers generally fall into 2 camps. One group argues that the only way to help the students is to identify their errors and gradually wean them away from them. The alternate camp holds that an "error-driven" approach is doomed to failure. It is simply more of the same medicine that has not worked for 13 years. What they suggest is that teachers emphasize motivation by assigning autobiographical stories and ignore criticizing the students about their grammatical and stylistic errors. I tried both techniques early on, and although I had some modest success at times with the autobiographical story approach, I found that the students usually only had 1 or 2 good stories in them, derived from deeply moving incidents in their lives, but the students generally lacked the ability to transfer their personal musings into coherent prose because this required the mastery of many grammatical rules. I also discovered this technique was not easily transferable to other classes which might require classical writing skills beyond an autobiographical scene. As a result, I began to concentrate on the classical approach which identified the errors, helped the students understand them as we discussed what was good and bad about the papers in theme conferences, and I tried gradually to help my charges grow into competent writers.

But to be honest I found myself again facing the same limits as before because I was not able to generate enough work to change the students' basic habits. As I mused about this dilemma, I began to realize that what I was facing was the inability to generate enough work in the time available to complete my responsibilities as a teacher. I began to view everything in terms of the amount of work it required to change the students. I noticed how others in my profession had already taken steps to help the work shortfall. For example, I saw that teachers did not have enough time to write a definition of a comma splice each time they discovered the error, so they invented letter symbols which could be placed in the margin quite quickly. They had also invented style guides and writing handbooks which the students could reference to find out what the symbols meant (such as "CS" for comma splice) that the teacher would write on the students' papers.

And then one day I realized that the problem I was facing with my students was that I could generate enough work to find their errors and note them, but not enough work to sit down with them and go over their errors time and again until they were mastered. I couldn't offer enough trials to my students because I did not have the capacity or time to provide sufficient feedback.

In the best of all possible worlds, students would greet each correction with an energetic and systematic plan to provide that practice for themselves. But this is not a perfect world, and I probably do not need to tell you that this almost never happened. What most male students did when I returned a paper to them was to count the red marks on their paper, curse their fate, and angrily throw the paper into the nearest garbage can. The girls tended to correct their mistakes, but then produce the same mistakes in their future papers.

For a time I stopped giving new themes and tried to have them spend time correcting the errors on their older papers. I soon discovered that they spent as few minutes as possible to make a correction and did not come to terms with the nature of the error. I concluded that it would be better to have them continue writing new papers rather than picking minimally at their old ones. New papers might focus on other skills such as topic organization, outline development, writing transitional statements between paragraphs and learning to prove an argument in each paragraph with specific proof from quotations or paraphrases from the materials.

I also tried summarizing the error patterns of each student in my notebooks so I could spend time clarifying important writing trends in their approach, but I found again that I was involved with a procedure that would take too much time for me to implement successfully. I was running out of options. I could see clearly the limits of my approach, and by extension, those of my profession as a whole.

No matter how I tried, I could not come up with a way of making up the work and time shortfall that was a preordained limit of the system. I spent hours trying to discover new sources of work that I could utilize. But I could find no other sources. I realized for the first time that books were invaluable because they were sources of stored work, but I could not motivate many of the students to use them. Furthermore, as a lowly university instructor, I had little access to support personnel who might assist me in working with the students.

Finally I realized one day that I needed a machine to help me. At that time I knew very little about computers. In fact, they had only been around for about 13 years, and a market study by IBM concluded there would only be a market for about 12 machines. Obviously there were only a few people in a hurry to push their development. I envisioned some sort of a machine with a TV screen and keyboard where a student would be required to work for 30 or so minutes a week. He or she would be focused on a personal interactive program that would help on the points I had identified that needed additional effort. This, I sensed, would be the way to provide the missing work and time component and close the learning gap.

At this point, however, I had left BYU to pursue a doctorate in English literature at NYU. I taught briefly at Vassar, returned to BYU for a year, then accepted a post as chairman of the English Department at Pine Manor, a women's junior college outside Boston.

There I made another interesting discovery that had little to do with my quest but taught me that there are other variables in play as students learn besides the learning of facts. I was forced to understand that learning is accomplished amidst silent but powerful societal assumptions that impact students' motivation and color their view of what they are learning. In other words, the local culture would impact their perceptions. The summer before I left Utah I taught a seminar on the American Novel and was surprised by a robust enrollment. When I asked why so many had taken the course, they answered that they had heard that I was leaving and they wanted to take a course from a "communist" before I left. Raised as an Easterner, I am generally thought of as centrist or slightly conservative, so this student response surprised me.

Three months later a group of students taking the same course approached me in Boston and asked me if I would become a member of a panel because they needed a conservative, someone who was sort of a "fascist," and I was the only one they could find in the Boston area. Here I discovered how much the culture warped our perceptions of data as the same course generated 2 polarized political responses. There was, and still is, a long distance between Provo, Utah, and Cambridge, Massachusetts.

Years earlier I had noted a similar cultural bias when lecturing my class at Vassar when it was still a women's college. I had said something about "mothers," and the class went berserk. A quiet girl in the first row, who rarely ever said a word, suddenly got red in the face and denounced her mother for making her go to Vassar. Others chimed in. I lost total control of the class and listened with astonishment as the young women paraded grievances, real and imagined, about their mothers. When the next class came in, I mentioned my astonishment to the students about the impact of discussing mothers in my previous class, and I had no sooner used the word "mother" then the second class erupted just as the first had.

I decided that, as a male, I had discovered a new universal truth: young women have strong feelings about their mothers, e.g. I overheard, "I am really mad at my mother! When I refused to do it, she didn't make me follow through. She knew she should have made me do it!"

Years later when teaching again at Brigham Young I made a comment about how mothers sometimes cause stress for their daughters because I thought it might help the males in the class understand this strange but universal principle. This time the girls in the class attacked me and expressed dismay at my cavalier tone about their mothers. They told me, in no uncertain terms, that they loved their mothers, that they never argued with them, and they were upset with my suggestions that daughters often felt stress concerning their relationship with their mothers.

Afterwards I invited the most vocal girl to have a root beer with me in the student cafeteria where she continued to berate me for my lack of sensitivity. She assured me that she never argued with her mother, and after awhile I decided that maybe I was in over my head, afloat in an area of conflicting data. Obviously, the conservative Western girls were different than the Eastern girls. But just as we were about to leave, I asked the student if her mother liked the dress she was wearing, and her face grew angry and she said, "No, she does not like it, and last week we had a screaming match, and I told her that her taste was terrible. I wanted her to stop telling me what to wear!"

Sometimes separating cultural from universal truths is difficult, whether it be about politics, religion, or the use of technology.

Chapter Three: "Reforms" and the Retiring Headmistress

In the fall of 1969, I moved my family to New York City and prepared to become Headmaster at the Spence School, a private girl's school that enrolled about 500 students from kindergarten through 12th grade. Founded by Miss Clara B. Spence in 1892, Spence had become one of the city's most respected independent schools under the tutelage of wonderful leaders like Dorothy Osborne and Barbara Colbron.

Shortly after starting my reign, I was invited to a retirement dinner to honor another private school head who was completing a distinguished career in education that had lasted over 50 years. While waiting for her remarks, I sat restlessly, charged with righteous energy as I planned the reforms I would implement at my new school in the months ahead. When it came time for the retiring headmistress to address the assembled guests, she stood erect, her shoulders back, and fixed us with a no-nonsense gaze that bred both an instinctive respect for her commanding presence and some residual guilt for vaguely remembered sins as we regressed back to childhood under her compelling spell. She addressed us with a slightly quavering, but firm, voice and said something like this:

> You probably assume that I am retiring because I have reached 4 score or so years and am pleased to have some time to rest and pursue less strenuous activities. While it is true that I am

tired, this exhaustion comes not from the children or the school community, but from listening to parents and trustees pushing the latest reform on me. Every time there is another book written with an exciting new approach to educational reform, I am swamped with demands to implement this new discovery that is guaranteed to improve our current instruction.

The problem is that I have lived too long and know too much; I have now seen these reforms cycle through our schools over and over again as the decades have flown by, and the thought of not having to face any more of them makes retirement seem like a privileged paradise.

She then went on to describe a number of reforms that kept recycling every decade or so. She would first describe the reform, give its initial title, and then describe some of its variant names that had been given during the more than half-century of her educational service. I noticed, to my embarrassment, that one of the reforms that I was planning to introduce at my new school had been tried 3 different times during this woman's years of service. She then concluded by stating that we should take great care when being assaulted by well-intentioned people who are mesmerized or enthralled by some new reform. "Don't let the bastards suck your blood dry!" she said, and then she sat down with a stiff back and ladylike firmness leaving me to digest an insight that has haunted me ever since.

Over the years I grew to appreciate this retiring head's insights about the general futility of pursuing educational reform in the traditional manner. Her compelling narrative review alerted me to the potential futility of relentlessly pursuing new reforms without studying their efficacy. At the same time, she left me with a hunger to understand why most reforms fail, and to identify, at the least, reforms that do work and possibly even a science of reform where cause and effect could be established to guide future efforts.

THE CYCLICAL NATURE OF REFORM:

Another way to understand how difficult it is to have a reform succeed in the school system is to trace the history of educational reforms over the past few decades and recognize how each reform seems to run through its own cycle that begins with hope and commitment, transitions to puzzled uncertainty as results fail to meet expectations, and then gradually collapses as administrators and teachers turn to another idea as the panacea. One scholar, Robert Slavin from Johns Hopkins University, paused to examine this phenomenon and wrote an article, published in the educational journal *Phi Delta Kappan* that documented the 12 phases that a standard educational reform follows before it disappears.[1] These phases are divided into 2 types: the Upswing and the Downswing. They are as follows:

The Upswing:
(1) Program is proposed.
(2) Program is piloted.
(3) Program is introduced in innovative districts.
(4) Program becomes "hot topic" among staff developers.
(5) Program expands rapidly.
(6) Controlled evaluations begin.

The Downswing:
(7) Innovative districts move on to other programs.
(8) Complaints surface in professional publications.
(9) Preliminary evaluations are disappointing.
(10) Developer claims that disappointing results are due to poor implementation.
(11) Interest in program flags.
(12) Controlled evaluation studies are published.

Reforms are generally initiated by articulate, university-based scholars who have a flair for leadership and persuasion. Their insights and concepts are usually very commendable and, although they manage to produce some positive data in their early sites, problems surface when the proponents attempt to replicate or scale up the reform for systemic distribution.

---

[1]Robert E. Slavin, "PET and the Pendulum: Faddism in Education and How to Stop It," *Phi Delta Kappan,* June 1989, 752–758.

INDIVIDUAL REFORMERS:

Now and then, in contrast with the major reforms that are well-funded and staffed, a dedicated and talented individual appears who is a great teacher or principal and thrills us with his or her dedication. Such is the extraordinary saga of Jaime Escalante who successfully taught calculus to inner-city children in Los Angeles and flummoxed the College Board officials who refused to believe that his students could perform well. Mr. Escalante's Los Angeles saga was highlighted in the movie "*Stand and Deliver*." Similarly, a great inner-city principal in New York, Debbie Meiers, relentlessly drove her students to significantly higher achievement levels against extraordinary odds. But unfortunately great individuals are rarely able to replicate their achievements at multiple sites and tend to burn out when pressed to scale their projects. Businesses such as McDonald's, Wal-Mart, or Starbucks have been able to build successful franchises helping them to scale their stores rapidly, but school leaders have never been able to accomplish this.

The reason for the success of these individuals has a heroic and tragic component because neither the individuals nor the public understand the reason for their success. In general, the public and educational leaders believe these great individuals have discovered a powerful new approach that others could profitably imitate, and yet nothing is further from the truth. What these extraordinary educators have unwittingly accomplished is the unusual feat of focusing all of the available time and work they can muster from themselves and the personnel available in the community on a sound educational goal that they can articulate for the teachers, parents, and students.

There is just enough manual work (people, not machine work) available in a family and school setting to provide educational success for most students if it is organized and utilized with almost perfect efficiency and motivation. Volunteers can be used as teachers' aides, parents can be inspired to help with homework, and time can be co-opted for additional instruction in the morning before school, the afternoon after school, and weekends. In some cases it is even possible to expand school hours and to encroach on long weekends,

Christmas and spring vacations, and even the traditional summer vacations. What all of these successful reformers accomplish is a strategy that focuses the students, teachers and parents on a very specific educational goal (such as reading or calculus) and then provides additional manual labor from themselves and/or the community for the required extra instruction and drill needed for the students to achieve academic competence.

Geoffrey Canada in his program "The Harlem Children's Zone" has—against all odds and with extraordinary leadership—produced a remarkably successful program for about 10,000 students. Beginning with prenatal training for the mother, it does not stop until the child finishes college. His approach has 2 components: (1) He provides dynamic growth metaphors for the parents and children to adopt in Harlem that encourages them to take their education seriously and assume that they will graduate from college and launch successful careers. For example, pregnant mothers are given a multi-week seminar in what is called "Baby College" in order to get them used to the idea that their children are expected to attend and finish college; (2) In his charter schools the day is much longer than in the public schools. In addition, students who are struggling are required to stay late and sometimes return on Saturdays for additional tutoring. Furthermore, the students only have 2 to 3 weeks of vacation during the summer.

Unfortunately, Canada's approach is difficult to scale because he has to, personally, raise over $50 million a year of private funding for his full service approach. In all probability others will lack his vision, fund-raising capabilities, and determination, and they will ultimately fail, just as those who tried to scale Jaime Escalante or Debbie Meiers have failed.

The tragic part of these accomplishments is that they are never replicable, partially because in not understanding the true reason for their success (providing additional instructional time), the would-be imitators copy the wrong blueprint and try, half-heartedly, to scale what they perceive to be the model. What never occurs to them to imitate are the insane hours that these leaders keep as they focus the community on generating additional work and frequently clash with work rules and district customs as they drive their reforms home. They also usually lack the vision of the importance of the specific reform and offer, instead, a more diffuse set of goals that rarely focus enough work on any academic topic. For example, the new head of the school may be interested in having the children enjoy the resources of the city rather than focus almost totally on a phonics reading curriculum. Or she may judge her teachers on their talents in providing lovely bulletin boards that impress visitors and parents.

In other words, the real cause for the success of a few reformers is their ability to generate more support (work) for the students in the educational delivery system instead of just using the available work paradigm more efficiently, as well as their ability to focus the community on tightly defined academic topics. This is accomplished through working longer hours and/or hiring more helpers to accomplish the educational tasks. Their triumph is a delivery system triumph generated by the presence of additional workers for the delivery system who provide extra work. Unfortunately, this approach is unscalable because it requires the extra expense of hiring additional personnel during the school year and for after school, weekend and summer programs.

Since my Spence days, I have tracked many reforms and have seen them rise, crest and slowly move off center stage. The first was a West Coast initiative called *The Program for Effective Teaching* (PET) developed by Madeleine Hunter. Some of the other scholars and educational leaders of the past few decades who have launched popular reforms are: Benjamin Bloom from the University of Chicago whose approach was called *Mastery Learning*; Marie Clay from New Zealand who has led a movement called *Reading Recovery*; Ted Sizer from Brown University who led an organization called the *Coalition of Essential Schools*; Marilyn Adams from Bolt, Beranek, and Newman, Brown University and Harvard who has edited a text series called *Open Court* that enjoyed great commercial success; Henry Levin from Stanford University with a program called *Accelerated Learning*; James Comer from Yale with a program called *The School Development Program*, and Robert Slavin himself from Johns Hopkins with *Success for All*.

All of these reforms, and many others, have received great attention and support for a season and, though they may be still around in various formats, they have never been effective, affordable, and scalable enough to be accepted broadly by the education community.

By the early 1970s over a decade passed since my lecture on "who" and "whom" had focused my attention on the limited effectiveness of traditional teaching strategies. During those 11 years I had become a department chairman at a junior college and then Headmaster at one of the nation's most prestigious independent schools. Sadly it seemed that no matter how hard I worked, no matter what resources I brought to bear on teaching the students that I loved, there was still an unbridgeable gap between what they needed and what the schools could provide. What I never could have foreseen is that in 1971 (the same year the first microcomputer chip was built by Intel) I was about to play a chess game with 2 of my daughters one evening snuggly ensconced in the Park Avenue apartment that the school provided for my family that would ultimately alter my life and provide the first glimmering clues about a solution for my quest.

Chapter Four: A Chess Game with my Daughters Kary and Kim

Becoming the new Headmaster of the Spence School at the age of 37 was a real shock. Although I had attended both the Bronx High School of Science and a New England boarding school called Mount Hermon, I had never realized what a phenomenal education was possible for children who were fortunate enough to be supported by a great academic tradition and could start their training as early as kindergarten and have a clear path ahead with a world class curriculum up through high school.

I had thought that the Wellesley public school system my daughters attended was outstanding because 80% of the tax base was budgeted for the public schools. That New England setting, with its beautiful red brick school buildings, had the appearance of a Hollywood movie set. But the experience my daughters had at the Spence School was significantly better. In fact, it was so much better, that I felt uneasy about directing a school that most children could never hope to attend. I would often wonder how I could ever replicate and scale Spence so all children could have the same educational opportunity that only the wealthy seemed able to afford.

One evening, as I was playing chess with 2 of my middle school daughters, I lost a $3 bet and won a life-changing insight. One of my daughters suggested that, instead of paying them the $3 I owed them, I pay them by putting a penny on the first square of the chess board and double it on each of the remaining 63 squares. After a moment of thought, I decided to encourage her entrepreneurial spirit and agreed to her suggested payment schedule. Imagine my shock when I discovered I now owed my daughters $92 million billion. I will not dwell on how I had to struggle to maintain any sense of fatherly authority, given this debt that I could not possibly repay, but I will note that I was left with an exquisitely developed sensitivity to the word "doubling."

As I thought about this explosion of potential through doubling, I was reminded of the work of the famous American intellectual Henry Adams. Like me, he was fascinated by the capacity of innovative technology to double production. In his case, however, the technology in question didn't involve bits and bytes but coal and steam.

Born in 1838, Adams had an interesting pedigree. His great-grandfather was the second President of the United States, his grandfather was the sixth President, and his father had been Minister at the Court of St. James in England during the Civil War. His mother's father, Peter Brooks, died the richest man in Boston, and his uncle, Josiah Quincy, was President of Harvard University. His circumstances allowed him access to all areas of society both at home and abroad. During one of his trips to Europe, he had a seminal experience at the Paris Exposition in 1900, when he was 62 years old.

In Paris, Adams was stunned by the sight of 40 foot dynamos humming away as part of the science exhibition. They seemed to him to constitute an elemental force that might change society. Fortunately his friend, the physicist Samuel Langley, guided him through important scientific exhibits such as Daimler's internal combustion engine, and made him aware of other sources for accelerating forces such as the steam engine. Langley also introduced him to Marconi's work on radio waves, the recent discovery of radium, and x-rays, as well as the work Langley himself had done on the infrared spectrum.[1]

Trying to make sense of this acceleration of force and energy that was becoming available to society, Adams calculated that the coal

---

[1] Henry Adams, *The Education of Henry Adams* (New York: Penguin Classics, 1995), 360–362.

output of the world had doubled approximately every 10 years from 1800 to 1900 as coal was burned to generate steam for steam engines and dynamos. This meant that, by 1905, an individual could be propelled across the ocean by a 30,000 horsepower steam engine. By working backwards Adams calculated that in 1835 individuals had had only 234 horsepower available to them.[2] By extrapolating the accelerating energy curve forward, Adams made the remarkable prediction that, in 100 years, "every American who lived into the year 2000 would know how to control unlimited power."[3] While it might be difficult to calculate how much power each individual controls in the 21st century, society as a whole certainly has access to almost unlimited power. Consider such technologies as rockets, jet aircraft, radio, television, cellular and standard telephones, atomic energy, satellites, the Internet, and computers that early 21st century people have at their disposal.

Adams was also intrigued by the growing number of physicists and scientists who were involved in the development of new discoveries and technologies. He noted, for example, that the population of scientists in America who would be laying the foundation for future scientific breakthroughs was growing from a handful at the beginning of the nineteenth century to hundreds and even thousands within a few decades. He foresaw the day when that number would rise to tens of thousands, not only in America but also throughout the globe; and he believed their discoveries would continue to fuel the acceleration of energy that was being introduced into society.[4]

Adams' insights are important because they alert us to a new phenomenon that is destined to have a growing impact on our civilization. As he predicted, there is an ever increasing tidal wave of energy being generated that will produce additional work. Some of this work will be useful, but some will be destructive. By 1945 a pilot using the technology of the aircraft to carry the technology of the atomic bomb demonstrated the capability to destroy an entire city and tens of

---

[2]Adams, 463.
[3]Adams, 469.
[4]Adams, 467.

thousands of lives within seconds of one bomb's detonation. Without trying to translate the amount of horsepower an atomic bomb generates, we can see that, true to Adams' prediction, there was a stunning increase in available energy in the 110 years between 1835 and 1945. Since then scientists have managed to fulfill Adams's remarkable predictions as they have continued to develop new technologies that are flooding our civilization with ever increasing energy.

Late one night a few months after the chess game with my daughters, I found myself in my office at school struggling to catch up on my paperwork. I was particularly frustrated with trying to digest an engineering article on computers that I had collected as part of a personal assignment I had given myself after 2 students had complained that they were going to graduate from Spence without knowing anything about computers.

The article I was reading utilized the usual engineering rhetoric where equations were offered, diagrams were displayed, and then a summary was given which began with the words, "Thus we see…" Somewhat frustrated I blurted out loud, "Only an engineer could write 'Thus we see' after offering only diagrams and equations instead of coherent English." Then in some embarrassment I realized I was alone at 11 o'clock at night in the building and talking out loud without other people around. Settling down, I thought to myself, "With a PhD in English, you should be able to understand a simple engineering paper." So, reluctantly, I started through the paper a second time carefully looking for words that I could understand and use for comprehension. Suddenly I saw the expression "doubling every 2 years," and broke out into a cold sweat. After that chess game, I knew what a powerful word "doubling" could be. I went through the article with great care and discovered that the engineer was pointing out to the reader that the number of transistors that fit on a computer chip would double every 2 years for the foreseeable future—all at no additional cost.

I knew enough to understand that transistors were like currency and could be used for a number of purposes. For example, an electrical engineer could use them to build a microcomputer on a chip the size of a fingernail as a replacement for large and expensive vacuum tubes, or as a replacement for expensive and bulky memory which had to be hand built with wires wrapped around small circular donut shaped metal cores for each bit of memory. The first modern computer (the ENIAC) had been finished in 1946 at the University of Pennsylvania. It had 18,000 vacuum tubes and weighed 30 tons. Twenty-five years later (1971), Intel built the first microcomputer (the 4004) using transistors in place of vacuum tubes. This computer had the same power as the ENIAC but it needed only 2,300 transistors and had shrunk in size from filling a room to ⅛ of an inch by ⅙ of an inch.

Suddenly I understood that, in the coming years, powerful microcomputers would be built which had billions of transistors in them. These would offer a stunning amount of power to add to our capacity to generate additional work for whatever tasks were desired. The engineering article I had read was by Gordon Moore who was a cofounder of Intel that developed the first microprocessor chip. We now call his insights "Moore's Law," which formalizes the doubling phenomenon he articulated.

In a flash, I realized that I might now have available a new source of work that would enable me to individualize teaching and scale my capabilities to allow all children access to outstanding instruction. In other words, there might be a way so as to scale Spence for all children by harnessing this new energy support for education. I could use the computer.

My chess game, Moore's Law, and Henry Adams's insights combined to suggest how a single worker, the teacher, using the emerging energy fueled by transistors with the help of the speed of light would be able to bring to bear extraordinary amounts of additional energy in the form of useful work to help educate children.

Our computers would be working with electrons that were moving at the speed of light. To honor this potential, Waterford has adopted the phrase, "Learning With the Speed and Energy of Light" as part of its logo. The key to accomplishing this would be the development of spectacular software that would continue to improve by keeping pace with the ever-accelerating potential of computer hardware.

Chapter Five: The Equation, the Walk, and the Death of the Pony Express

In the weeks after digesting Gordon Moore's article, I mused about energy, life, and education whenever my duties at Spence allowed. Slowly I confirmed my intuitions as I realized that the lessons of history and my own experiences during my years on earth suggested that the quality of life and the statistical chances for human survival are frequently determined by access to energy. But at the same time, as an educator, I had learned that the quality of life and the statistical chances for human survival are frequently determined by access to education. I could not help wondering what the connection was between education and energy.

Over the next few months I often found myself doodling on pads and the blackboard in my office as I tried to find the relationships between them. One morning, as I was trying to simplify my thinking, I suddenly wrote a simple equation on my blackboard that clarified the connection between education and energy. That equation provided a framework for my thinking that continues to guide me to this day. This was my personal epiphany, my Einstein energy moment, my equivalent of his famous $E = MC^2$ equation where he recognized that energy and matter were interchangeable forms of the same entity.

I began to realize that the new sources of energy might be harnessable to help alleviate the manual work limitations that most teachers face as they try personally to provide enough useful work to educate each child successfully. I realized that despite my best efforts that I had personally hit unsolvable limitations no matter how hard I worked to teach my English students because I had run out of time, energy, and work before I could provide enough support to succeed in my teaching. Thus, I was full of excitement and enthusiasm as I now sensed that there was a new source of inexpensive additional work coming on stream that could provide me (and by extension, all teachers) enough new capacity to individualize instruction and insure that each child learned successfully.

To clarify this insight I wrote a box on the right side of a board. This expressed what a solution would require, i.e. enough available work to insure that each child learned effectively.

> TOTAL USEFUL
> WORK

Thus I knew where I wanted to end up: I had to have enough additional work available to me as a teacher to help me solve most of my instructional problems.

Once I had this, I struggled to identify the variables that were the sources for work. The first obvious source of work was the teacher or person providing the instructional work. Thus I started with what the teacher could offer through her work.

Recognizing that not all workers are equally efficient, I had to add an "Efficiency" factor to the equation in order to capture the difference between "good" and "bad" teachers as workers.

Unfortunately, efficiency never adds any potential to the work; instead it measures how much potential can be saved and how much is lost because of inefficiency. Since no one is 100% efficient, there will always be some loss. Perfection is expressed by multiplying its number by 1.00. For example if I said that 6 was the full potential of something, and I multiply that by 1.00, I retain 100% of the potential, or 6. On the other hand, if I multiply it by .50 (representing 50% of the potential) then I end up with a new usable potential of 3.

In analyzing the faculty of a good school, I would guess that the school might average a .70 (or 70% of perfection). On the other hand, a poor school might only average a .30 (30% of perfection) because a poor school would not salvage as much useful instructional work as a good school. Looking at the data in terms of standard educational reform, we would say the obvious thing is to train the faculty to become more efficient and raise their average up to .70 or .80. But, as we shall see in the book, most of the problems of a .30 school are caused by the poor preparation the children of low social economic status experience in their families. This, in combination with the way they spend their time during holidays and summer vacations (as contrasted with the experience of wealthy families), helps generate the less than satisfactory profile of most low SES (socioeconomic status) schools.

Unfortunately, as I would later learn, almost every single educational reform (current or past) is obsessed with increasing the efficiency box which unfortunately does not add additional work to the system; instead, it tries to salvage as much efficiency as possible from whatever the current system contains.

However, Moore's Law allowed me to introduce a new "leverage factor" that would add more work to the system. It was this knowledge that I found so exciting because it meant that I might actually reach my original goal, which was to somehow discover an approach that could add desperately needed additional work and could allow the teacher to succeed in most teaching situations. Such is not generally the case.

Though compared to Einstein's, my modest insight was trivial, I was still so stunned by the importance of energy to education—and what this insight might mean to education—that I slipped out of my office on East 91st Street and wandered down Fifth Avenue in a daze, trying to digest the implications of this new understanding. I was so engrossed that I walked all the way south, down past Wall Street to Battery Park at the southern tip of Manhattan, and somehow returned to my home in the Upper East Side at night, a journey of many miles. I don't remember any of it.

I sensed that the doubling in Moore's Law could eventually offer unbelievable amounts of additional support to a teacher' s work tasks (just as the doubling from the chess game ultimately offered unbelievable amounts of money starting with a single penny). This energy might be harnessable to help alleviate the manual work limitations that most teachers face as they try personally to provide enough useful work to educate each child successfully. I realized that, despite my best efforts, I had personally hit unsolvable limitations no matter how hard I worked to teach my English students because I had run out of time, energy, and work before I could provide enough support to succeed in my teaching. By the time I arrived back at my apartment, I was completely exhausted but my mind was still bursting with excitement and enthusiasm. Finally I had found a new source of inexpensive additional work coming on stream that would continue to grow which could provide me (and by extension, all teachers) enough new capacity to individualize instruction and insure that each child learned successfully.

I soon realized that my new equation could be generalized far beyond teaching and applied to all human efforts. In order to understand this, I first had to realize that humans naturally organize themselves into delivery systems in order to deliver goods and services to others. Education is just one delivery system, but there were many others. Transportation, communications, agriculture, medicine, entertainment, and the military all come to mind.

Even more importantly, each of these delivery systems usually has made fundamental breakthroughs in their capabilities when they harnessed animals first and then technologies in an effort to improve their effectiveness (using some new leveraging factor such as the animals or technology). For example, in the communications delivery system for a period in the 1860s the fastest way to transmit a message across America involved using the Pony Express from St. Joseph, Missouri, to Sacramento, California. There were 400 horses, about 160 weigh stations, 120 riders and approximately 400 personnel involved in delivering the mail. This system averaged about 10 miles per hour and took about 10 days to deliver a letter. Riders could not weigh over 125 pounds.

Two days after the telegraph was connected in Salt Lake City on October 24, 1861, the Pony Express was closed because it was unable to compete with the telegraph. This was one of the fastest collapses of a business in history and highlights the potential technology has to improve a delivery system. The person delivering the message (doing the work) was no longer using an animal-supported delivery system (the leverage factor), but was sitting and transmitting the information using a new delivery system (the improved leverage factor) utilizing the speed of light instead of the speed of the pony. The communications system using the horse delivered its product at 10 miles an hour (its useful work limit); whereas, the new delivery system, harnessing some portion of the speed of light (the fastest known entity in the universe), delivers its useful work at speeds approaching 670 million miles per hour, roughly 67 million times faster than the Pony Express.

The rapid demise of the Pony Express is a particularly poignant example of what happens when technology is able to harness a significant portion of the speed of light which appears to represent the ultimate limit given our current knowledge of the universe. There is no manual worker who can compete with it.

This is significant because both the Internet and the microcomputer harness the speed of light and are able to complete useful work cycles at an ever increasing speed that has no end in sight. In fact some scientists believe that when we are able to harness quantum theory and someday build a quantum computer that the potential number of useful work cycles will be increased a billion times.

THE CONCEPT OF A MATURE DELIVERY SYSTEM:

As people work in delivery systems to provide goods and services to others, their new technologies, such as the cell phone (as part of the communications delivery system), will grow wildly at first, but after a period they become mature, growth slows, and then the workers concentrate on becoming more efficient. The educational delivery system is mature and has not substantially changed over the past 550 years since the invention of the printing press.

One symptom of a mature delivery system is the painful recognition that adding additional capital to the system makes little difference. For example, had the United States government decided to invest $50 billion to improve the horse at the time of the demise of the Pony Express (an example of a mature delivery system) to add more work to the system, then the following scenario could have been likely: $10 billion would be budgeted for the National Science Foundation (NSF) to improve the technology of the horse, $10 billion for NASA to incorporate space science and aerodynamically improve the horse's air resistance, $10 billion budgeted to the National Institutes of Health (NIH) to work on the horse's diet, and $20 billion budgeted (education always costs more) for the Office of Education (OE) to develop training algorithms for the horse and rider. Clearly, the funds would be wasted.

This investment would have been wasted because the horse is basically, by definition, heredity, and breeding, a one horsepower entity. Despite the fact the National Science Foundation could develop titanium or composite graphite shoes for the horse; NASA could aerodynamically work out how best to arrange the horse's mane to minimize wind resistance; the National Institute of Health could calculate an ideal diet with supplementary vitamins and shots; and the Office of Education could develop a superb curriculum for the horse and rider which might include national exams to insure fairness and accountability, regional training centers to dispense knowledge equitably, and hiring policies free of political patronage; there remains an unsolvable problem: Still the horse will basically remain a one horsepower creature. In fact the word "horsepower" has become a universal measure of one unit of work first articulated by James Watts to help the potential users of steam engines understand how much more powerful a steam engine was than a horse. This suggests a certain limitation of effort that a well-trained and well-taken-care-of horse can achieve. It also suggests that, if the United States had spent $50 billion on improving the horse, most of that investment would have been wasted. After centuries of effort, just as the delivery system utilizing a horse has matured past the point where we can wrest more work out of the beast by trying to make him more efficient, so pouring more capital into the current educational delivery system would generally be a waste because it, too, has matured and reached its natural work limit as defined by the amount of work a teacher can accomplish. Unfortunately, the desire to improve education drives us to invest more and more money in this old educational system. For example, in the past few decades we have tripled our per pupil expenditure in constant dollars in the educational delivery system without improving our test scores. This is a key symptom of a mature delivery system, i.e. further investment in the system will not significantly improve the delivery of its intended goods and services. On the other hand, if new technology can be developed as a new leverage factor, then the delivery system can deliver much more "Useful Work." We can see this illustrated in the evolution of the communications delivery system which culminated in the development of the telegraph after centuries of using less efficient approaches that evolved through smoke signals, pigeons, pennants from masts viewed by telescopes, and the Pony Express.

The equation I worked on the blackboard at Spence is illustrative of this.

The "worker" is the individual who provides the manual work component. Naturally each worker can be an efficient or inefficient performer. The leverage factor is the work actually produced by the addition of technology, and it too can be used both efficiently and inefficiently. Different technologies produce different usable work levels of energy. In combat, for example, a soldier using his own arm and hand can strike an enemy directly, or he can use a rock, stick, or sword to do this. Alternatively the soldier can introduce a significant energy leap by introducing a bow and arrow. Then he can graduate to rifles and cannons evolving right up to the quantum leap of an atomic bomb. Each process, i.e., striking, hurling, and using the energy of a bow, gun powder, or the atom, leverages a soldier's efforts to a higher and more productive energy/work level. Changes in the transportation delivery system offer another excellent example of the way delivery systems evolve into using more advanced technologies.

What this equation below makes clear is that different processes generate different energy levels, and thus impact capabilities to accomplish human goals. These additional capabilities are a direct result of inventing more methods of harnessing new sources of energy to address transportation needs.

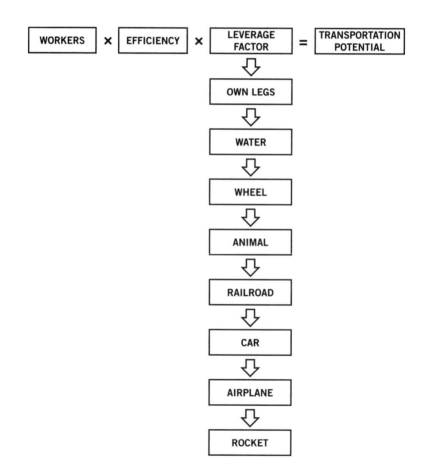

While effective training may help improve the efficiency of a system, inevitably there are inefficient users who will drag down the average performance of any delivery system. The following diagram represents the minor fluctuation possible, depending upon the skill of the worker, during a period when new technologies are not available and most of the efforts for improvement depend upon the worker's ability to use the available technologies more efficiently.

FLUCTUATING CAPABILITIES OF A DELIVERY SYSTEM

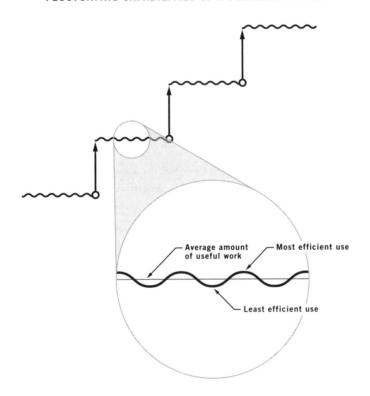

In the diagram above, in the upper left quadrant, there are 3 vertical lines that, after rising, generate a wavy parallel line like a sine wave going from left to right. The left to right movement depicts epochs in time when the delivery system is static. It should go without saying that some workers are more efficient than others as they deliver their goods and services in their jobs by using the tools and technologies that are available to them. The middle of these epochs is enlarged in order to demonstrate that, although good and poor workers are included in each delivery system epoch, the amount of work they are able to deliver averages out over time. This is indicated by the horizontal line running left to right through the up and down sine wave.

The top of the fluctuating line represents the peak of efficient use of the available work possible in a delivery system, while the valley at the bottom of the fluctuating line represents the efforts of a poor practitioner. Thus, the wavy line represents the fluctuating capabilities of any delivery system using either manual labor or some mature technology. The straight line is the average amount of useful work that can be harnessed by combining human effort with any fixed technology in a delivery system.

What is important to note is that the amount of fluctuation available is miniscule in comparison to the huge pop that is produced when a new technology is introduced to the delivery system. Thus, as illustrated below, there is always a huge "pop" when new technology is introduced into a static delivery system. This almost washes out any standard improvement that can be attained by using the traditional efficiency approaches that train people to become more efficient in their performance while using old and static technologies to support their own manual efforts.

ADDED WORK FROM NEW TECHNOLOGY

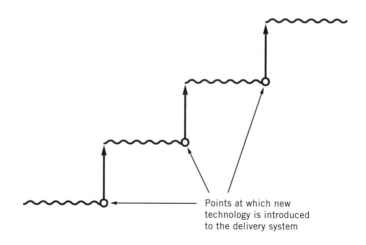

Points at which new technology is introduced to the delivery system

This becomes even clearer as we graph the earlier equation (see page 54) representing the evolution of technology in transportation. In the diagram below, we see that new technologies (a car or airplane) offer a quantum leap in additional capacity for the workers compared to the modest gains possible by becoming more efficient or using an earlier mature technology such as a bicycle.

MAJOR ADVANCEMENTS IN TRANSPORTATION TECHNOLOGY

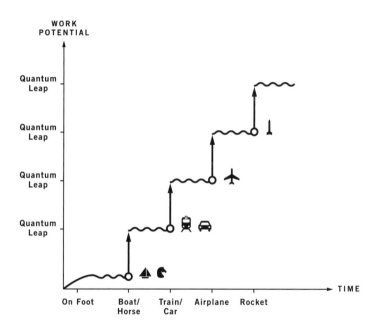

Notice that the minor differences in energy on a fixed level, shown by the fluctuations from good and poor usage, represent only a tiny fraction of the potential that exists between new technology introductions. Specifically this means, in analyzing the potential of a horse, that no amount of careful breeding, attention to diet, training, conditioning, etc. can bring it even close to the work potential of a poorly driven, mediocre car. The car will always be 100 to 500 times more effective and powerful than the horse.

The diagram above helped me to realize that most of man's efforts to accomplish work have to do with improving his efficiency in whatever processes he is using, but, once a quantum leap is made through the introduction of a new technology, no amount of polishing the previous process will enable it to compete with the amount of work the new process can generate. In other words, man is foolish to concentrate on the "efficiency" variable once a new "leveraging" variable has been discovered. Surely a more efficient and better-trained archer will lose to a rifleman just as an efficient cavalry will be defeated by tanks.

Unfortunately, in striving to improve education, government agencies, school districts, foundations, and philanthropists are all fixated on the current delivery system. They want to wring more efficiency from it. I say "unfortunately" because almost every possible reform has been tried and found wanting. However, even if there is a moderately successful reform, unless a technological "pop" can be introduced to support the workers, the sponsored reforms will have a negligible effect. Below I have illustrated some of the "pops" in the history of educational reform using the "Useful Work" equation.

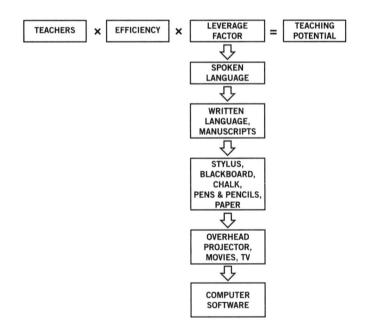

Perhaps the most interesting insight that emerges is just how few quantum leaps can be found in the history of education as seen in the following diagram:

MAJOR ADVANCEMENTS IN EDUCATION TECHNOLOGY

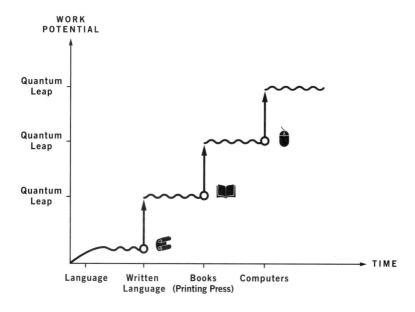

Because there have been so few quantum leaps in education, society, more or less, is still using the same teaching process that has been followed for over 550 years since the invention of the printing press. We have added a few frills such as overhead projectors, tape recorders, videotape cassettes, television, and an occasional movie, but the instructional process is basically the same as it was in the 1400s. If we were to remove books from the schools, the process would be the same as we have known for all of recorded history. Thus—except for the printing press, which allows a teacher to leverage his or her work into a portable and permanent form that others can use without the author's presence—education has become almost totally stagnant in terms of work improvement strategies.

As I continued to analyze education in terms of work requirements, I realized that not only have few technologies been implemented, but society has not understood that there is too much work required of teachers in most classroom situations. This lack of work capacity handicaps our ability to produce effective instruction. In my attempt to teach English at the university, I ran into severe problems because the work requirements were greater than I, as one person, could produce. And, in fact, for the most part I failed my students despite optimum teaching conditions and a great will to succeed. An understanding of work, its sources and applications, I determined, was the key to understanding and implementing successful education.

These are the thoughts that I was fixated upon after working on the blackboard and taking my journey through New York's jostling crowds until I ended up late at night in my home. What I kept returning to in my thoughts was that the centuries-old educational delivery system is primarily a manual one where teachers are responsible for most of the work. Aside from the technology of books, which represent a useful and inexpensive source of stored work, teachers are given very little technical support and are limited by the amount of useful work they can accomplish through their physical and mental efforts in a 6 hour school day using slightly less than half the days in a calendar year.

I came to believe that all the reforms that had been introduced to improve the educational system were only "efficiency reforms" using the available work in the system more efficiently rather than offering new technological breakthroughs to add more work to support the teacher's manual efforts. Thus while other delivery systems, such as communications, agriculture, the military, transportation, and construction, used the benefits of an extraordinary array of ever improving technologies that had flooded and enhanced their systems' abilities to perform more effectively, schools had not.

Chapter Six: Michael, Math, Work and the Computer

The great cycles of history have a way of dwarfing our private ambitions, and unknown to me, I was entering my stewardship at Spence at the onset of 2 of them. The first was a great year of student unrest; I had an interesting first spring that aged me between 5 and 10 years. It was, in the vernacular of the trade, a "learning experience," as students and young faculty forcibly occupied my office and demanded that I close the school as a protest to the Vietnam War which was escalating and threatening to draft young faculty members. As a product of the New York City Melting Pot approach, I believed that the glory and strength of our democracy depended on having schools always open and never closed because of unreasonable political pressure.

As I refused to close the school to meet their demands, I decided that my tenure of a few weeks was going to be the shortest in educational history because I was not prepared to close the school to satisfy the student protestors. As I expressed my opinion and said we would not close down, the opposition was so negative I assumed the worst and prepared to be fired. I expected student protests to accelerate. Heads of independent schools serve at the pleasure of their Boards of Trustees, and I knew the trustees were already furious that I had allowed this chaos to happen. But suddenly the students and faculty changed their mind and withdrew. It certainly was a confusing first experience for a new head of school.

The second revolution started much more quietly but is apt to have a more profound impact on our society. This was the feminine revolution. As part of my new responsibilities I had to be certain that the young ladies at Spence would receive an education that would prepare them for careers in the new society that was emerging. This meant, of course, I had to work both on the curriculum and on student attitudes towards such courses as mathematics and science.

A survey of our curriculum had indicated we were not doing very well in these disciplines. I constructed new laboratories, added to the science curriculum and accelerated the mathematics. The science efforts were successful. By the time the class of 1975 graduated, about 25% of the girls were headed toward college as probable science majors. For the first time, 2 of our graduates matriculated at MIT.

The mathematics also seemed successful at first as our brighter students were soon finishing Algebra II by the end of the 8th grade. The science department had suggested some modifications of the math materials to enable them to teach certain topics earlier. The Director of Studies wanted to introduce a new math curriculum that would include more modern math topics from the fifth through the 12th grades. At the end of the first year of this curriculum, and while we were exuberantly proclaiming its merits, someone politely pointed out that the students computational scores had fallen disastrously. Everywhere in an orgy of blame assessment, we immediately expressed consternation. The list of the guilty included, as I recall, teachers, students, parents, alumni (for letting it happen), test makers, trustees, myself, rock music, Communists, and President Nixon. Vice-President Agnew had already left office, or I'm certain he would have been included in the list.

To understand the depths of this emotion, one must recognize that, like motherhood, baseball and apple pie, math computation scores are a sacred part of the American culture. Mathematicians are fond of pointing out that an obsession with computation, rather than the general topics of mathematics, has probably done more damage to the math profession than the Salem Witch trials did to Christianity. But mathematicians are also known to be impractical theoreticians who have never "met a payroll," so their feelings are generally ignored. The advent of the calculator would sharply impact this debate in the years ahead.

In any case, I had a problem I was going to have to solve. As I studied the situation and listened to the elementary school teachers, I realized that we were spending years teaching computation skills to the children. Each spring the students were doing quite well after months of drill, but over the summer their skills would begin to atrophy from disuse. A graph of the cycle looks like this (Fig. 1):

MATH COMPUTATION SKILL RETENTION FIG.1

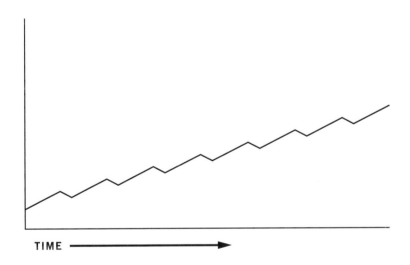

Over a school year the children again improved their computational skills, and then each summer they lost some of these gains because of lack of practice. What we had inadvertently done at Spence by continually pushing more complex mathematical topics further down to the lower elementary grades was to take away a great deal of computation time from the children. At the turn of the 20th century, elementary schools had 8 years to teach computation; whereas, we were trying to do it in about 4½ years. Note the lack of progress when time is subtracted (Fig. 2).

MATH COMPUTATION SKILL RETENTION FIG.2

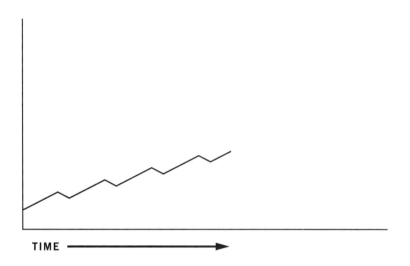

TIME

However, our new policy worked well for some of the students who had started to become bored, so we did not want to abandon it entirely. The question became how to individualize the curriculum in order to allow the students to keep working on the more profound and complex material while at the same time ensuring they kept their computational skills alive. We recognized that the slower students would need extra help, and all students would need their computation checked occasionally.

Rather than tear the new curriculum to pieces just as the teachers were learning to handle it, I decided on a more conservative approach: we would have the students take a mathematics test in the fall to pinpoint their particular problems in computation and comprehension. Then, whenever we identified a weakness, we would arrange to have the student work with remedial materials in our Learning Center which was staffed by remedial personnel.

My first surprise came when I discovered that, in order to schedule, grade, and administer these diagnostic tests to the children during their math classes at the opening of school, we lost almost 2 weeks' worth of instructional time. This I had not anticipated. This loss was particularly critical at the beginning of the school year when the children were fresh and eager to learn. Still, I hoped that the testing and remediation policy would vindicate itself.

Every few days students who were identified as having a particular problem would stop by the Learning Center, pick up the assigned remedial materials, do the work, hand it back in, and then return the next day to see the results and get a new assignment. I was delighted as I followed this apparent solution. The only unexpected symptom I noticed was a certain strained enthusiasm when it was discussed at math meetings. Then finally, one day, the whole policy became unhinged in a controlled but slightly hysterical meeting of the math department.

What had been happening, I learned, was that some of the math department members were working until 2 in the morning to stay abreast of the remedial work. And, instead of feeling proud of their efforts, they were conflicted because now they never had time to visit with their students and offer them the traditional individualized instruction they were accustomed to. As a result, I had to discontinue this policy, a chastened leader who asked too much of his people and neglected noticing that he had assigned them more work than their schedule could allow.

After hours of reflection, I realized that I was facing the same problem with my faculty that I had personally experienced at Brigham Young, and it was a simple but profound problem: teaching requires a great deal of work, and every educational goal, no matter how worthy, must be analyzed in terms of its work requirements. No amount of enthusiasm or sentimental hope can transcend the cold realities of a policy's work requirements for the personnel. I was tempted at this point to make a study of education in terms of work, but my daily responsibilities as head of school impinged on my philosophical interests. Besides, I was now facing a crisis: how was I going to be able to roll math back to a slower, manageable pace at the expense of even minimal individualization? Could I somehow salvage a system that would keep computational skills alive with a richer curriculum and at the same time not overwhelm the capabilities of my excellent staff to accomplish the necessary work?

The solution came in a most unexpected manner. Due to the backing of some remarkable foundation personnel,[1] Spence gradually raised the necessary funds to build an outstanding computer center and start a program that could be networked with other schools.

During the summer of 1974, we decided to write some math "drill and practice" materials using the template from the outstanding work of Pat Suppes of Stanford University. In the back of my mind I was hoping that we could have our children spend time working on the 16 terminals we had attached to our new computer network. Developing the programs on our minicomputer was going to be a substantial task, I recognized, because we lacked a budget for programmers. Fortunately, one of the schools on the Spence computer network had a remarkable teacher by the name of Bruce Alcock who brought us Michael that summer from the Riverdale School. Michael was a 14 year old student of Bruce's who was "drafted" somewhat reluctantly to help us write the program during the summer.

Following Michael's drafting, there ensued one of the most unorthodox and interesting educational experiences I had ever encountered. As the teachers gathered to discuss their needs, Michael sat quietly in the back of the classroom and listened. As outside experts were brought in to tell us what the Stanford "math strands" were like, Michael once again quietly listened. I went out and bought books and materials published on the subject and made them available. Then we stepped back to let Michael write his program. Bruce had other programs and responsibilities to work with, so he could talk in general with Michael each day, but the project was really Michael's from start to finish.

Naturally there were problems, but not the ones I had anticipated. Since we were located in New York City, we had a transportation problem because Michael had to be put on and taken off the bus each day in order to commute between Spence and his home. Furthermore, his parents had set up sensible curfews, and these frequently tangled

---

[1]William Fowle of the Edward E. Ford Foundation, Doris McGowan and David Thomas of the Charles E. Merrill Trust, and James E. Koerner of the Alfred P. Sloan Foundation.

with his creative thrust. Then, too, we worried about his suddenly finding new interests, as one of his friends had done when he "got into tennis." Furthermore, Michael was very handsome and beginning to relate to the opposite sex. Imagine the guilt we felt hoping Michael would fail to find either another interest such as tennis or a romantic attachment for the 6 to 8 weeks we needed him during the summer. No adult wants to rob a 14 year old boy of his childhood.

Our luck held. By the time school opened we had a math program that met our highest expectations. The program worked as follows: A student would give her name and then she was assigned a terminal. Immediately a mathematics computation problem was generated for her. The genius of the system was that each problem generated for the child was almost precisely at the level of difficulty she could handle in 1 of 10 areas, from simple addition, subtraction, multiplication and division right on up to the use of exponents. The problems would be randomly generated, that is, no 2 were likely to be alike, and the student would be assigned any of the 10 types that her age and ability qualified her to handle. Although she would have a great deal of variety while working on the problems, the computer would keep a record of her scores on each session and carefully generate either easier or harder problems in each of the areas depending on how well she was doing. In addition, a complete and up-to-date record was available for the teacher for all of her students at any given time.

We were delighted to see the intensity and concentration that each child exhibited while working at the terminals. There was no boredom, only excitement and interest. They gave their answers and found out immediately how well they had done. We noted an interesting contrast that frequently occurred when the whole class came to work on the terminals at once. Since there were not enough terminals to go around, a few children would always work on problems from worksheets while waiting their turn. The dynamics of working with a worksheet are not as inherently interesting as working on the terminal, however, and when we watched the children with the worksheets we noticed that in the absence of a response to their answers they would soon tire and do 1 of 3 things:

- Daydream

- Walk around the computer room, talk with others, and interrupt their work.

- Stand in line to see the teacher, work in hand, to see how well they had done with their answers.

In each of these responses the students ceased productive work and taught us another interesting lesson: the computer not only helped the faculty to solve a work problem, but it also helped the students to work more efficiently by individualizing instructional sequences.

Our mathematics dilemma was solved during the new school year. We were able to keep our advanced math curriculum with the certainty that each child was also getting a great deal of practice in computational fundamentals. We also found we could now individualize the curriculum still further and during the 1974–75 academic year our leading math sections, working on volume 4 of a new 6 volume series, had two 7th graders, four 8th graders, four 9th graders, and two 10th graders in the same section.

As I reflected on this interesting experience, I realized that, while struggling to give my students a satisfactory learning sequence, I myself have had a profound and definitive learning experience about the nature of education. I was starting to understand at least 3 important concepts:

- There is a great deal of work involved in education, and any attempt to manipulate the educational process must take into account the total work available to complete the tasks of any reform, or the reform will soon be abandoned along with the thousands of other experiments that have failed.

- Technology in the form of a computer can accomplish a great deal of work and thereby extend the teacher's efforts.

- This new technology is so powerful that a few weeks worth of work from a 14 year old boy accomplished more than my entire math department could perform during the school year.

This was my first opportunity to test my hypothesis that computers could leverage the amount of work available in a typical school setting, and I was so excited by Michael's unqualified success that I told my family that, within 10 years, education would be entirely revolutionized. Unfortunately I was to learn it would take me decades to overcome all the obstacles that I did not even then know existed.

Chapter Seven: The Graduate Dean and the Speed of Light

One day, one of my trustees who was the president of a university asked me to have lunch with the Dean of his large graduate school of education and alert him to what might be happening with computers and education in the future. This trustee had noticed how successful the work in math had been and was astute enough to sense that, if the potential of the computer was as exciting as it first appeared, then the graduate schools of education could begin to prepare curricula for the teachers and administrators in this new field.

As we met in the university's dining area I was surprised to find there were 4 or 5 key members of the graduate faculty also present. We sat at a long rectangular table with the Dean at one end and me at the other. Obviously the dynamics of the meeting were going to be fascinating, for these faculty members wanted to know about my credentials, and in discussions of high technology, the headmaster of a private girls' school with a background in English has, at face value, a severe credibility problem. Thus I was anxious to avoid concentrating on my credentials. After toying with my soup, discussing the weather, and generally stalling as long as I could, I was finally forced to begin the discussion as the Dean cleared his throat and suggested that I "tell them" about computers.

I tried to talk about computers, but the group wanted to know about me and kept pulling the conversation back to a discussion of my training, credentials, and current responsibilities. In any case, rather than prolong the jousting with the Dean's faculty, I quickly established that I had a PhD in English, not computer science, and I was currently headmaster of a private girls' school. The sense of strain lasted for only a moment, and then the faculty visibly relaxed as they changed their expectations for the luncheon and prepared to squash this enthusiastic amateur who had strayed into their professional domain. To their credit, they started in on me gently as they asked about our hardware and were visibly impressed when I named our powerful minicomputer, described our 7 school network, and explained how the 30 terminals were being used. They were noticeably concerned that my private school experience with girls could not be translatable to rough and tough inner-city public schools, and mentioned that New York City had already tried computer instruction in the late 60s, and it had been a multi-million dollar debacle.

I countered by explaining that I had visited installations in the inner-cities of Philadelphia and Chicago and discovered that their terminals were treated with more care by their students than ours, and that their planning had benefited from the mistakes made in the New York City project. Furthermore, Chicago would soon have over 1000 terminals connected to their central system, and they were having outstanding results. I then sketched for them what I had seen all over the United States in my travels on an Alfred P. Sloan Foundation grant, particularly the work by Pat Suppes at Stanford, John Kemeny at Dartmouth, Don Bitzer with "Plato" at Illinois, and Vic Bunderson with TICCIT at Brigham Young University. I also told them about the creative work I had seen Seymour Pappert of MIT and Tom Dwyer of Pittsburgh accomplish with children in mathematics. I reviewed the creative public school work at Freeport, Long Island, and Montgomery County, Maryland, where the districts were showing outstanding results using technology for their struggling students.

Then I sketched in the brilliant work of Alan Kay and his attempt to construct a "Dynabook" or portable computer the size of a book at the Xerox research center in Palo Alto (PARC) where Steve Jobs from Apple later borrowed his ideas for the Macintosh Windows computer and afterwards the MacBook and other Apple devices such as the iPad.

This cleared the air and we got back to basic issues. The professors opened with an attack on the economics of computers, suggesting they would always be too expensive for common use. I reminded them that prices for minicomputers have been dropping an average of 30 to 40% a year for the past 10 years, and projections were that this would continue for at least another 10 years. In the meantime, I noted that the outstanding work with microcomputers using the newest technology developed by Intel and others was going to drive the price for small computers down dramatically in the coming decades.

I explained that the newer microcomputer technology allowed as many as 6000 transistors in an area only a fraction of the size of a small fingernail. (As I write this some 35 years after that meeting, we are putting billions of transistors on these chips as Moore's Law continues to play out.) I also noted that the new calculators had been the early beneficiaries of this technology, but they were only the tip of the iceberg in relation to the ultimate potential of the field. In not too many years, I noted, we would be putting very powerful computers inside the student terminals because the new computer chips would be only 1 to 2 inches in size.

The faculty members then turned the discussion to teacher resistance to computers, a popular topic in the field because such resistance is reputed to have destroyed many projects. Here I reported some surprising findings. Using the best advice in the field, at Spence we had paid many teachers to be trained on a voluntary basis during their vacations, and to my disappointment, not one really became interested enough in the computer to use it as an integral part of his or her class. On the other hand, once we had developed a math program that actually helped the teachers and their work, these same teachers were delighted to use it. In fact, my latest political problem was how to distribute the usage fairly among the many interested teachers. During our last educational policies committee meeting, the faculty trustee group had enjoyed some heated discussions along these lines. So many children were coming in on Saturdays that the center was flooded with activity and needed clearly defined usage policies to monitor and control the traffic.

During the luncheon the Dean actively evaluated each of his faculty member's comments. They obviously were being competitively evaluated by him based on their questions to me, and the luncheon was developing into a contest where they competed for approval. They tried to best one another by attacking me. After each sally, the Dean would either smile or frown depending on the cleverness of the thrust. I wondered how I had managed to drift into this surreal mess, and I was frustrated that we were souring a great topic with mundane sniping.

Fortunately, after a while, the Dean paused and had each member give a description of his research interests. I believe the intent was to suggest to me what real work was going on in the frontiers of a great graduate school where there was no place for gadgets and toys.

I listened politely to their individual scholarly interests, but as one of the faculty members was describing his work in linguistics, I suddenly understood that my concern that education had become a mature delivery system was indeed correct, even though none of the players at the luncheon realized it. This scholar was particularly interested in helping improve the quality of spelling instruction, so he had labored for a number of years in linguistic theory, concentrating on the work of one linguist who, true to the code of his specialty, wrote with the smooth consistency of broken glass in unintelligible, but apparently profound, prose. I admired the amount of work this scholar was spending on his project and his commitment to his cause, but I realized that he had a very naive view of schools and no understanding at all of the delivery systems that served them.

Most spelling instruction is done at the lower elementary school level and trails off as a student gets older. Spelling is not a complicated process to master and does not require a graduate degree in linguistics to administer or improve. While a few students may have suffered from problems with poor spelling, their real problem was more apt to be a lack of vocabulary. This has fatal consequences for many students learning to read because it generates comprehension problems when they are unable to recognize enough words in the text to follow the author's line of reasoning.

There was little chance that no matter how hard he worked this scholar's spelling program could be very useful in schools. First of all, the teachers already have many traditional workbooks and materials to guide them in their spelling instruction. Having another from him would make little difference.

- Most teachers feel very confident of their spelling policies and have no burning desire to implement a serious spelling reform movement. They understand the importance of spelling, see it as a simple problem, and have a routine worked out to handle it. In the absence of compelling evidence, they will not be motivated to work hard and introduce new changes.

- At best this scholar's work could convince a few teachers to adopt his program, but first he would have to convince a publisher that there is a significant market for his ideas.

- There is a serious question as to whether a relatively simple task that is only performed during a small percentage of class time can be improved by polishing the way the topic is presented.

- How would a scholar leverage his or her findings to reach many teachers? The training of teachers and the dissemination of his ideas would be very difficult.

- Would other graduate departments of education accept this dogma and preach it to their new teachers? Probably not!

- His approach assumed that teachers were not teaching spelling properly. He missed that the problems of teaching spelling are more apt to be a "limited time problem" than an "approach bound problem." If a student is genetically a rapid learner, he learns; if not, he struggles and needs many trials with each word. If the teacher had more time and could stand over students as they learned, and carefully check each student's work, then more could be accomplished. However, even after the presentation, the student still has to learn the correct spelling and later review words in order to remember how to spell them.

  Thus the presentation technique is a minor task in comparison to the actual task of learning and retaining the spelling knowledge. Polishing the presentation technique might help a little, but, since spelling is such a simple concept, it would probably help very little; whereas, if more individual time could be spent with each student, drilling him or her individually on specific spelling words to fit the individual needs, then quite an improvement might be possible.

Without the use of technology, such a level of individualization is impossible. Quite naturally as we talked I thought how useful the computer would be for spelling drill and practice and how much more helpful this would be to the profession than trying to find a better way to teach a student the spelling of a word. I realized that if I worked with computers on improving spelling while the teachers worked on instructional theory and new ways of teaching spelling manually, I would have such an advantage that there would be no contest.

I would be able to track every student in real time, give each one precisely the instruction appropriate to his or her spelling knowledge level, offer intervention to offset learning decay on the words as the student learned them, and keep a rich record of the status of each student, all of this without my being present. Furthermore, I could scale the program to millions of students in a few days without expensive training and travel demands and provide daily or weekly status reports. As I compared our theoretical tasks, I was reminded of stories I had read of horses trying to compete with trains and cars just after they had been invented, or of the cavalry charging tanks. Give me the necessary computational power and the speed of light in my corner, and there is no way the standard delivery system can compete with my system any more than the Pony Express could compete with the telegraph.

To this day I cannot recall many of the details of the end of the luncheon except for my feeling of sadness that my thoughts were being treated patronizingly rather than taken seriously. Obviously, life for these graduate school faculty members lay along a different track.

After the luncheon I walked for quite a while to crystallize what I was beginning to understand in order to clarify it. Back at school I talked to my classes, peers, friends and family (not to mention my golden retriever on long walks in Central Park) about my thoughts until gradually they became clear.

I recognized, first, that my advantage over other teachers would come because with the computer I could do more work than they could, and I had already become sensitive to how much work needed to be accomplished in education. But I also sensed that this insight was only the gateway to a much more powerful insight that I felt uncomfortable about pursuing. What concerned me was the realization that the research efforts of the young faculty members under the Dean's tutelage would probably never make a contribution to any school. Instead of introducing reforms that would add to the capacity of their delivery system, faculty members would become embroiled in projects that were inefficient squanders of potential energy and work.

What concerned me the most was the thought that there were thousands of scholars under the directions of Deans doing educational research in the humanities, and this work essentially would be of little value to the elementary and secondary schools of our nation. In fact, there was a danger that they would make things worse if they failed to recognize the problem as a delivery system work limitation and began substituting new reforms for ones that were already in place and functioning as well as they could given the manual limits of the teachers. This already had happened in the "Reading Wars" when for centuries scholars and educators fought over whether a phonics or a whole language approach was a better way to teach children reading. In the mid 1800s Horace Mann had come down on the side of whole language so we know it is an old debate.

The whole language approach is very attractive to teachers who have grown weary of teaching a dry phonics-based curriculum to beginning readers. For a quarter of a century, beginning around 1930, this dominated American elementary school reading instruction and was called the look-and-say method, a method of teaching beginners to read by memorizing and recognizing whole words, rather than by associating letters with sounds (phonics).

Unfortunately, this reform became one-sided, and its practitioners developed a questionable thesis that argued that students who were exposed to excellent literature would automatically learn to read without having to resort to phonics-based drills. They believed that,

if the students were socially engaged in class reading activities involving interesting stories and books, they would automatically learn the
necessary skills required to read. As one advocate wrote:

> In print-rich early learning environments, reading and writ-
> ing are incorporated into every aspect of the day. Children are
> encouraged to explore print materials in the same enthusiastic
> manner that they approach sand, blocks, and outdoor games.
> They attempt to use literacy for their own purposes just as
> they see it being used by the adults around them. Because the
> learning is so joyful and natural, the development of specific
> skills may not be in evidence.[1]

This argument was so compelling and the proponents in favor
of the program were so persuasive that, after Bill Honig was elected
Superintendent of Education for the State of California in 1982, he
allowed whole language enthusiasts to implement the program statewide. The results over the next few years were disastrous, and California fell from one of the best performing states in reading to one of the
lowest. After Honig retired from being State Superintendent in 1993,
he took the time to review the latest research on reading and to meet
with many of the leading scholars. As an outside consultant, he tried
to undo what had been implemented in whole language during his
tenure. He even wrote a book (*Teaching Our Children to Read: The
Role of Skills in a Comprehensive Reading Program*) which reviewed
the research and recommended policies and procedures in reading instruction favored by the latest research. Unfortunately, the damage
was already done.

This is a clear example of what can happen when enthusiastic
scholars initiate a poor program in order to improve a frustrating
reading problem that is destroying the academic trajectory of many
poor children. They succeed by offering an approach that teachers
instinctively liked and were loathe to give up, no matter how devastating the data might be. It never occurred to these dedicated faculty

---

[1]Marilyn Jager Adams, *Beginning to Read* (Cambridge, Mass.: MIT Press, 1990),
428.

members that the real problem might be a work shortfall in the educational delivery system, not a bad instructional approach.

We also need research professors to take the time to understand the potential of technology so their data can guide the new delivery system and quickly scale their findings. They need to be working in conjunction with technologies and recognize that new algorithms alone are not going to solve the educational problems of America. In fact, these will have very little impact if they are delivered manually. On the other hand, if scholars can identify a number of efficient algorithms that might provide a fractional advantage in working with students, then if these can collectively be delivered and scaled rapidly on the new technologies as a series of modest improvements, they might add up to a substantive contribution to education. This will be especially true when individual instruction can be provided to handle the plight of students who do not fit the average mold. It is here that individualization is extraordinarily valuable.

Chapter Eight: Judy's Impact:
From Approximation to Precision

As I reviewed the classes at Spence and analyzed the limitations we faced as teachers, I again came to the same realization of how overwhelming the work problem was for a teacher who desired to teach each student with an approach that fits the student's needs at that moment. Because of the limited work a teacher can personally provide to each student, the teacher is denied the opportunity to address individual student concerns and has to settle for an approach that seems best for the class as a whole but is of little value for many of the individual students.

I found that a good rule of thumb is that students in an average elementary school class will have about as many years of ability difference in their section as the grade level of the class. In other words, a 4th grade class will have an approximate range of 4 years in student abilities. Students in this 4th grade class may be reading from the 2nd to the 6th grade level, a 4 year spread. By the 8th grade the 8 year spread might stretch from the 4th grade through the 12th grade level. Obviously the labor problem presented to a teacher who is trying to effectively teach students with this broad an ability range is beyond any simple solution for there is not enough time to teach all the students individually to fit their current level of knowledge.

Even if a teacher is presenting the materials at the right level for a particular student, there is still the possibility that her instructional strategy may be inappropriate for the learning style of the student. I learned this important lesson in an unexpected epiphany with a student named Judy. Most of the time in a school setting we do not notice our inability to address individual needs because the system is one we have been raised in and seems immutable. We cannot imagine any alternative.

But once in a while the façade cracks open, as it did one day in my headmaster's office when I had an appointment with Judy to discuss her lack of effort in my English class. I was concerned because I was preparing to write a letter of recommendation for her to college and noticed that she never bothered to take any notes in my class. When I looked up her school records, I discovered that she had either "A"s or "C"s for her grades. But what really stunned me was her I.Q, which was one of the highest I had ever seen. Given this data, I decided it was time to deliver what I call "Headmaster Lecture A" to Judy. "Headmaster Lecture A" included the usual litany of topics that a headmaster would be expected to present (with a stern demeanor) to a recalcitrant student, including a charge to work harder and to take notes in class. The lecture seemed to work. She burst into tears and promised she would do better in the future. But then just after leaving my office, she came back through the door sobbing and said there was one thing of which she was innocent. She told me, "I don't have to take notes because I remember everything you say."

"Don't lie Judy; You will only make it worse!"

Still sobbing she replied, "Test me! Ask me a question about one of your lectures."

"O.K." I replied skeptically. I asked her some questions about an earlier lecture which she answered with total recall. I was stunned at this tour de force. But I was also a bit intimidated at meeting a student with this level of talent, particularly since I have a very poor memory. I did not know what to say and was a bit flustered by a talent that seemed almost supernatural to a man with serious memory issues.

Finally I stammered, "But how come you only got C's in a number of your classes with your memory?"

"Oh that's easy," she said. "Those were the classes where I couldn't ask questions!"

Her response stumped me. I could not understand the difference asking questions might make.

She explained that, "Since I can remember everything, I never know what is important and use questions to get hints from the teacher by watching his face and listening for clues about how to order the materials. I can usually get a C when I haven't been able to ask questions by just quoting back what the teacher said when I don't understand the materials. I get A's when I can use my sorting technique by asking the teacher questions and watching his responses. This gives me clues about what he thinks is important."

As I digested the implications of what I had just learned, I realized this was an incredibly important lesson.

As students, Judy and I were near opposites. I needed help remembering information, but had no difficulty making sense of it once I knew it. Judy didn't need any help at all remembering, but was lost when it came to making sense. Had we been 2 members of a class of 25 students (or even 15 students), a teacher instructing us in her class would have no idea of our differences. But even worse, even if the teacher did discover them, there were limits to what she could do to accommodate these differences during a 50-minute class period. Indeed, this knowledge began to torment me because I wondered what the learning profile was of my other students and how I might be failing their individual needs as well.

- I realized that only an accidental incident where the teacher and his student met outside of class in an emotional exchange uncovered this serious learning problem that Judy faced. Who knows what other problems we were missing in our students? Had my own teachers ever noticed that it was almost impossible for me to memorize items rapidly, that I struggled mightily in foreign languages (before finishing my doctorate I had to learn to read Old English, Middle English, Latin, French and German which I scarcely mastered and quickly forgot).

- We all have such different learner profiles that it is a miracle that we learn effectively at all. And for those students whose family backgrounds fail to provide them with robust vocabularies and a healthy diet of encouraging "growth metaphors" extolling the virtue of education and the importance of it in their lives, there was little hope of helping them to increase their learning pace, much less maintain a positive view of education as they faced daily humiliation and uncertainty in their classes. How could I ever offer the individual instruction each student needed and the encouragement to persevere despite their stress?

Daily exposure to the realities of a school's inability to individualize continued to haunt me as I interacted with the faculty. Researchers such as Howard Gardner have sensitized all of us to the variety of ways that students learn. At that time, however, it was not a topic most people had considered, and I quickly set about trying to introduce a climate conducive to individual needs. But the school's efforts were stymied by the shortage of work available to teachers. For example,

- I was very encouraging to a family that wanted to discover the learner profile of their daughter in order to improve her performance in the 5th grade. They had the means to pay a number of experts at Columbia University to test their child with a battery of exams to see how she might best learn in a school setting. Their results were conveyed to me with great excitement, and I scheduled a meeting with the girl's 5th grade teacher to discuss how the school might best implement them. What a shock I had in that meeting!

  After listening politely to my recapitulation of the findings, the teacher smiled pleasantly and asked me if I had been smoking something "illegal?" Or perhaps I was experimenting with some "pills" with pretty colors?

  She went on to outline the daily schedule of her class, where she was in charge of 18 students, and then asked in a warm and unthreatening manner which periods she should cancel so she could work with the child to accommodate the recommendations of the scholars to give "Prunella" her ideal instructional sequence? Oh, and by the way, "What would you like me to do with the other 17 students while I am working with her?"

- Noting the validity of her comment, I realized that since it was difficult to individualize instruction for students in a standard class setting, little progress could be made for a child whose unmet needs were blocking her mastery of the materials. As I mused over this problem, I decided to build a center where experts could provide the needed individual support. After considerable effort I carved out space for this "learning center" at Spence and staffed it with 3 full time PhDs, 5 part time graduate students, and 24 parent volunteers who offered to tutor assigned topics.

   My experiment in providing additional manual labor was a devastating failure because even this extraordinary investment could not dent the individual needs of most students. Just as the math department had burned out trying to individualize computational skills, I watched the enthusiasm of the learning center personnel begin to wane and dim under the relentless assault of student need.

Suddenly I was reminded of my experience in teaching English at Brigham Young University to 4 sections where I was forced to limit the individual attention I could show to my 100 students. At best I could meet with them individually in my office a couple of times a semester for a few minutes, and I was also restricted by the number of papers I could assign and grade, and the number of comments I could write on each paper, etc. This led me to search the literature to see what scholars had said about the amount of individual instruction a teacher could offer.

I found that Eaton Conant had recently published a book (1973) tracking the amount of instruction that occurred in an early elementary school classrooms in Portland, Oregon. He discovered that only 26% of a typical school day (93 minutes of the 360 minutes) was instructional, and that most teachers had difficulty giving more than a minute a day of individual instruction. This suggests that a minute a day of instruction will provide a student with about 3 hours of individual instruction a year (180 days = 180 minutes = 3 hours). Three hours is ½ of a school day a year, so the 13 years of attendance from K-12 will total 6½ school days of individual instruction.

This of course demolishes our favorite image of a lovely and caring teacher working one-on-one with her students as part of a child's daily fare. Parsing this out for K-12 suggests that most students have less than a week of individual instruction during their elementary and secondary years.

Since then I have become concerned about the efficacy of any individual instruction which is given in a class where the other students can observe the interaction between the teacher and the student being helped. This school year (2010–2011) I taught a high school honors English class to just 9 students at our research school and found that when I tried to dialogue with them individually in class they froze up at the public display of their answers and comments. They were only prepared to listen, analyze, and try a new approach when this was all done privately without the possibility of public judgment or ridicule. I enjoy the thoughts of the advantage of a small section, but I found that contrary to standard thinking, students do not necessarily get more helpful individual attention in small classes!

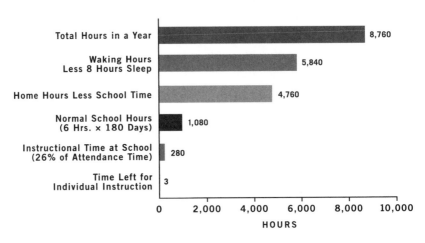

CONANT (1973) IDENTIFIES LIMITS OF INDIVIDUAL INSTRUCTION

In analyzing instructional time in general, I am surprised how little of this there is in most schools. Against the background of this limitation, notice how significant 15 minute bursts of individualized interactive instruction are for improving total individual instruction. At a minimum the students working on the computer materials receive 15 times the average daily individualized instruction as students without it. The graph (see page 86) portrays the average use of the hours in a year in terms of sleep, time in school, time at home, and time available for individualized instruction.

TIME AND TECHNOLOGY:

One of technology's greatest gifts is that it increases our ability to use time more efficiently. In short, technology allows us to do more useful work in a given time period because it increases the number of instructional work cycles that we can complete in a given time frame. For example, in delivering physical cargo the Pony Express averaged 10 miles an hour, ships about 20–30 miles per hour, cars usually about 65 miles per hour, airplanes about 570 miles an hour, the telephone about 186,000 miles per second, etc. As the graph below illustrates, 15 minutes a day at home on the computer provides over 20 times as much individual instruction as the child receives at school during a one year period.

COMPARISON OF HOURS AVAILABLE FOR INDIVIDUALIZED INSTRUCTION IN DIFFERENT SETTINGS

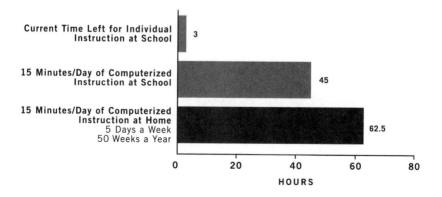

THE STANDARD SCHOOL MODEL:
APPROXIMATION INCARNATE:

Successful education requires excellent teaching and curriculum, but because the "standard school model" has a limited amount of work available in the system, schools are forced to operate in a quagmire of approximation. This compromises their ability to offer educational excellence because the standard model can only approximate an ideal instructional sequence for each child. This forced strategy of approximation leaves the individual needs of many students unmet. Until technology is introduced to add work to the system, the standard model will be unable to produce more than a rough approximation of excellent teaching and curriculum.

"The standard model" is the educational approach that most of the educated world has adapted after centuries of experimentation. This model generally includes a teacher, a building to house the school, classrooms with 15 to 50 students, some books, blackboards (or whiteboards) and assorted technologies depending upon the economic level of the population. The school year usually lasts approximately 180 days, which is slightly less than half the days in a year, and the students attend school for approximately 6 to 7 hours a day (which represents less than 20% of their waking hours per year) and at a grade level assigned by age.

The students first matriculate in school when the month of their birthday matches an arbitrary schedule published by the local school district (e.g. all children who turn 5 before November 30th will begin kindergarten that fall when school opens in September). Of course this means that a student born a day later on December 1st will have to wait almost a year longer and may end up with classmates the following year who are almost a year younger than he or she is in the kindergarten class. In some cases, then, a child will have lived almost 20% more than a classmate which will insure that the teacher will be facing a broad range of skillsets when addressing the class.

This assignment by age is the first serious approximation of many to follow in the instruction of the child. The problem starts long before the children enter school. As will be discussed in chapter twelve, there are many children who have been spoken to 32 million words less than their classmates by the time they are 4 years old in preschool. This means that some of the children entering the 1st grade will know twice as many words as their classmates. The difference will spread to 4 times as many by the 12th grade. There are also significant differences in intelligence and learning disabilities. One child in 5 will need tutoring. Thus, whether we like it or not, the teacher has a serious instructional problem that will force her to teach to some approximate level to the class as a whole.

Historically the only way to take a task from approximation to precision is to add to the amount of work that the system has. This sounds abstract, but what it simply means is that when there is a limited amount of work available in a delivery system, it has to be shared among the components. This limitation will force approximation into the delivery system it serves because of the cost parameters always limit the amount of labor available to support the delivery system goals. Obviously we could individualize instruction providing one teacher for every child, but the cost would be prohibitive.

Technology is a great help in adding additional inexpensive work to support delivery system goals. Over time its cost/benefit ratios will insure its deployment, but there are 2 other advantages which will hasten its acceptance: (1) Its potential is doubling every 2 years, and (2) its cost continues to decline. These benefits initiate a righteous cycle that will gradually move education from approximation to precision.

An example of this cycle can be drawn from military history. One of the important goals of the military delivery system is to drop bombs from planes onto targets below. The introduction of technology improved the accuracy of bombing because the additional work provided by the technology enhances the effectiveness of the delivery system by moving it from approximation to precision. In the First World War, we threw bombs manually over the side of the aircraft without a great deal of precision. During the Second World War we improved accuracy by using a new technology called the Norden Bomb Sight to guide the release of the bombs from carefully locked-in bomb runs at a fixed altitude, and in the War in Afghanistan and Iraq, we used intelligent bombs that found their targets with astonishing precision. Some of them even locked-on their targets and chased them. In these cases additional work added to the system by the technology of microprocessor chips and lasers provided additional precision to the delivery system. As we will see, the only way to improve precision in schools will be to introduce technologies that can add exponentially more work to support the teacher's efforts at individualization.

Similarly, a teacher may have a number of students whose parents failed to provide any preliteracy training before the child entered kindergarten or 1st grade. The teacher may sense that the child needs extra drills in some basic areas (such as achieving automaticity of the alphabet, understanding print concepts, or mastering phonological awareness) but other students in the class have had 3000 hours more exposure to these skills since birth and are influencing the pace of the class. Here again, instructional approximation will be devastating to the slower cohort that needs extra instructional time the system cannot provide. Because of her work limits, the teacher has no option except to progress at a pace that is appropriate to the class as a whole. Unfortunately, this strategy dooms the brighter students to passivity and boredom and exposes the slower students to frustration, anxiety, fear, and above all else as documented in studies by The National Institute of Health to a devastating and debilitating sense of shame. This cripples their motivation, drives them into print flight, and insures that by the end of 3rd grade they will avoid any situation that has to do with working with words. The youngest students are particularly vulnerable to the dangers of approximation that surface as a natural result of the limited amount of available work time in the standard school model.

But presenting the material at any level, as I had learned in my English classes, was just the first part of the teaching process. In order for students to master this material, they must actively attempt to learn to use the material; and the teacher must respond to these efforts with guidance and encouragement. Here again we run into a serious elementary school labor problem because the teacher will be unable to monitor the students' efforts. If a teacher works with 1 student, she can have from 20 to 30 other students either waiting to see her or trying to learn without guidance.

Aside from the difficulty of keeping students on task when they are unsupervised, there is also the potential risk that they will learn something in error and have great difficulty in the future trying to eradicate the faulty learned response which is now part of the brain's wiring. For example, if someone was confused and learns the direction of "left" and "right" improperly when she was young, she will forever lack a quick, intuitive response to the command, "Turn right!" After a brief pause, she will be able to turn in the proper direction, but she will make mistakes if she tries to respond rapidly since her brain wiring is confronted by 2 options instead of being clearly tuned to just 1. I have a daughter that has this left/right problem. I have a similar problem that is a remnant of my amateurish efforts to teach myself touch-typing because I confused myself on which middle finger to use for the "I" key or "E" key. To this day I continue to confuse them whenever I type too rapidly. These problems can last a lifetime because we have wired the brain in a way that insures they do.

Fortunately we are entering an exciting new era for education where we will be able to harness the speed of light to provide additional work to help children learn more efficiently, effectively, and pleasurably. Also at the same time the new technologies will provide additional support for the teacher who has traditionally been workbound and forced to adopt approximation strategies fitting a group approach in lieu of being able to offer her students instruction tailored to their individual needs.

In an unexpected way my experience with Judy at Spence and my subsequent analysis of the difficulty of providing individualized instruction for my students such as Judy reaffirmed for me the potential that technology could offer to solve the educational work problem. I found myself thrilled and suffused with a sense of hope as I realized that not only would my students at one of the elite schools benefit from technology, but all students, no matter their economic status or location, could also be given access to the finest education imaginable. When services are delivered manually, only those with capital, political power, or extraordinary talents (which can generate scholarships) can gain access to the best, but when services are delivered by technology, all receive identical benefits. Every song played on the radio and every TV program on the air waves is identical for all users. That is the strength of technology; it scales inexpensively and accurately, and it is identical for the wealthy and the poor alike. It offers both excellence and equity to its users.

So long as educational access to excellence is restricted to those with money, political power, or extraordinary talents, then we inadvertently introduce a type of aristocratic unfairness that encourages a type of class warfare. Thus only those with money, political power or extraordinary talent can go to the head of the line and gain access to its services. The general population, which is biased in favor of democratic ideals, recognizes that this is not fair and disparagingly labels the process "elitism." While this may be true, this elitism is also an unfortunate byproduct of producing excellence in a manual system that cannot scale the services except by adding expensive new workers who (because of the demand for their services) will keep raising their costs.

Miss Spence was a wonderful teacher and leader who devoted her life to providing young girls with an outstanding education. Ironically, her services were sought and sponsored by the wealthy because they desired that their children receive the best, and they had the capital to insure this would happen. Her goal had never been to establish an "elite" institution. What I found so hopeful in my work on technology, and delivery systems, reinforced by my experience with Judy, was an insight that said it would be possible to break up this elite monopoly for the few to make excellent individualized education available for all. As I recollected what Judy had taught me, I realized in a hopeful haze that this would become possible, and I wanted to help make it happen.

Chapter Nine: Devastating Data

Once I understood the implications of my insights about energy, the limits of manual work, mature delivery systems, technology, leveraging factors, Moore's Law, the speed of light, and approximation to precision, I recognized that if I focused my efforts and worked hard I might be able to contribute a process that could ultimately provide every child access to a Spence quality education in the decades ahead. The key would be software: it would determine what and how the child was taught. But if this was true, then I would have to leave the educational nest and begin to develop software.

This insight came to me one freezing Sunday morning in 1976 in an upstairs room at the Hanover Inn in Hanover, New Hampshire, as my wife Nancy and I huddled over a radiator overlooking the Dartmouth Green while waiting to take a flight back to New York City. We had been part of a group of VIPs at Dartmouth College hosted by President Kemeny over a weekend. I was there because I had requested information from the president about the Dartmouth computer program.

President Kemeny was an outstanding mathematician whose father had moved his 14 year old son from Hungary to New York City in 1940 where he graduated as valedictorian at a public high school prior to entering Princeton in 1943.

Before graduating from Princeton in 1947, Kemeny spent a wartime year at Los Alamos working under Richard Feynman on punch card machines to help develop equations for the Atomic Bomb project. Later, while working on his PhD at Princeton, Mr. Kemeny was Einstein's research assistant and was also influenced by the brilliant mathematician John von Neumann, Einstein's colleague at Princeton's Advanced Institute. Kemeny had been impressed by a lecture he had heard von Neumann give at Los Alamos about the theory of computer design. At that time John von Neumann was involved in the development of the Atomic Bomb and also was consulting on the design of the first electronic computer at the University of Pennsylvania (the ENIAC) which was finished in 1946 just after the war ended.

Back at Princeton after the war, von Neumann built his own electronic computer to expand his insights. This project inspired Kemeny who was working on his PhD there. After teaching mathematics and philosophy at Princeton, in 1953 Kemeny moved to Dartmouth to teach mathematics, becoming chairman of the mathematics department 2 years later in 1955. Recognizing the potential of the computer, Kemeny worked on making its capabilities available to undergraduates. To accomplish this he realized that he had to provide 2 things: (1) access to a computer for each student and (2) a simple new computer language that would allow students to interact and write programs for the computer. In 1964 he and a coworker named Kurtz built the first commercially successful timesharing computer at Dartmouth and a new language called "BASIC" that allowed the students to write programs for the machine.

Up until that time, very few people could interact with a computer because they cost millions of dollars to build and could only be accessed by one person at a time running a program which was stored on a large deck of punch cards with holes placed in them from a keypunch machine. The advantage of the timesharing machine was that many users could use it simultaneously as if they had their own machine. And instead of requiring decks of punch cards, the users could work from terminals with keyboards wherever they were located any time of the day or night.

By the time I visited Dartmouth, some 12 years later in 1976, the college had a flourishing program that was generating a great deal of national interest because of its timesharing machine as well as the

BASIC computer language. The leadership formed the Dartmouth Time Sharing System (DTSS) which began to generate a significant income from leasing its terminals to distant users over telephone lines. In 1965 they began placing them in high schools as well as leasing their operating system to businesses that wanted access to their time sharing capabilities.

I had experimented with time sharing terminals in 1971 for a few students shortly after taking over the school and quickly realized that they were too expensive to lease very many of them. This concern about expense led me away from the large timesharing machines toward what were called "minicomputers." These were the new generation of computers that were smaller because they replaced bulky vacuum tubes with tiny transistors and were stored in cabinets rather than filling a room as the "mainframe" machines did. Through parent and foundation support over a 3 year period I gradually built up Spence's capabilities using a powerful new DEC minicomputer that supported a 16 terminal classroom at Spence plus another 14 terminals connected to 6 additional private schools: Riverdale (5), Masters (2), Lenox (2), St. David's (2), Nightingale (2), and The Day School (1).

The Sloan Foundation awarded me a $14,000 grant to travel and become educated about computer technology and the university scholars who were developing this new field. The program officer, James Koerner, had infinite patience and the talent and perseverance to make the difficult sale to his foundation leadership to convince them to support my proposals. Typically the foundation gave grants to scholars at the graduate schools of the world's leading research universities. They were not impressed by a proposal from the head of a private elementary and secondary girl's school, particularly since he had a PhD in English.

In the end, Koerner convinced them to give me a travel grant to help train me and make them feel more comfortable by exposing me to some of our nation's leading experts. With the grant I visited 11 universities throughout the United States, 10 large school districts, 4 federally supported research centers, and I also attended 9 computer conferences. I also met with 10 leading experts, some of whom we paid to consult at Spence and others who devoted a significant amount of time training me at their institutions. Finally I visited with 4 corporations that were involved with state-of-the-art research. The most significant was with Intel where I was introduced to the latest central processing and memory chips just 2–3 years after the company had built the first microprocessor in 1971.

These new chips stunned and amazed me! More importantly they demonstrated that the new state-of-the-art minicomputers I was working with were going to be replaced by microcomputers within the next decade. The 1970s would turn out to be the decade of the minicomputer, but the 1980s would see the emergence of the micro-computer and the personal computer.

What I failed to see, or even sense, was the advent of the Internet which would begin to dominate the 1990s and destroy the tradition-al barriers of distance. Discussing the implications of the linking of these technologies, Thomas Friedman wrote a wonderful book, *The World is Flat*, that alerted us to what is coming in international trade and competition and stressed the need for Americans to educate their children so they can compete in the new international markets. The barriers of distance would be destroyed by the Internet which would connect us through fiber optics and wireless technology at the speed of light.

As Nancy and I huddled over the radiator at the Dartmouth Inn that Sunday morning digesting the implications of what we had seen, I realized that I wanted more than anything to help harness the edu-cational potential of this new emerging delivery system, and in order to give Spence to all children, I would have to leave Spence!

Kemeny had shown me what great leadership could accomplish, but oddly enough, he also clarified what not to do. By concentrating on generating revenue from its inventions in order to fund further research at the college, the leadership was forced to freeze and defend the mainframe approach because it was the source of its revenue. The future of education belonged to the new microcomputers, not even the exciting new minicomputers, and certainly not in the large main-frames that were enriching Dartmouth.

I sensed that, even though I had just outfitted Spence with the newest generation of minicomputers and constructed a 7 school timesharing network with the help of a $300,000 grant from the Sloan Foundation, I would have to start all over again with microcomputers and be free of the administrative requirements of running a school. I had a taste of the potential of software to individualize and provide efficient instruction to students in our math experiment with Michael's programming skills, and I realized that the future lay not only with microcomputers, but more importantly with educational software development.

I also sensed the danger of trying to link rapid profit-making goals with an appropriate development strategy in the decades ahead when the technology would be changing rapidly. I will always be thankful for Dr. Kemeny for inviting me for a visit that fired my imagination and insights because of his magnificent efforts to democratize the educational potential of the computer which he understood and fought for. I owe much to him even though in the words of another Dartmouth product, the poet Robert Frost, I chose a different road and left academia.

> Two roads diverged in a wood, and I,
> I took the one less traveled by,
> And that has made all the difference.

All of this coalesced over a radiator on a freezing Sunday morning at the Dartmouth Hanover Inn.

Thus in the spring of 1976 I gave the Spence Board of Trustees a 1 year notice so they could conduct a search for a new head. While waiting I organized a nonprofit legal entity and board of trustees on September 1st 1976. On July 1st 1977 I moved to Provo, Utah, in order to anchor a team of leading scholars from Brigham Young University. They were in danger of losing their positions because a large grant from the National Science Foundation (NSF) involving computer-assisted-instruction (CAI) was running out and would not be renewed. NSF believed the prototype was successful and ready for others to support it. Also, the Dean who had been the architect of the program had died of cancer and there was no spokesman for the project at the university.

I moved west to the team rather than trying to recruit them to move east to New York City. The next 4 years were a struggle to find nonprofit funding from individuals and foundations that would enable us to conduct our software development. But because of the cutting edge nature of our work, we also began to win training contracts from government and industry organizations. We developed the first educational videodisc in history for McGraw Hill, the first computer based training modules for Ford Motor, flight training for United Airlines, computer testing for General Electric, training modules for Boeing, studies for AT&T, and the first training videodiscs for the Army. The list went on and on.

However, the road to nonprofit funding was not as easy as I had anticipated. I believe I was turned down at least 600 times in soliciting grants from individuals and foundations during those first years. I found myself holding Intel chips in the palm of my hand trying to explain to skeptical donors what was coming in technology and its implications for the future of education. Clearly, I was too far ahead of my time. For example, when presenting to the head of a large bank foundation that had the director of their data processing center present to verify my claims, I noted while holding up the new microcomputer chip set, "You may think that minicomputers are exciting, but this microcomputer is the future and will open up undreamed of educational opportunities if we can build appropriate software for its potential." I knew I was in trouble when the head of the bank's data processing department interrupted and said, "What is a minicomputer?"

After 4 years filled with frustrating efforts to convince the nonprofit community of the potential for this new delivery system, I decided also to open a "for profit" entity where I could appeal directly to the profit motive of capitalism rather than to the higher more abstract attraction associated with nonprofit causes. The idea was successful, but I was to find out that, with outside investment, came a reasonable set of expectations from the investors about quarterly earnings and also close scrutiny from the government once we "went public." I had left Spence so I could work on developing the finest educational software possible for the new technologies such as the microcomputer, the laser, videodiscs, fiber optics, etc. without the daily administrative duties that kept me from this work. After a couple of years of "for profit" fundraising, I had successfully raised about $100,000,000 in private placements and a public offering (1983), but I now had no time to work on the software. During one fall period I was only home 4–5 days between Labor Day and Thanksgiving as I crisscrossed the globe and met with investors.

After 8 years of working for this for-profit organization, I decided to resign and return to running the nonprofit Waterford Institute full time. During my years at WICAT, the Institute had been quietly growing a research school called the Waterford School.

About the time of my resignation in the fall of 1989, I received a call from a former Spence parent that dramatically altered my life. The phone call from Ezra Zilkha, an outstanding business leader in NYC, asked politely whether Nancy and I were by chance going to be in New York on a Sunday 2 weeks hence, and I of course said that as luck would have it we would be. And of course after much scrambling of calendars we were.

Years before, after my daughter Kimberley, then a junior at Spence, had given me $10 as the first donation to the new Institute I was forming, Ezra wrote a substantial check that enabled us to begin operations. He was also the gentleman who had once asked me whom I would like to meet at his home for dinner. Knowing that he was a trustee of a university, I replied that we would enjoy meeting the president of the university. When we arrived for the dinner, he said he had forgotten to ask me whether we wanted to meet the former president or the new one, so he had invited both, and of course they both came.

Thus, years later, my wife and I found ourselves at a delightful luncheon on Fifth Avenue in a restaurant with a pleasant view of the Metropolitan Museum of Art where the Zilkhas explained that they would like to do something to help "Barbara" who was interested in improving the reading of our nation's children. We agreed that this was a worthy goal (since this was one of the purposes of the Institute) although for about half an hour we were not certain who Barbara was until a comment about their recent visit to Washington D.C. revealed that this was First Lady Barbara Bush that we were discussing.

The upshot of the luncheon was that I agreed that with their help we would begin a "New York City Project," The Waterford Institute would provide 30-terminal classrooms staffed by paraprofessionals who would work daily with classroom teachers as their classes were rotated through the computer labs. This would transfer the computer portion of the Waterford Model we had developed at our research school in Utah to the New York City public schools. My wife Nancy agreed that she and her school faculty would travel regularly to New York City to train the teachers and the laboratory aids. Having recently resigned as Chairman of the for-profit corporation, I believed that this was an excellent opportunity to transfer the knowledge we had gained using computers with great academic success in the early elementary grades in our research school in Utah to the New York City public schools. Thus I unwittingly signed up to spend at least half my time in New York City working on this project for the next few years.

Most of my time was spent in fund raising. With the help of the Zilkhas and Liz and Felix Rohatyn we were able to raise $10,000,000 over a 4 year period and installed 1 or more labs in 10 schools in Manhattan, the Bronx, Queens, and Brooklyn schools. We worked directly with the new Chancellor of Education for New York City and his deputies and formed a partnership with a nonprofit entity called New Visions for Public Schools which provided oversight for the business and foundation community. With careful advice we organized a panel of distinguished scholars and experts who would oversee the evaluation of the project.

Originally we placed the labs in grades 2–5, but not long into the project we had a rude awakening that taught us we would have to start the labs with kindergarten children rather than 2nd grade students. The light went on for us when a group of scholars convened in my office in Utah in front of a large blackboard and sketched out with chalk diagrams our preliminary results. The meeting taught me a lesson that left me in tears, which is not a traditional scholarly reaction.

A number of different trainers reported that the 2nd grade was too late to begin the program because, if the children had not learned to read by then, their frustration began to interfere with all of their subjects and their attitude toward school. As the Institute began to analyze the problem, some research scientists from Brigham Young University who were part of the project reported a learning rate problem that clarified for us the need to begin serious instruction and remediation in the youngest grades. The scholars' calculations showed that, if the kindergarten and 1st grade students were not well-trained, they would be unable to stay up to standard with their classes because it would be impossible for them to increase their learning rate adequately. Asking the poorest learners to learn many times faster is a questionable, if not impossible, task.

This problem can be understood by studying the following illustrations. Figure 1 depicts the national average student growth where children advance 1 grade level for each year in school.

FIGURE 1

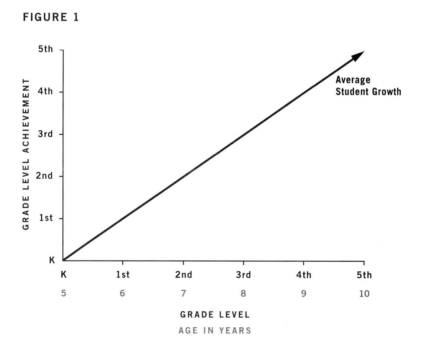

Unfortunately, many students have trouble learning to read, particularly those who are in at-risk populations such as inner city or rural poor. Typically, (see Figure 2), these at-risk children tend to learn only half as fast as their more affluent counterparts.

There are various ways of stating this learning problem. Some experts generalize and say that for every year they are in school the at-risk students fall half a grade level behind, while others measure the academic year in terms of months of growth. When I visited Chicago to study their data at that time, for example, the children were expected to grow 10 months a year, and the at-risk children tended to grow only 5 months a year.

FIGURE 2

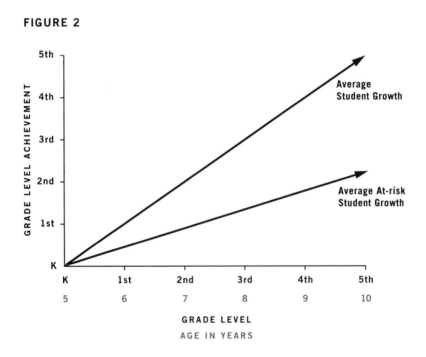

In the past, what educators generally have overlooked is the importance of early intervention in the child's reading problem. For example, if an intervention program, such as computer-assisted learning, were successfully introduced in 4th grade and increased the student learning rate to the national average, then the students' learning would be as illustrated in Figure 3.

FIGURE 3

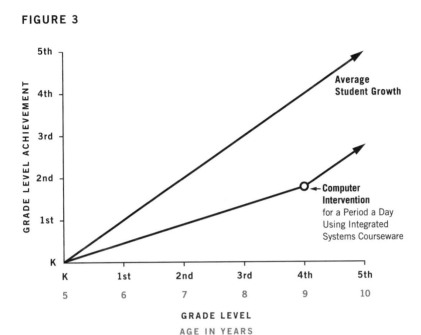

The problem with this apparently successful intervention strategy is that even though it has the students learning much faster, this intervention only arrests the students' tendency to fall further behind. It still leaves the at-risk students 2 years behind the normal population. In order to have the students catch up, we would have to have them learn even faster than their peers. This is depicted in Figure 4.

There is a fundamental problem with this approach. As Figure 4 shows, we are probably putting too much pressure on these learners in expecting them to catch up. Notice in Figure 4 that, in the first intervention, we are asking our worst learners to suddenly double their learning speed (2x) over their earlier performance. Then in order to catch up, we are asking the children to double their learning speed again, and learn 4 times faster (4x). Tears began streaming down my face when I realized it would be impossible for most of them to ever become successful academically because it is unrealistic to assume that the worst learners in school are going to be able to begin to learn 4 times faster than they have learned previously in order to catch up with their peers. My romantic dream of providing encouragement and success to children with difficult backgrounds was shattered by the mathematics of the problem. The practical consequences of my insight were that generations of children were already in a system that had failed them and more generations were on the threshold. The realization that too many children in the world have their fates decided before the 1st grade was devastating to me.

FIGURE 4

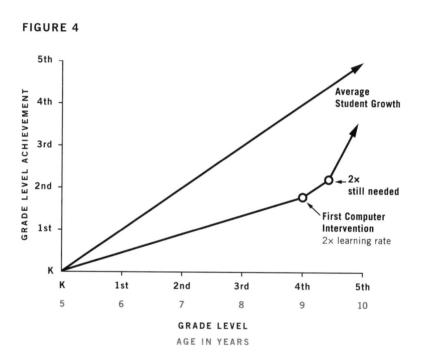

The secret to avoiding this almost unsolvable problem is to bring additional work support to bear for preschool, kindergarten and 1st grade students. This will help to make up for the deficiencies that are a function of too little preliteracy training from their families. According to our earlier equation on generating work, people can also be hired to add work in a manual mode such as in the excellent programs developed by Marie Clay (Reading Recovery) and Robert Slavin (Success for All,) but these programs are extremely expensive and have problems maintaining quality when replicated rapidly. Thus the ideal is to concentrate a great many resources which add significant work potential to the kindergarten and 1st grade in order to insure that the children stay on grade level. Figure 5 illustrates this strategy.

FIGURE 5

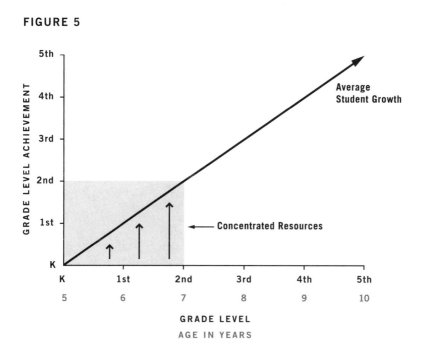

But there is another subtle problem which must be faced in order to execute a strategy that helps the kindergarten and 1st grade classes stay on grade level. The problem is that there is a significant difference between the way a knowledgeable mother works with her child on pre-literacy training from birth compared to the less knowledgeable parents who are stressed and/or are living in isolation, which is typical of inner city and rural poor populations. Marilyn Adams suggests in her book *Beginning to Read* that, while the average parent may spend up to 3000 hours in preliteracy activities with his or her children from birth to the 1st grade, by contrast the inner city parents may spend as little as 20 to 200 hours.[1] Figure 6 suggests the implications of this discrepancy.

---

[1]Marilyn Jager Adams, *Beginning to Read: Thinking and Learning about Print* (Cambridge Mass: The MIT Press, 1990), 85–90.

FIGURE 6

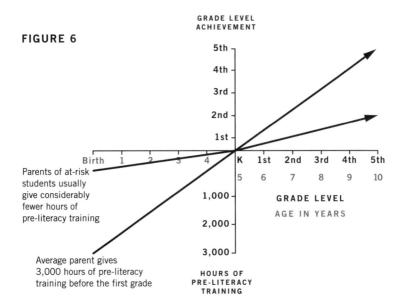

Read this graph by starting at the lower left where it says "Average parent" and follow the line rising upward to the right corner where the child's status is depicted at the end of the 5th grade. Note that this line is a function of the 3,000 hours of preliteracy training that most students would have as represented in the lower left quadrant.

Now compare the "birth" line with the one above it that illustrates the progress of the children from "Parents of at-risk" students who usually provide considerably fewer hours of preliteracy training. This is the line that shows the academic growth of those students who only receive between 20 and 200 hours from their families before they enter the 1st grade. Over time, the graph demonstrates how they fall farther and farther behind. This is the penalty they face when, at best, they only have about 7% as much preliteracy training from their families as the more prosperous families.

Reflecting on this phenomenon in terms of education, note that a school year produces about 1,000 hours of classroom time, so many of the inner city students who have the equivalent of a fraction of 1 year of training from their families (20–200 hours) are competing with students who have an average of 3 years of preliteracy training (3,000 hours) from their parents by the time they enter 1st grade and begin formal reading instruction. As the line goes from the upper right quadrant with the at-risk students back to the lower left at their birth, the reader can see that the low SES (socioeconomic status) students have only had a fraction of the preliteracy training of the high SES students.

This diagram also suggests that children who have experienced the least preschool training will probably constitute a fair percentage of those children who are not performing well in their 1st grade reading skills. As we have already seen, once students are behind, they find it almost impossible to catch up. Please note that this is not a literal diagram, but one that suggests the nature of the problem.

Some children may catch up with their peers, but the odds of this happening are not favorable. Because the greatest single predictor of how well a child will read in the 1st grade is the degree of proficiency the child has mastered in being able to identify letters accurately and automatically, those children who have had 3,000 hours of preliteracy training before the 1st grade should outperform the children who have not.

The Institute became sensitized to this problem when the developers discovered that, although they were using state-of-the-art reading software that had been built by a commercial vendor, some of the weakest students were failing to gain even after having been exposed to it. This puzzled them because the children were obviously confused when given a very simple and clear instructional item. For example, they found that the students were not learning the letter "A" successfully when presented with a screen with the letter A shown in bold black lettering with a voice saying in the background, "This is the letter A."

No matter how many times the students went through the sequence, many of them failed to learn to recognize the letter "A." Without realizing it, the developers had designed the instruction at a level of approximation that was inappropriate for the needs of the least-prepared inner city children. For months we had puzzled over the problem. We could not understand what was wrong with the presentation. The graphics were clear and interesting, the voice was very easy to understand, and yet, for some reason, this cohort of students was unable to learn what the scholars perceived to be a well laid out instructional sequence. Finally the developers discovered that the children's vocabulary background was so lean that they had never heard of some of the words such as the word "letter" or "A." Thus even though they understood the first part of the sentence, "This is the," they had never heard of the words "letter" or "A," and they sounded like gibberish to their untrained ears. The solution was to teach the students that there is something called a "letter" and an "A" before teaching them the alphabet.

Once we understood the problem, we introduced new units which taught the concept of a "letter" and a "word" and the problem disappeared. As scholars themselves begin to become more precise in their research, the information they reveal begins to clarify further actions that we must take to transition away from approximate strategies to more precise ones which directly address the student problems. For example, we have just detailed how the software developers had to learn to become far more precise in their reading instruction for young students from the inner-city families who had never heard of words such as "word" or "letter." But at the time it was far more than a scholarly exercise to me as I sat despondently with tears streaming down my cheeks overwhelmed by the realization that generations of children were being unwittingly slaughtered academically before they even entered school and this would continue despite heroic manual efforts until we developed the software and traditions of usage for the current delivery system.

I mention the phrase "traditions of usage" because, although we thought we had found the solution for the students' failure to learn in their lack of vocabulary training, there was another approximation problem lurking in the data that we failed to identify and which did not surface for another decade. This was the problem of student usage. We all saw the students working away when we visited and felt certain that they were using the materials in the carefully scheduled computer labs where the students were spending a period a day under the supervision of their teacher and a full time laboratory paraprofessional who oversaw the system and scheduled the activities and reports.

In reality, however, over time the teachers rarely worked with their students during the sessions and used the period as a break from their labors. Or even more damaging, they began cancelling the computer classes in order to work with the children on other activities such as practice time for student assemblies or as time to have the class work on a project such as celebrating birthday parties, Mother's Day, or some historical or contemporary figures or worthy causes.

Sometimes there was also a subtle hidden competition going on between the teachers as to who had the most beautifully decorated boards that were displaying student's work in their rooms and in the hall outside the room. Many a computer lab session was sacrificed for the proud presentation of student work on classroom and hall bulletin boards. We only discovered this years later, after an evaluation by a careful scholar of the impact of student usage in a Tucson, Arizona study turned up the fact that students showed little gains until they had used the materials for 1,100 minutes during the first few months. After this there were strong and steady gains that then continued on without flattening or reaching a shoulder. Over a decade later we went back and dug out the usage logs from the New York City project and discovered that only a few classes had reached the 1,100 minute level. None had reached 1,200 minutes even though they were scheduled for and reported over 2,700 minutes in each discipline.

At the time the New York City project ended and was evaluated, the evaluators had concluded that although the project showed some positive gains, the student improvement was far below what we had expected. And although there were a few implementation problems, we believed that in general those students had received a reasonable exposure to the materials, although years later we discovered that most had not.

At the time the test data reviewed by our distinguished scholarly panel revealed the limits of the current software. With this clear message at hand, I packed my bags and returned to Utah to start the development of a new generation of software which I assumed would solve the problem. What I had failed to notice was that I had deeper problems than the quality of the software, problems that would take another 15 years to discover.

Chapter Ten: Hart and Risley:
30 Years in the Wilderness

I first became aware of the devastating statistics from Hart and Risley's research when I was eavesdropping on 2 scholars during a "Poster Session" at the annual meeting of the Society for the Scientific Study of Reading (SSSR) in 2001. A Poster Session is held in the evening and displays the research results and experimental findings that have not been featured by speakers in the daytime sessions. Typically, Poster Sessions are reports by graduate students which display their research after the senior scholars have presented their papers in sessions during the day. The senior scholars usually walk the aisles in support of their graduate students' work as they check on the progress of their protégés, stay abreast of new research trends, and look for possible recruits for their graduate departments. I was staying close behind 2 distinguished researchers hoping to gain some insights by eavesdropping on their comments as they discussed the various exhibits, and was surprised when one said to the other, "How is my favorite graduate student that I sent you doing in your program?"

He answered, "I'm sorry to report that she has had a nervous breakdown."

"How in the world did that happen?" was the immediate response.

"Oh, unfortunately she discovered Hart and Risley!" he responded.

To which the other scholar replied, "Oh, I'm sorry to hear that, but I certainly understand the problem."

Intrigued to the point of near madness by this extraordinary exchange (scholars are never supposed to wallow in emotion) I raced home after the conference and read some materials by Hart and Risley. I particularly enjoyed their book *Meaningful Differences* (Brookes Publishing) published in 1995. In them I found a new world of insights opening to me as I read their work and listened to taped interviews of one of the authors, Todd Risley, by David Boulton. His interviews helped clarify the remarkable insights that they had gathered as they studied why the Great Society educational reforms were not working for the low SES and welfare families. Above all else Hart and Risley's work clarifies why so many children from low income families have difficulty learning to read despite enormous expenditures and our best efforts to teach them.

But their information is also devastating because it suggests that it will be extremely difficult, if not impossible, to solve the problem. The public schools appear to be incapable of making up the vocabulary shortfall that students from economically disadvantaged families face because their family circumstances determine the level of vocabulary they are exposed to for the first few years of their lives even before attending preschool.

Recognizing the seriousness of the problem, the scholar who heard that his protégé had been exposed to Hart and Risley's work understood immediately that their apparently unsolvable findings might be emotionally unsettling to a sensitive and idealistic young scholar.

Hart and Risley's saga began in 1965 when, at a university in Kansas City, they began working with grants from the Great Society legislation initiated by Lyndon Johnson in his well-financed "War on Poverty." Over the next few decades, along with other scholars, they found, with some consistency, that their research projects were failing to solve the reading problems of their young disadvantaged charges.

Year after year scholars from all over the United States worked on school research projects hoping to improve reading for children in the public schools, particularly those who were from low SES (socioeconomic status) backgrounds. For years scholars had claimed that if they only had enough money to initiate their new particular reform, they would be able to dramatically increase student learning.

Nolan Estes, the superintendent of the Dallas school system, who was well-situated with his Texas connections to Johnson's administration, wrote a poignant article years ago describing a whirlwind ride from exuberance to despondency as his District received funds, implemented programs, and then measured the results. Initially they were delighted at finally having an opportunity to fund various research projects they had fantasized about during their administrative years, but then came the wrenching heartbreak when research indicated that these new programs were not having any significant impact on student learning.

Nolan Estes moved on to other interests, but Hart and Risley worked on reforms for decades; year after year trying to understand what was blocking the learning of the students from the poorer homes. Finally, some 30 years later, they reported on a brilliant experiment where they finally developed some data that clarified what the problem was. They turned up the clues by directly recording samples of the speech in families from different socioeconomic classes starting about 7 to 9 months after a child's birth and kept sampling the family speech patterns for the first 36 months of their children's lives. This helped them clarify what the meaningful differences were between students who developed enough vocabulary to become successful readers and those who were not. Their findings were summarized in a book published in 1995 entitled *Meaningful Differences*.

The "meaningful difference" they discovered was that the volume of a family's spoken vocabulary to which the child was exposed from birth through age 3 or 4 generally determined that child's future academic success. Notice this is speaking vocabulary, not written vocabulary. Their finding is both marvelous and terrible: marvelous because they identified a critical variable that others had not noticed; and terrible because it suggested that children's futures were determined long before they entered school and at an age when they were essentially isolated from any external influences that might mitigate their severe vocabulary deficits. In the words of Hart and Risley:

The boost-up from early intervention during the War on Poverty did not solve the problem of giving children the competencies they need to succeed in school. We recognize now that by the time children are four years old, intervention programs come too late and can provide too little experience to make up for the past.[1]

Hart and Risley found that the major difference "between families was in the amount of talking that went on." They also discovered that "the family factor most strongly associated with the amount of talking was" their SES (socioeconomic status). In examining families' talking patterns for children who were 11 to 18 months old, and barely beginning to say words, they divided the families into 4 SES categories and discovered the following:

(1) In the lowest SES of the group, those eligible for welfare, parents averaged 197 utterances an hour to their children.

(2) In the next highest SES status, families involved in construction, factory work, and service industries, the average was 283 utterances per hour.

(3) In the next highest SES status involving office and hospital workers, who averaged 321 utterances per hour.

(4) Professional and managerial families averaged 482 utterances per hour to each child.[2]

As they continued to track the children up through age 3, completing a 2½ year observation cycle, these researchers found the difference accelerated even more. They divided the SES classes into 3 areas:

• Welfare Class

• Working Class

• Professional Class

---

[1] Betty Hart & Todd Risley, *Meaningful Differences in the Everyday Experience of Young American Children* (Baltimore, Maryland: Paul H. Brookes Publishing Company, 1995), 2.
[2] Ibid, 62–63.

Over the 2½ year period the number of words (higher than the number of utterances because each utterance usually includes a number of words) heard by the average child in each of these categories was as follows:[3]

Welfare Class	616 words per hour
Working Class	1,251 words per hour
Professional Class	2,153 words per hour

These findings are quite powerful in their own right, but Hart and Risley also make 2 other important observations:

(1) There is a cumulative impact over a number of years that is quite remarkable. By the time a child has lived for 4 years, we can see the following break-downs:[4]

Welfare Class	13 million words
Working Class	26 million words
Professional Class	45 million words

In other words, the average child in a professional family could be expected to have heard 32 million more words spoken by his fourth birthday than a child in a welfare family. No matter how we twist and turn and calculate and recalculate the importance of these words, clearly a child who has heard 32 million more words by his fourth birthday will be in a much more powerful position to use and understand language than a child who has not.

(2) Another significant finding by Hart and Risley is that the nature and quality of the discourse between the parents and the children

---

[3]Ibid, 107.
[4]Ibid, 198.

had some important characteristics that would impact the children's future academic competence. These characteristics are:

- Prohibitory (negative) vs. affirmative (positive) comments to the children from the parents:

  - Welfare Class   2:1 negative comments

  - Working Class   2:1 positive comments

  - Professional Class   6:1 positive comments

Closely examining the first 4 years of life, Hart and Risley found there were 560,000 more instances of encouraging feedback in a professional family; whereas, in a welfare family the average child has had 125,000 that are more discouraging than those that are encouraging.

- They also noted an added advantage introduced by the professional family that was not utilized in the other 2 SES groups. In their words:

We saw virtually all of the professional families preparing their children for symbolic problem solving from the very beginning of the children's lives. We saw them devoting time and effort to give their children an experience with the language diversity and symbolic emphases needed for manipulating symbols; we saw them using responsiveness and gentle guidance to improve problem solving; we saw them provide frequent affirmative feedback to build the confidence and motivation required for sustained independent effort. We saw how strongly related the amount of such experience was to the accomplishments of children from working class families. But we saw only one-third of the working class families and none of the welfare families similarly preparing their children.

In fact they were so impressed by this aspect of language interaction that they hypothesized about the emergence of a new subculture:

The nearly uniform advantages received by the children of the college-educated professionals suggest the evolution of an increasingly distinct subculture in American society, one in which adults routinely transmit to their offspring the symbolic thinking and confident problem solving that mark the adults' economic activities and that are so difficult for outsiders to acquire in midlife.[5]

They were so taken by the inequalities that they recommended that young children be given an opportunity to receive appropriate remediation to help them stay up with their peers. But the problem is that their recommendation faces the traditional work problem wherein the standard manual delivery system is not able to generate enough work to alleviate the need. By their calculations, to give a welfare child equivalent exposure to language interactions as the working class child (not even the professional class,) the children would have to be taken out of the home after birth for 8 hours a day, 5 days a week and given a carefully scripted language experience similar to what a professional child receives. This would require a sophisticated group of caretakers, since in addition to the vocabulary training, the children would have to be given a large percentage of the comments with positive feedback to make up for the negative commentary from their families.

The Hart and Risley analysis is an important and interesting one because it details the difficulties in trying to teach children in circumstances where not enough work is being performed on their behalf. This has the dreadful effect of providing a loose approximation of appropriate instruction to children who are never supported with enough specific vocabulary training to achieve the more precise mastery available to their more affluent contemporaries. Note the words of Marilyn Adams, one of our greatest reading scholars, discussing the assumptions of her duties as a parent to her young son and daughter.

Discussing her young 5 year old son, John, she writes,

Since he was 6 weeks old, we have spent 30 to 45 minutes reading to him each day. By the time he reaches 1st grade

---

[5]Ibid, 203–204.

at age 6 and a quarter, that will amount to 1,000 to 1,700 hours of storybook reading-one on one, with his face in the books. He will also have spent more than 1,000 hours watching "Sesame Street." And he will have spent at least as many hours fooling around with magnetic letters on the refrigerator, writing, participating in reading/writing/language activities in preschool, playing word and "spelling" games in the car, on the computer, with us, with his sister, with his friends, and by himself, and so on.

Marilyn's point is that John was a normal boy approaching his fifth birthday as she was writing her book, *Beginning to Read*, and was acting as a normal mother, but the cumulative effect of John's exposure to preliteracy activities will have a positive impact on his ability to read and become successful academically. In her words,

> John is just approaching his fifth birthday. He has been able to recite the alphabet since he was 2 and to recognize all of the capital letters nearly as long. He still has trouble recognizing some of the lowercase letters although he is quite interested in them.... I have only recently and only on a couple occasions caught him inventing spellings in the effort to teach his sister (who is almost 3) how to write.... Since he was 3, he has derived great pleasure from figuring out the first letter of all manner of words; it is one of his standard car seat diversions.... Has John shown extraordinary interest in learning to read? Not particularly.... Has John been extraordinarily pressured to read? I don't think so. We encourage his interest but have never sat him down for a lesson or exercise.... Is John unusually gifted in his prereading abilities? Apparently not. He is about average in his middle-class daycare center.

But as Marilyn points out, because John has had all these hours of preliteracy training and support from his family, "He will learn to read on schedule because he has nearly learned to read already." Marilyn's healthy attitude concerning parental responsibility is summarized in a lovely final paragraph of the chapter in which she discusses John's start.

> But even before children enter grade school, we must become universally committed to developing their appreciation of and familiarity with text. We hug them, we give them treats and good things to eat; we try to teach them to be clean and polite, good natured, thoughtful, and fair. We do these things because it is the best way we know to set them off on happy, healthy lives. We must do as much with reading. In our society, their lives depend on it.[6]

In a poignant interview with David Boulton who has developed a priceless and wonderful organization on the Internet called the *Children of the Code*, Todd Risley offers some interesting clarifications of their research. The *Children of the Code* materials can be found on the Internet and are an invaluable resource for those interested in reading and/or listening to taped interviews with some of the world's greatest experts on reading.

One important and subtle insight offered by Risley is that although reading seems to be a sociological phenomenon (low SES children have difficulties learning to read while high SES children do not), in actual fact the key element is the number of words spoken to children, and not their economic class. Although low SES families tend to talk less to their children, in those low SES families that are talkative, the children are as successful as those coming from professional families. Similarly, if a professional family is taciturn and talks very little to their children, the family will have the same difficulties as the taciturn low SES families.

If the problem is being caused just by poverty, then it would be very difficult to solve because the solution would have to await the elimination of poverty. What is hopeful about these data is that they suggest the problem is not poverty, but conversation.

---

[6]Adams, 83–85, 91.

Risley also notes that talkative families tend to introduce another element called "engagement" which also helps to generate a richer vocabulary. A talkative mother will chat with her baby while looking intently at her face. She then will give the child the opportunity to respond. The parent and the child will take turns, and talkative parents take extra turns responding to what a child has just said or done, elaborating on it, caring, making extra effort to extend the interaction with the child, "not abbreviating it."

As a parent, I never noticed this phenomenon as my wife and I raised our 6 children, but I have had in the past few weeks the wonderful experience of watching what Risley calls "the dance" as one of my daughters is interacting with her new baby. As Risley notes, the child craves this relationship and is sending a signal saying, "Stay and play. Dance with me. Stay and play!" And as they talk and play in turn, Risley notes how their interactions mimic a dance where 2 partners continued to interact and influence one another as they extend the complexity of their steps.

But under this pleasurable interactive veneer there are important processes being constructed in the child's brain as the child is enmeshed in a wave of vocabulary—or not. The amount of vocabulary spoken will have a significant impact on the child's intelligence and future success. Risley notes that every family has a minimum amount of vocabulary used to conduct the "business" of the family where the parents might say "pick up your room" or "eat your peas," but in the families that go beyond "business talk" to "extra talk" the children receive a serious advantage that surfaces over time. In fact, Risley was stunned to find an almost perfect correlation between the amount of "extra talk" beyond the "business" words and the Binet IQ test. Summing up this point, Risley reinforces his finding that there is no correlation between SES and a child's future academic success. He found that "all variations in outcomes are taken up by the amount of talking," (just talking!), "before babies are 3."

Hart and Risley also counted what they called "affirmations" contrasted with "prohibitions." They discovered that, since most of the conversation that went on in welfare families involved business words, roughly two-thirds of the comments made in welfare families were prohibitory or critical in nature. In contrast, professional families spoke so many "extra words" beyond the business words that their children were exposed to 6 times as many positive affirmative comments as prohibitive ones. Thus not only were the taciturn families underwhelming their children with vocabulary, but they were also providing a very negative atmosphere with few positive affirmative comments for the children (2:1 in favor of prohibitions over affirmations) while the talkative families were providing primarily positive comments (6:1 affirmations over prohibitions).

In his interview with Boulton, Risley noted the truly horrific psychological implications for those children who have been raised in families with too little speech. He notes that the impact of a taciturn family on children is frequently hidden from adults as they struggle in the early elementary grades because their reading efforts are crippled by an inadequate vocabulary. But inside the child a robust sense of shame is emerging that causes him or her to begin to flee from print activities lest their shortcomings be made public in a classroom in front of their peers. As Boulton notes, when the children have difficulty learning to read, "They feel they have a fault in themselves," and "this triggers shame." Summing up the implications of this problem, Boulton notes that the children then face "a preconscious shame aversion to confusion which decapitates learning!" In fact, like a jet engine that suddenly flames out, they "shame out" of the system.

Finding a solution to this problem will be difficult, but it may not require a huge expense to provide children with an appropriate vocabulary environment in their homes. We know that some experts have spent a great deal of capital working with young children and their parents in their homes from birth through age 3 and been successful in helping these children. The problem with this direct manual approach is, of course, the expense and the difficulty of maintaining a high quality of participation. A PhD working with every child would certainly help, but this would be prohibitively expensive. Fortunately, we realize in Risley's words that "it's not about just the things you talk about; it's about how much talking is going on." As the distinguished brain scholar Patricia Kuhl has noted, just providing conversation from video or TV will not help build the child's vocabulary. To be effective the process must be interactive: we need Sesame Street on steroids; moreover, the interactive vocabulary training must be accessible daily because it cannot be built up overnight. There are too many words that children have to learn. Some experts believe they have to average at least 10 new words a day to stay in the hunt for literacy.

Fortunately, as we will see later how an affordable technological solution is slowly coming into focus, but first we need to examine the confusion that has been generated over the past few decades because we have sought to treat the school as the sole responsible party for the success of the child's education.

However, the Schools are not the only players in the education of a child. In summary, Risley notes that: (1) There is a strong correlation between the amounts of "extra talk" a family gives a child and that child's IQ. (2) Similarly there is a strong correlation between the "extra talk" that a child receives by age 3 with the child's score on a Peabody vocabulary test administered in grade 3 when the child is 8. (3) Risley comments that he agrees with George Farkas's view that 80% of the variation in public school performance results from family effects, not school effects.

With their important 1995 research, Hart and Risley called our attention to the significance of the family's influence for the first 3 years of the child's life. They focused our attention on working with even younger children long before they start school, and on the family as well as the child. They also taught us how important it is for parents to make an effort to talk with their children. Finally, they taught us that the schools are facing hidden psychological time bombs unwittingly produced by taciturn families that destroy self-esteem, enhance a sense of personal shame, and encourage the desire to drop out of the system that is causing such intense personal pain. Learning to decode print is a necessary skill for young children to acquire, but it is not sufficient. Without the backing of the vocabulary, decoding is an interesting, but futile, pastime on the journey to literacy. While the last few decades scholars were involved in "reading wars" trying to prove that either "whole language" or "phonics" was the better approach, very few scholars were noticing the implications of an inadequate vocabulary. Decoding, it is turning out, is necessary, but not sufficient!

Chapter Eleven: Summer Slides, Schools and ALT

There is a riddle that has always intrigued me, but it has a fatal bite to it because it is destroying the education of many of our poorest children.

Question: How can 2 friends from an early elementary class leave their class testing at the same skill level in June and return to their class in September 6 months apart in skills?

Answer: The child from a home with a poor verbal environment may lose 3 of the 9 months she has gained during the school year. At the same time, the child from a strong and robust verbal environment will continue to learn during the summer months as her family challenges her verbally and involves her in stimulating academic learning opportunities. Thus she will experience 12 months of academic learning while her friend will have lost 3 of the 9 months she learned during the school year and be at a 6 month skill level, and approximately 6 months behind her friend in September.

This phenomenon is called the summer slide, or slump. Scholars have identified it as a powerful educational effect that works against low socioeconomic status (SES) students who (unlike the higher SES students) are unable to involve themselves in academic learning activities (academic learning time or ALT) during the summer months.

THE RISING INTEREST IN SUMMER PROGRAMS:

Inevitably the 3 month block of time in the summer has led to extensive research that has some very interesting and potentially helpful findings. Over 30 years ago in 1978 Barbara Heyns published a book entitled *Summer Learning and The Effects of Schooling* which documented the impact of summer learning for about 3,000 6th and 7th grade students in 42 Atlanta public schools. She was careful to divide the child's year into 2 separate segments: the school year and the summer months. This division revealed some startling information when the child's SES was taken into account. Dr. Heyns found that, contrary to expectations, both the poorest and wealthiest children grew cognitively at the same rate during the school year, but very differently during the summer months.

In a perceptive review of her book, Bruce Eckland of the University of North Carolina noted that "Heyns's Atlanta study is the first to compare school and summer learning and to study the results of race and social class on cognitive development during each time interval," and "the main finding of the book then is that most of the disparity in test scores between children from different socioeconomic families, as well as between African Americans and whites, develops not when schools are in session but during the summer."[1]

Despite the fact that she was working with middle school children whose reading habits were far more fixed than those of younger students who might not be able to read at all, Heyns's findings were extraordinarily useful in suggesting 6 major points:

(1) The importance of tracking and clarifying the impact of academic learning time (ALT). She did not define the students' learning experiences strictly in terms of academic learning time, but she called our attention to noting whether or not the children were involved in activities that were contributing directly to their education.

---

[1] "Schooling Does Make a Difference", *Contemporary Sociology* Vol. 9, No. 6 (Nov., 1980), pp. 799–802.

(2) When assessing student growth over a calendar year, Heyns pointed out the importance of differentiating the learning impact of the formal school year (9 months) from the summer vacation (3 months) because many of the low SES children cease learning during the summer months.

(3) The recognition that, during the school year, the schools were successfully performing their mission and all children (both rich and poor) grew at roughly the same academic rate.

(4) The summer months, however, provided a different learning outcome for the children of the low SES families (who did not learn during the summer and sometimes regressed) as contrasted with the high SES families (who continued to learn during the summers).

(5) The low SES families were unable to schedule useful academic time during the summer and relied totally on the schools for their children's education.

(6) The summer activity for middle school children that seemed to have the greatest impact on their cognitive learning was the number of books they read and the amount of time that they spent reading.

Her analysis also demonstrated that middle school children from the Atlanta area who read a number of books over the summer did not experience summer learning loss. Unfortunately, the implications of this excellent study were missed by most scholars as librarians seized and publicized the data as a rallying cry for the support of public libraries and to convince parents to have their children read at least 6 books a summer. State library associations all over the United States began proselytizing the same emotional message, citing Barbara Heyns's work. Her research gave them a simple understandable message for parents that valued the librarians' services and provided them with a powerful research-based rationale for their existence that could also be extended to legislatures that determined their budgets. Now they had an argument for extending the number of libraries so that access would be facilitated for low SES families.

Unfortunately, the data from Heyns is for middle school children, and scholars realize that by middle school too many children have already experienced a level of reading failure that guarantees they are on the way out of the system. Future dropouts suffering from print flight are not going to be found in the vicinity of a library.

Also, while the use of the library can be helpful to young elementary school children, there can be serious access issues for families of young children who are reluctant to let their charges use a library unless it is very close to their homes. Similarly access may be difficult for those families who do not have the time or ability to escort their members because of work or family commitments, or who might be unaware of the advantages of summer reading, or fearful of having their children travelling from their homes for safety reasons. Thus many of the lower income children lack both access and motivation to use the libraries.

Another disadvantage to this suggested library approach is that, by definition, the library's role is not one that offers specific, carefully sequenced, sustained, intense, and interactive instruction, which is critically needed by many of the low income children who have not learned to decode properly or lack access to a sound academic vocabulary.

Robert Sampson, who was chairman of the sociology department at Harvard, showed in an extensive study published in 2008, young African American children in their early elementary years lose 4 IQ points because their parents tended to isolate them for reasons of safety. This, in combination with a limited family vocabulary, makes it difficult for them to acquire an academic vocabulary. Four IQ points represent almost 2 years of schooling. Unfortunately, even children who moved from the inner city to the suburbs never recovered the 4 points in their new and safer settings.[2]

THE BALTIMORE SCHOOL STUDY (BSS):

In 1982, some 4 years after Heyns's book was published, Karl Alexander, Chairman of the Sociology Department at Johns Hopkins

---

[2]Robert Sampson, Patrick Sharkey, Stephen W. Raudenbush, "Durable Effects of concentrated disadvantage on verbal ability among African American Children" (*PNAS*, January 22, 2008, vol.105, no.3), 845–852.

University, launched the Baltimore Beginning School Study. He and his colleague Doris Entwisle began studying about 800 students from 20 of Baltimore City's elementary schools and concentrated on following the data of 1st grade students through high school, college, and their working careers.

Using Heyns's model, they initially measured the academic status of a group of incoming 1st grade children, taking into account both their socioeconomic and racial status. They then carefully tracked the children's progress both through the school year and the summer months. Then, just as Heyns had earlier, they discovered that most children learn at the same pace during the school year. But then during the summer disadvantaged children who live in families and neighborhoods where there is little access to academic stimulation and quality learning time tend to either cease to grow academically or even fall behind as much as 3 months.

However, their peers from higher SES families continue to progress because they have access to knowledgeable parental tutoring and training as well as neighborhood activities that stimulate their academic growth. For example, their families read to them and encourage their summer reading, schedule activities in community centers, perhaps travel with their children or send them to camps or to summer school or clubs where they will work hard to master new skillsets. And, while they are at home, they will continue to be exposed to a rich and varied family vocabulary as noted by Hart and Risley in an environment that will be enhanced by games that require an extension of vocabulary and cognitive reasoning. Games and activities such as music lessons, Monopoly, Boggle, Checkers, Chess, card games, Magic, and Dungeons and Dragons introduce them to new knowledge domains that help them to build up their vocabularies. In addition, for those with capital, some will be provided with Microsoft Xboxes, Sony PlayStations, and Nintendo games, and for those who have computers and access to the Internet, there also are whole simulated worlds that they can join, or even invent.

Alexander and Entwisle tested the children twice a year using the Reading Comprehension subtest of the California Achievement Test (CAT-R) in grades 1–5 and then gave a final summarizing test in grade

9 that showed that after the first 9 years of schooling the achievement scores of the high SES students were 73.2 points higher than those of the low SES students. They also noted that at the beginning of 1st grade there was already a 26.5 point gap, representing a little more than a third (36.2%) of the total discrepancy which in turn represents the impact of the family, neighborhood, and any preschool experience on the cognitive growth of the child prior to 1st grade. Almost the entire additional gap is generated by the cumulative effect of the summer months when the low SES students tread water and either cease learning or fall behind.

Thus they came to believe that almost all the difference between schools labeled as "good" or "bad" can be explained by the summer ALT slump, which is more a function of parent training and neighborhood environment than school quality. Those schools with low SES students will suffer from a summer slide and produce scores that suggest they are not teaching their students effectively when in reality their students are probably learning reasonably well during the school year.

An interesting interpretation of the data suggests that, instead of blaming the schools for poor performance with disadvantaged children, critics should understand that the data show that schools are successfully teaching children during the school year when all children grow. It is during the summer that the difference in access to learning opportunities (ALT) causes the ever growing disparity in reading scores between those who have access to summer resources and knowledge and those without them. This means that we must have a renewed sensitivity as to how important it is to carefully schedule the use of summer time for the low SES children.

In other words the problem, as Alexander and Entwisle summarized in 2007 some 15 years after starting their Baltimore School Study, is that the educational carnage caused by a combination of being raised in a poor family/neighborhood environment prior to starting the 1st grade as well as only having poor learning opportunities (ALT) during the summers, generates almost the entire academic gap that separates low SES students from their peers. Their family environment prior to starting school in the 1st grade causes about ⅓ of their learning gap by the 9th grade. The other ⅔ is caused by the unequal learning opportunities during the summer.

However there is some good news in the data as well. It shows that:

(1) All students learn at about the same pace during the school year. Neither race nor economic status appears to make a difference. Poor and minority children are not inherently inferior. They learn just as rapidly when at school!

(2) Schools are successfully fulfilling their mission. They do not need reforms to straighten out their weaknesses. Most of the problems that the children of the low SES families face are a function of their family's inability to generate sufficient academic learning time for their children during the preschool years and during the summers of the school years. The question is what kind of structures we need to build to generate better and more ALT, particularly in the summer months.

(3) Now that we know that the school works we can concentrate on strategies to enhance the students' Academic Learning Time (ALT) both in schools and during the summers.

The only discouraging issue with the Baltimore School Study is that despite the many positive aspects of the study in terms of reaffirming the value of public schooling, there are 2 difficult issues that may cause concern:

(1) The children arrive in the 1st grade with a 26.5 point gap on the California Achievement Test that has been caused by their family and neighborhood background. This 26.5 point gap is over a third (36.2 %) of the 73.2 points deficit that they will have by the end of the 9th grade on the California Test. Thus although they are learning during the school year, this deficit is never made up, and in fact increases despite the school's best efforts.

(2) Even though the students seem to learn at a similar rate during the school year, and even though the remainder of the gap can be

attributed to the summer slide, the school system seems incapable of stopping the carnage. Part of the problem appears to be the metaphors the students adopt as a way of life. Scholars do not measure the metaphors that guide their students' decision making, but we know they are not very healthy because, as Alexander laments in discussing what he has learned, 40% of the students from the project are dropping out of school. In this sense the public schools may be doing their best, but the carnage goes on.

THE SUMMER SLIDE:

Similarly, a 1996 University of Missouri study by Harris Cooper and his colleagues reviewed over 39 studies from 1904 until 1987 concerning the impact of the summer slide to see if there was any consensus among scholars. Dr. Cooper found that students in general lost about a month of schooling each summer. But, like other scholars, he also found that the low SES students fared worse where there was "an annual reading achievement gap of about 3 months between the students from middle and lower-income families." While the low SES students were losing 3 months of achievement, the middle-class remained constant or improved during the summer months. The graph on the following page displays this phenomenon.

Writing about this phenomenon, Allington and McGill-Franzen labeled these "Lost Summers" for the lower income families. Summarizing their findings, they stated that in the elementary grades "a summer loss of 3 months accumulates to become a gap of 18 months by the end of 6th grade. By middle school, summer reading loss plus an initial achievement lag at the beginning of 1st grade...produces a cumulative lag of 2 or more years in reading achievement even when effective instruction during the school year is available."

**THE EFFECT OF SUMMER EFFORTS ON A TYPICAL
CHILD'S ACADEMIC GROWTH OVER ONE YEAR**

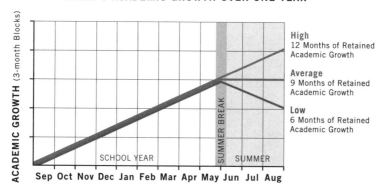

High (Continual Growth): Students with substantial effort during summer months in a **stimulating verbal** environment

Average (No Learning Decay): Students with modest effort during summer months in a **moderately-stimulating verbal** environment

Low (Learning Decay): Students with no additional effort during summer months in a **non-stimulating verbal** environment

Although all students continue to grow at a steady rate during the school year, by September, when students enter a new grade, some will have fallen up to six months behind, without parents realizing this has happened.

With very little effort, parents can determine which course of academic growth their children will follow.

The following graph displays what can happen when students from 3 SES categories are tracked over a 6 year period. Please note that while they represent the same phenomenon reported by Alexander in his Baltimore schools study, Cooper in his summary of many decades of studies, and Allington and McGill-Franzen in theirs, these data do not apply specifically to any of their findings but are intended only to portray visually the general phenomenon.

CUMULATIVE EFFECT OF SUMMER EFFORTS ON A
TYPICAL CHILD'S ACADEMIC GROWTH OVER SIX YEARS

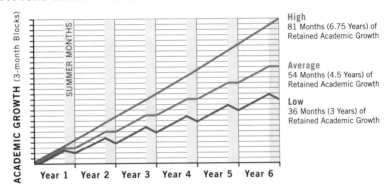

High (Continual Growth): Students with substantial effort during summer months in a **stimulating verbal** environment

Average (No Learning Decay): Students with modest effort during summer months in a **moderately-stimulating verbal** environment

Low (Learning Decay): Students with no additional effort during summer months in a **non-stimulating verbal** environment

Notice that three children from the same class will learn at the same pace each school year and still have a considerably different long-term outcome when the "Summer Learning Decay Effect" takes place. After six years, the child who has little verbal stimulation during summer months (**Low**) will be almost four years behind the child who uses those same months effectively (**High**). The child who lives in a moderately-stimulating verbal environment (**Average**) can avoid summer loss. But this student will still be up to a year and a half behind the student with optimum conditions (**High**) who continues to progress throughout the summer.

In the summer of 2009, over 30 years after Barbara Heyns began to note the impact of summer vacation on learning, the Harvard Graduate School of Education sent out an education letter describing the potential danger of the summer slide to low income families. They entitled their Harvard Education Letter "Putting the Brakes on 'Summer Slide.'" The letter warned that research confirmed that many students could be adversely affected by a 3 month vacation from their studies. For those students who were allowed only a short break, "98 percent of the students maintained their reading level over the shorter summer break. But those students who took the full vacation and followed the traditional calendar, they typically dropped 1 or 2 reading levels."

The Harvard letter goes on to discuss the history of research on summer education drawing on Harris Cooper's work, and stating there "is a body of literature going back to 1904 that includes 39 incontrovertible and unequivocal studies on summer learning loss, or summer slide." Having carefully reviewed the data, the Harvard scholars reached a conclusion similar to the other scholars and "show that while the reading skills of middle-class children actually improve slightly over the summer, children from impoverished or limited-English backgrounds lose ground. These students begin school behind their middle-class peers in kindergarten, and though both groups of students tend to learn at the same rate during the year, disadvantaged students never quite catch up. Each succeeding summer break only makes the losses that much greater and the gap that much wider."

Summarizing the research, the data suggest that (1) The influence of a low SES family has a greater impact on the children's academic success than the schools they attend. (2) Children of low SES families are helped by the schools and learn almost as well as the other students during the 9 month school year. (3) Although the schools try to supplement their limited time with the students through homework, afterschool, and summer programs, the students from the lower SES families usually lose ground during long summer recesses because they are exposed to less academic learning time (ALT) than their higher SES peers. (4) Because most schools do not maintain a full summer program or afterschool program for their students, the students from these schools suffer from an ongoing cumulative summer slide effect.

Clearly scholars have identified an important issue (the influence of family and neighborhood) that goes a long way toward settling a puzzling series of research findings beginning in 1965–1966. During this period Daniel Moynihan and James Coleman wrote very important studies which stunned the Johnson Administration and were either hidden or distorted until the war in Vietnam shifted attention away from civil rights legislation and implementation. In both cases the scholars found that the family unit was the most important variable in predicting educational success, and the Moynihan Report emphasized the disintegrating characteristics of the family.

- The Moynihan Report (1965) was written as a government labor department report directed by Daniel Patrick Moynihan who later became a Senator from New York. In it he noted the disintegration of the African American family was becoming a crisis where almost a quarter of the families were having children out of wedlock. He was concerned by the data and wanted to provide a strategy to halt the progression of the problem. Unfortunately, the report was misunderstood and labeled as "racist" so the report was buried, and research on the African American family was put on hold. At the time Moynihan wrote the report the white families had slightly over 3% of their children born out of wedlock, or about ⅛ of the rate of the African American families. Now, 45 years later, the African American families have over 70% of their children born out of wedlock and the whites over 25%. What was viewed as a crisis for African Americans in 1965 is now the norm for whites in 2010!

- The Coleman Report (1966) was commissioned by the Johnson Administration as justification for initiating the Great Society reforms for American elementary and secondary schools. Contrary to everyone's expectations, however, this impeccable scholar from Johns Hopkins found that there was not a great deal of measurable meaningful difference between schools. This finding shocked the public, from the scholars to the politicians, who were certain that many public schools had inadequate resources, and the way to attack educational inequality was to add resources to these schools.

  Instead, Coleman found that family background was the most critical predictor of educational success, although, in some cases, low SES children performed higher than their peers if they were integrated into classes with wealthier students. This finding led to "bussing" as an attempt to have the schools compensate for the family differences. Bussing has not been a very successful policy. This suggests that family background is hard to overcome by simply mixing and moving children to different schools. In some cases the family's and neighborhood's influence is so strong that at times the low SES families can overwhelm the resources of the local schools because the children are already significantly behind their peers. Recall that the Baltimore school study reported that, by the 1st grade, there was already a 26.5 point gap in reading comprehension between the low and high SES students. Even though many students might learn in school at the same rate as their peers, every summer adds to the learning gap they started with until by the 9th grade they are a few years behind.

• After decades of futile experimentation with educational reforms using Great Society funds for low SES children, Hart and Risley (*Meaningful Differences*, 1995) discovered the level of family conversation (number of words spoken) by the age of 4 was the major predictor of educational success or failure. The family, not the school, had the greater influence.

• Following Coleman's startling findings in 1966, decades of research from other scholars such as Heyns, Alexander and Entwisle, Cooper, Allington and McGill-Franzen all confirmed the strong influence that families and neighborhoods have on children, but they also noted that, unexpectedly, the schools are not the culprit that many educational reformers believe they are. In fact they taught us that the schools in general are doing a reasonable job in educating their students (even in an urban schooling system such as Baltimore) and identified the problem as the family and neighborhood which (1) starts the children behind their peers as they enter school and then (2) adds to their learning gap for a third of a year when their children are back with them every summer.

As I mused over these findings, I turned up some hope in school performance data that indicated that during normal schooling hours all children seemed to learn reasonably well and that our public schools seem to be performing their mission better than we think.

An objective graphing of student learning (as shown above) suggests that the culprit is both the family and neighborhood influence which sends the low SES children to school already behind which increases it for the ⅓ of the year the children are with their families during the summer.

But I also felt some significant unease with this comforting metaphor because: (1) I had worked for 4 years with some of our worst inner city schools in New York City and had been appalled by the atmosphere of the failing schools. I knew what a good school was like; I had led one in NYC for 8 years and then started one in Utah that has been successful for more than a quarter of a century, and I was certain that some of the NYC schools were not run well despite what Coleman and other scholars reported. More could be done for these children. (2) There was too much confusion and too little understanding of the sanctity of time and curriculum. Time was wasted and used indiscriminately without understanding the very specific curriculum objectives that should be presented and practiced each day, week, or month both in school or home in order to achieve academic competence.

For example, one fall a school we were working with had such poor scores that they were awarded another $300,000 over the summer to help improve their results. The delighted teachers and administrators spent enthusiastic hours reorganizing the school. They spent the first 3 weeks of the school year rearranging their courses and responsibilities. To free up planning time, they scheduled the students to watch cartoons in the auditorium most of the first 3 weeks of school. They also placed new-hires as homeroom teachers and released some of the best senior teachers from teaching duties to become advisors to guide the other teachers. The only teacher with an advanced degree in reading was assigned to deliver mail to the district headquarters once a day to collect district gossip and to provide a positive image of the school to district headquarters.

As I observed the school's use of the additional funds, I realized how difficult it was for taxpayers to insure that poor schools were improved by adding additional funds to improve their dismal standings.

In addition, I found that what seemed at first glance to be peripheral issues, such as the scheduling of substitutes, could destroy the best intentions of the administration if the leadership was too busy to produce a schedule for a sound substitution policy and did not understand how this decimated the curriculum. For example, when 6 teachers called in sick, instead of having a ready cadre of knowledgeable substitute teachers ready who understood what to teach, they separated the classes of the absent teachers into 2 groups and added them to other classes. Thus the 6 classes would be separated into 12 groups that would be added to 12 of the scheduled classes for the day effectively destroying the educational momentum of 18 of their classes.

Other curriculum time bombs were found in the enthusiasm for classes diverting the scheduled time for computers to other activities such as "theme holidays" or "special assemblies" that were scheduled to honor and appreciate some individual, tradition, or class of people through bulletin board exhibits, skits and songs, and even a student assembly on the topic. Teachers' reputations were often secured by their ability to provide a colorful bulletin board displaying the students' work demonstrating these theme materials.

These activities were often supplemented by frequent class trips throughout the city to enrich the students' lives. While I was beguiled by the excitement and enthusiasm these activities produced, I was also concerned about the zeal and excess time spent in lieu of daily disciplined instructional activities, or academic learning time (ALT). When I delicately suggested that some of the academic areas that were slipping in arrears might be bolstered by some modest graded daily homework, I was instructed that this was not a possibility because it added extra grading time to the teacher's day.

The question that never seems to be in the forefront of the administrator's minds (and which should be their guiding metaphor) is: "What is it that I have to offer in my school that is so important that I have the right to say to parents that I need your students for 6 hours a day so I can share my important information with them and even take time from their evenings and weekends at home because this information is so compelling and important for them to learn?" The answer of course is "curriculum and the skills associated with mastering curriculum." Lacking this metaphor of the purpose and sanctity of learning, schools will drift and damage their charges.

In an almost Darwinian sense, humans have spent millennia learning that their ability to master abstract symbol sets such as reading, writing, mathematics, equations, foreign languages, musical annotation, and chemistry and physics with their symbolic equations have the power to give their users a serious statistical advantage over their less well-trained counterparts in society. Thus, the primary activities of a school must reflect this insight, or else they are serving a watered-down version to their clients.

A NEW SENSE OF HOPE:

As I struggled with the reality of failing students, I hoped that I might provide, through software, a capsulized source of academic learning time (ALT) of such precision, beauty and scope that I could enhance the speed and efficiency of learning. The most important byproduct of the new technologies and their software will be their ability to make up for the inefficient learning time that is a function of the summer slide as well as some of the built-in inefficiencies of home and school instruction. When prepared properly, educational software is an ideal source of instruction that avoids the emotional baggage generated by the faulty metaphors that permeate the lives of students who are raised in less than ideal environments in less than ideal schools. We must do all we can to insure that, above all else, each student will receive a fair portion of ALT (academic learning time) to insure future success and avoid the consequences of insufficient instruction as detailed and diagramed in this chapter.

Chapter Twelve: The Vocabulary Police

As we will discover in this chapter on vocabulary, the construction of a child's vocabulary is one of the most important and formidable responsibilities we have as adults. The scholarship of the past few decades has unexpectedly highlighted vocabulary's critical role in developing functional literacy for our children. Thus one of the most important contributions of the new technologies will be the development of products and distribution strategies to insure that all children have a sufficient knowledge of words as they enter the early preschool and elementary years.

Unfortunately, most of us have missed the importance of vocabulary in learning to read, and we view vocabulary with a bit of ambivalence born of years of being corrected for misusing words or being frustrated by our inability to understand them. We reserve our utmost contempt for the intellectuals who use words as weapons to assert their superiority over the rest of us.

While parents may prattle on about the importance of vocabulary, they are rarely in a position to provide a carefully sequenced curriculum for the family, and they are usually unaware that the initial size of their children's vocabulary is set by the amount of words they speak to them for the first few years of life. My father's sole oration on vocabulary was a constant lament that even though he had invested heavily in my education, I was no use to him when he asked for help in doing his crossword puzzles.

Without access to a rich vocabulary, children's minds are handicapped by a serious deficiency that can remain hidden until about the 3rd or 4th grade. After this their ability to stay up with their class's reading level suddenly disintegrates and leaves them frightened, lonely, confused, and riddled with a strong sense of shame that they often keep hidden. Up until this point, in order to cover their inability to read grade level books as they fall behind their peers, they resort to strategies such as memorizing whole words and even whole stories, or trying to find clues from the illustrations or comments by their classmates. However, over time, as the number and complexity of their assigned stories keep growing, they find the experience so painful that they engage in what scholars call "print flight" and will do anything to avoid being put into a situation where their shortcomings can be exposed.

Despite the ambivalence many of us hold concerning vocabulary, my review of the research has convinced me that there are few subjects as important. I find it hard to ignore Hart and Risley's findings and recognize that they have articulated a serious vocabulary problem that stems from the family's influence during the first few years of a child's life.

One of the first scholars to address the importance of vocabulary in relation to reading was a scholar named Jeanne Chall who identified a 4th grade slump caused by a lack of vocabulary in many of the low SES families. She explained the slump as a logical consequence of entering the 4th grade without an adequate knowledge of words. Jeanne Chall was a faculty member at Harvard who worked as an expert on reading for decades and quietly but firmly developed amazing insights about the status of reading instruction in America's public schools. Born in Poland in 1921, she immigrated to NYC where she became part of the great melting pot of distinguished contributors to American democracy. She graduated from City College in 1941. After working as the assistant to the director of educational research at Columbia's Teachers College, she moved to Ohio State for graduate work and became a research assistant to Edgar Dale, receiving her master's degree in 1947 and a PhD in 1952.

Chall's relationship with Dale was fortuitous. He sensitized her to the importance of vocabulary as well as worked with her to establish readability levels for children's textbooks. She and Dale developed the Dale-Chall Readability Formula in 1948. This determined the readability of texts by combining vocabulary complexity with sentence length to determine the appropriate grade level of the reading material. Readability is defined as reading ease, and it is important for the child because if the vocabulary is too difficult or too easy, the child becomes a less efficient, interested, and committed reader. The background information she had acquired on readability by doing research for Dale led her in 1958 to publish her own monograph at Ohio State on the topic entitled *Readability: An Appraisal of Research and Application.*

At the same time, Dale continued his research on vocabulary and coauthored a national vocabulary inventory with Joseph O'Rourke entitled *The Living Word Vocabulary: A National Vocabulary Inventory.* Beginning in 1954, Dale and O'Rourke began testing students' ability to understand the meaning of 43,000 words. They measured students in grades 4, 6, 8, 10, 12, 13, and 16 and published their findings 22 years later in 1976. The book is a compendium which identifies the percentage of students at a given grade level who are likely to be familiar with a particular word's meaning and is useful to publishers who are interested in norming their textbooks and children's books for schools and parents. Even best sellers (the blockbuster hits) are normed (to our eternal shame) to be certain that they do not use a vocabulary level above the 7th grade level lest the big words irritate readers.

Chall's time at Ohio State sensitized her to the importance of working with children at an "appropriate level" when teaching reading. She was able to see that children required different levels of interaction at different ages as they moved through different stages, and she constantly exhorts us to understand that there was not one way or one method to teach reading effectively since each stage worked on different skills. In other words, she believed that young readers might require not only a different level of vocabulary but also a different instructional approach than the more mature students. For example, when they were young students, they might need training in phonics, but when they were older, they might need instruction in fluency and comprehension. Her views were codified into 6 stages of childhood reading development and published in a book, the *Stages of Reading Development (1983)*.

Her calm assumption identifying the necessary and different stages through which a child evolves from preschool through the college years was developed even as the great reading war between "phonics" and "whole language" advocates was swirling about her.

In 1955, Rudolph Flesch's wildly popular book *Why Johnny Can't Read- and What You Can Do About It* burst onto the American scene. Flesch argued that reading was best taught by breaking words into phonics, rather than relying on "look-say" strategies (what we would call today "Whole Language"). In 1961, the Carnegie Corporation of New York gave Chall a grant in order to study the research data and establish which of the 2 approaches was the most effective.

She spent a few years reviewing the data, visiting classrooms, analyzing textbooks, talking to experts, and interviewing teachers. In 1967 after carefully digesting the data, she published her findings in a book called *Learning to Read: The Great Debate*.

Jeanne Chall's findings generally supported Flesch's phonics position, but her sophisticated understanding of the stages of learning that children go through kept her from agreeing that there was only one way to teach beginning readers. As Diane Ravitch notes, "she concluded that no single method had completely solved the problems of teaching reading; some methods were better than others, but none was a panacea."[1] In her research, according to Ravitch, Chall discovered that

> Teachers who had been trained since the 1930s had never learned to teach phonics and were likely to fall back on what they knew best, which was the look-say method.
> Chall found that from 1930 on until the early 1960s, there was a pervasive professional consensus on the best way

---

[1] Diane Ravitch, et al, "A Tribute to Jeanne Chall," *American Educator* 25 (1): 16–23.

to teach reading. This consensus de-emphasized the use of phonics and concentrated on teaching children to recognize whole words and sentences. It stressed silent reading, rather than oral reading (oral reading was associated with phonics because it demonstrated the child's knowledge of the sounds of letters and syllables). Children were encouraged to identify words 'at sight' by referring to pictures and context clues; the sight vocabulary was carefully controlled and repeated often in the primaries. While phonics was not necessarily banned, it was relegated to a minor role in learning to read.

This orthodoxy, Chall discovered, was not supported by research. In reviewing reading research from 1912 to 1965, Chall found that the studies of beginning readers over the decades clearly supported decoding. Early decoding, she found, not only produced better word recognition and spelling, but also made it easier for the child eventually to read with understanding. The code emphasis method, she wrote, was especially effective for children of lower socioeconomic status who were not likely to live in homes surrounded with books or with adults who could help them learn to read. For a beginning reader, she found, knowledge of letters and sounds had more influence on reading achievement than the child's tested mental ability or IQ.

At the same time Chall was careful not to overemphasize the use of phonics (which she found critically important in the students' early years) as the sole solution for effective reading instruction. Recall that she had found 6 distinct stages in learning to read, which she labeled phases 0–5. The phonics or decoding years were assigned to level 1 which traditionally included grades 1 and 2 but did not address other skills such as fluency, vocabulary, and comprehension that the child would have to master in order to become a competent reader. In fact, she was concerned that if phonics were overemphasized and treated as the primary or sole approach to reading that there would be an intellectual backlash against phonics.

Her caution and prediction were uncannily accurate. Unfortunately this is precisely what happened as Whole Language swept back in and again became the dominant teaching method during the 1980s. Ironically, the prophet was blamed for the prophecy, and for a couple of decades Chall was vilified and attacked as a purveyor of a conservative and intellectually untenable position. Before her death in 1999, however, she was fortunate enough to see her position accepted. By the year 2000, a 5 stage process that was less explicit by grade level than hers became the generally accepted norm and includes (1) Phonemic awareness, (2) Phonics, (3) Fluency, (4) Vocabulary, and (5) Comprehension.

In the ongoing furor of the reading wars, many people ignored Chall's critical finding relating to what she called "the 4th grade slump" as part of stage 3 in her 6 stage development reading model (stages 0–5). Her "0" stage is prereading. Then stages 1 and 2 (grades 1–3) relate to learning the letters, their sound-spelling relationships, and then learning decoding and fluency.

Stage 3 (grades 4 through 8) represents a critical transition for children as they move from "learning to read" to "reading to learn." Up through the 3rd grade children are "learning to read" after which they must transition to "reading to learn." These are far more than attractive phrases, for they clarify that after students have learned to read, that reading becomes an important tool for their future learning. In fact it will become their most important tool and gateway to future learning because for many of them it will be their only tool for advancing their vocabulary and knowledge of various subjects and disciplines, partly because there frequently is no other source of new vocabulary words in their lean home and school environments.

Chall discovered that many low SES students face a "4th grade slump" where they stop advancing in certain critical reading skills. The first casualty is in "word meaning" or vocabulary. "Our population seemed to do well on measures of basic language abilities through the 3rd grade. After the 3rd grade, they began to decelerate firsthand knowledge of the meanings of words…especially the less common, more academic words found in books used in the intermediate and upper elementary grades and higher…. By grade 11, their reading scores were in the 25th percentile considerably below their achievement in grades 4 through 7."[2]

Here was the Hart and Risley time bomb exploding! Those students who had started with an inadequate vocabulary were able to function reasonably well in the early elementary grades without having this vocabulary deficiency impact their learning. The actual vocabulary in the books the students use while learning to decode is very simple, but by the 3rd grade the serious reading begins. Here we can see the validity of Chall's warning that only using phonics to develop excellent decoding skills is not sufficient. In order to transition into comprehension the children need also a robust academic vocabulary in addition to their decoding skills.

Andy Biemiller is a professor emeritus of reading at University of Toronto in Canada who worked closely with Chall during the last 2 decades of her life. About twice a year he would take a day or 2 and visit with her, and they would compare their mutual insights on the importance of vocabulary. He writes, "Both of us had come to the conclusion that vocabulary growth was inadequately addressed in current educational curricula, especially in the elementary and preschool years."[3] What they noted was that, over time, the lack of a robust vocabulary continued to be damaging even to the children who had learned to decode successfully. As Marilyn Adams notes, although learning to decode with phonics is "necessary, the problem is that phonics is not sufficient," and vocabulary is "very important for sight-word acquisition; yet it is still more important to understanding and learning."[4] Gradually Biemiller and others such as Isabel Beck began to quantify the specifics of the children's vocabulary world and look for a way that could address the Hart and Risley conundrum with the help of insights from other reading scholars.

---

[2]Jeanne S. Chall, Stages of Reading Development (2nd ed.) Fort Worth, Texas: Harcourt Brace, 1996.
[3]From a personal conversation with Andrew Biemiller, July, 2010.
[4]Marilyn Jager Adams, "The Limits of the Self-Teaching Hypothesis," in Susan B. Neuman, Educating The Other America, Baltimore: Paul H. Brookes Publishing Company, 2008, pp.277–300.

Vocabulary has been a prickly issue for many scholars because they recognize that children on their own learn about a 1000–3000 new root words a year. A root word is a word whose core meaning and form can be used to generate many related forms of the word, a word that can generate additional sets of words by adding affixes (pre and post suffixes such as pre- or -ing) or even in the middle. "Affixation is, thus, the linguistic process speakers use to form new words by adding sounds (affixes) at the beginning, the middle, or the end of words" (Wikipedia).

For example, the root word "bear" is different than the derivative word "bears" which is a plural form that suggests there's more than one bear present. They are separate words because there is a critical difference between one bear and a number of bears. Your life may depend on recognizing the plural form.

When my daughter shouted to me as a bear tore a hole with its paw through my screen door in the wilds of Vermont to get at the birdseed stored in my bedroom, I quickly changed my planned counterattack when she mentioned that there were "bears" involved, not just a "bear." My new strategy included putting down the chainsaw I was trying to get started and running madly, slamming doors behind me. Who would have thought that my humble effort to feed the lovely and harmless birds would lead to such a catastrophe? Here is further proof of the great credo that "no good deed goes unpunished."

Scholars have been reluctant to overemphasize the teaching of vocabulary because it seems futile to teach a few words a day when the schools are open less than half the days in the year and the students will quickly forget their word lists unless by chance they are exposed to them frequently in the months ahead. One vocabulary scholar from Pittsburgh, Margaret McKeown, suggests it takes a minimum of 12 exposures to the same word to solidify it into our personal lexicon or internal dictionary. But even beyond these problems, there is also the problem of establishing which words the students should learn first to help build a personal lexicon which includes the words they will most likely encounter at their age and in their settings to help them cement a vocabulary through regular exposure to most of the words. At best such a program would help the students retain either tens or hundreds of words by the end of a school year when thousands are needed.

Biemiller estimates that, by the end of the 2nd grade, the advanced students know about 8,000 root words, the average student knows about 6,000 root words, and the lower performing students know only about 4,000 root words. The core of his concern relates to the lower performing students who are now 2,000 words behind the average as they enter the 3rd grade. Since students generally learn about 1,000 words a year, this means that the lower performing children are 2 years behind the average students and 4 years behind the high performing students who are accelerating their knowledge.

This has left scholars wondering how, during the K-3 years in school, they can design a program that will teach the lower performing students 2000 new words to keep them on track academically and avoid Chall's 4th grade slump. Assuming that they will retain only about 25% of the words they are taught directly (which is at the high end of most research findings), this means that every day of a school year from kindergarten through the 3rd grade they would have to be successfully taught more than 11 new words. Teachers are willing to spend 30 minutes a day trying out different strategies to teach vocabulary to the children during a research trial, but they find the time commitment and the organizational efforts to handle almost 2,000 new words a year a logistical nightmare and are quick to drop the project once the trial is over.

Unfortunately, although there is a clear understanding of the importance of teaching vocabulary to aid comprehension, there is no simple way of accomplishing this goal. Some fortunate children have their vocabularies enriched naturally at home, and in many cases they are being encouraged by their parents and peers to embark on a reading binge that starts to accelerate their vocabulary and knowledge skills in a righteous cycle that produces what scholars have labeled the Matthew Effect.

In 1983 Walberg and Tsai, after reviewing many studies (conducting what is called a meta-analysis), discovered an interesting effect about learning which they called the "Matthew Effect" from the scripture in Matthew 25:29 which reads: "For unto every one that hath shall be given, and he shall have abundance: but from him that hath not shall be taken away even that which he hath." In 1985 Stanovich published an important study[5] that applied Walberg's Matthew Effect to reading. Stanovich found that, like the parable in Matthew in the New Testament, those who are raised in a rich word environment where they are exposed to millions of vocabulary words more per year than their peers in poverty (11 million to 3 million) statistically learn to decode, read fluently, and achieve comprehension years ahead of their counterparts. Stanovich reported that the practical consequence of this accelerating ability to read was that some students were beginning to read many millions of words a year while others were limited to as few as 100,000 as they struggled to achieve fluency in their decoding.

The discouraging implications of Stanovich's findings are that children seem to fall into 2 categories: either they start an acceleration of learning which naturally extends their exposure to vocabulary, fluency, and comprehension, or they flatten their learning trajectory and subsequently dwindle in motivation and competency. Many of the dwindlers then become the dropouts. Thus, independently of Chall's 4th grade slump insights, newer scholars have verified the identical vocabulary problem from different sets of data and assumptions.

Even though the students learned to decode, they were already too far behind in their oral vocabulary or store of words. Recall that in order to recognize a decoded word, the child has to already have it in his or her oral vocabulary. As Biemiller describes it, one of the problems of teaching vocabulary is the necessity of having "heard words" before learning to decode them. In fact he argues "If you haven't heard a word, it's unlikely that you'll learn it." This means that if families are unable to provide a rich vocabulary for their children at home or in their neighborhoods that only books or the teachers and the school community are left to teach the students these words as part of the learning process.

---

[5] Keith Stanovich, "Matthew Effects in Reading: Some consequences of individual differences in the acquisition of literacy," *Reading Research Quarterly,* Fall 1986 XX14 pp. 360–406.

In 2008 Marilyn Adams also addressed the complexity of trying to teach children vocabulary. Adams is one of the most influential scholars in the history of American reading education. Her book *Beginning to Read* (1990) is a brilliant summary of the latest reading research which calls attention to the importance of phonics as part of a balanced instructional approach and offers appropriate warnings against blindly following a straight "whole language" approach.

In addition to documenting a new frontier of educational research, Marilyn Adams also served the government in a number of roles on influential panels, developed an outstanding curriculum (Open Court) which modeled her research findings, served on a number of professional boards, conducted research on speech recognition for children at Bolt, Beranek, and Newman, was chief scientist for the development of reading products (Soliloquy), taught classes at an Ivy-League college (Brown), is the Senior Literary Advisor for PBS's *Between the Lions,* was the senior author of a literacy assessment kit, *Fox in a Box,* and was the lead design consultant for the Waterford Institute as it developed its *Early Reading Program* for computer-based instruction.

Adams also helped inaugurate a successful reading revolution at the early elementary level and now is concerned with moving from phonemic awareness and phonics to fluency, vocabulary and comprehension. In a subsection (entitled PHONICS IS NECESSARY BUT NOT SUFFICIENT) in one of her articles,[6] she rejoices in the importance of phonics in contributing to decoding automaticity.

> Decoding automaticity is rooted in the reader's cumulative knowledge of spelling patterns and their mappings to speech correspondences; in effect, this complex of knowledge provides a support structure by which nearly **every new word is partly learned already**.
> Although the most obvious benefit of having learned to decode may be that it enables readers to sound out the occasional unknown word they encounter in print, it is not

---

[6]Marilyn Jager Adams in Neuman's *Educating The Other America,* pp 287–288.

the most important benefit beyond the beginning stages. Instead, the most pervasive and invaluable benefit of phonics is that, through experience, it creates the infrastructure in memory that enables readers to identify new words with ease and to retain them distinctly and enduringly as sight words. Phonics provides the infrastructure for acquiring sight words, and, reciprocally, the acquisition of many, many sight words enriches that infrastructure and affords decoding automaticity.

But Dr. Adams believes that, in order to read fluently and with comprehension, the student's vocabulary must expand, and assuming that the child is restricted to the vocabulary in his home and neighborhood, this will probably only happen in 1 of 2 ways: the students will be taught vocabulary directly by their teachers, or the students will begin to read extensively on their own and become acquainted with a larger pool of words.

Unfortunately, a direct teaching approach has some limitations for children in lean vocabulary settings. As Adams notes, Nation and Ware's 1997 study estimates that only 4,000 basic word families account for 97% of oral language." At first this statistic sounds a bit hopeful. After all, mastering 4,000 words doesn't sound like a prohibitively difficult task. But a more thorough consideration suggests many children will be limited to hearing only a minor subset of vocabulary (the 4,000 words) in their homes, from their friends, and from TV right up through high school. Thus Nagy and Anderson (1984) estimate that the number of distinctly meaningful words expected of the average 12th grader may actually be closer to 40,000, or "10 times more than needed for—or available to be learned from— typical oral discourse."

Another even more sobering statistic is the estimate that the body of children's literature written for grades 1–8 includes over 600,000 different words. Obviously many of the children will discover a plethora of words that they cannot recognize, and this leads to comprehension problems: "The prospect of inferring a word's meaning from context depends on understanding the context itself, and research shows that adequate comprehension of a text depends on understanding at least 98% of its running words." In fact, "The actual probability of learning the meaning of any new word through reading is quite small in any case." As Anderson (1996) writes, "The overall likelihood ranged from better than 1 in 10 when children were reading easy narratives to near zero when they were reading difficult expositions."

Although, at first glance, neither of the approaches (learning vocabulary through direct teaching or by reading broadly with an inadequate vocabulary) is without problems, scholars are now investigating a series of approaches that may help solve this vocabulary and reading comprehension problem. Some of their suggestions are:

(1) Begin serious vocabulary instruction as early as possible in the preschool or early primary years so the children are ready to learn to read from the time they start kindergarten. Toward this end, according to Biemiller there should be a teacher-centered effort to promote vocabulary development, especially in the kindergarten and early primary years. In arguing the case for direct vocabulary instruction early in a child's educational career, Biemiller has noted that Cunningham and Stanovich have reported that "vocabulary assessed in grade 1 predicts more than 30% of grade 11 reading comprehension" which clearly signals its importance. Unfortunately, as Cantalini reports in another study, vocabulary acquisition by children in school in the K-2 years is practically non-existent. He bases his claim on findings that young 1st graders have about the same vocabulary as older kindergarten children, and the same results are found also for the 2nd grade. This suggests that preschools and the early primary elementary schools should include direct and specific vocabulary instruction.

(2) The key point to understand here is that, although we cannot assign most words to a specific age, we can assign a group of words as the ones that children are most likely to encounter at any given age from frequency studies of both oral and written language.

I like to think of a child's (or indeed anyone's) vocabulary as a vocabulary cloud that he carries with him, almost like the voice bubble in a comic strip, where the size and density of the cloud's particles represent the size of the individual's current vocabulary. Biemiller's important point here is that most children's clouds grow in reasonably predictive sequence in the same order, which means that word lists and literature can be developed to fit each age range. This is a comforting thought when we consider that the total English vocabulary is approaching a million words and growing more each year.

(3) There appears to be a critical period in the preschool and early primary years when the size of children's vocabulary is not too great and where it is possible to directly teach enough oral words to keep the children close enough together in order to avoid the vocabulary crash and burn crisis. There are a few positive facts to support this hope. They include:

- We know within a manageable number what words these children should know at every grade level within a word cloud of 1,000–3,000 words. In other words, there is a predictable sequence of words they are ready to learn, and we can highlight them in our instruction.

- We have learned how to teach these oral words through techniques developed in various research projects. Scholars such as Steven Stahl, P. David Pearson, I.S.P. Nation, Linnea Ehri, Isabel Beck, Margaret McKeown, Linda Kucan and Andy Biemiller have successfully developed strategies to teach elementary children vocabulary.

Isabel Beck has been a persuasive champion in articulating the importance of offering the students a "rich" instructional vocabulary sequence as part of their daily fare in schools. Early in her book *Bringing Words to Life* she notes that:

The practical problem is that there are profound differences in vocabulary knowledge among learners from different ability or social economic (SES) groups from toddlers through high school. Consider that:

- First grade children from higher SES groups knew about twice as many words as lower SES children (Graves, Brunetti, and Slater, 1982; Graves and Slater, (1987).
- High school seniors near the top of their class knew about 4 times as many words as their lower performing classmates. (Smith, 1941).
- High-knowledge 3rd graders had a vocabulary equal to the lowest performing 12th graders (Smith, 1941).

Most chilling, however, is the finding that once established, such differences appear difficult to ameliorate (Biemiller, 1999; Hart and Risley, 1995). This is clearly very bad news! But to put it in perspective, we need to consider the present situation of vocabulary instruction in the schools. To sum up that situation—there isn't much. All the available evidence indicates that there is little emphasis on the acquisition of vocabulary in school curricula (Biemiller, 2001; Scott, Jamieson, and Asselin, 1998; Watts, 1995). That may sound like bad news, too, but there is an upside. That is, the fact that early differences in vocabulary remain through the school years is understandable if little is being done to change that situation during the school years. So, perhaps it is not so much the case that those differences cannot be changed, but rather that little has been done to focus on making them change. Thus taking on the task of providing effective vocabulary instruction is a very high priority for our educational system. And it is my position that the operative principle for the orientation of that instruction is that it be robust—vigorous, strong, and powerful in effect. A robust approach to vocabulary involves directly explaining the meanings of words along with thought-provoking, playful, and interactive follow-up.[7]

Just as Chall was greatly influenced by Dale's interest in vocabulary and his sense of dividing learning into stages of development, so Beck notes the validity of Dale's 4 stages in developing the knowledge of a word:

---

[7]*Bringing words to Life: Robust Vocabulary Instruction*, Isabel L. Beck, Margaret G. McKeown, & Linda Kucan, (New York: The Guilford Press, 2002) 1–2.

- Stage 1: Never saw it before.

- Stage 2: Heard it, but doesn't know what it means.

- Stage 3: Recognizes it in context as having something to do with...

- Stage 4: Knows it well.

Beck also points out that, in deciding which words to learn it is helpful to divide the vocabulary into 3 tiers. Tier One consists of the most basic words (about 8,000) which are not worth concentrating on because the students will probably learn them ultimately on their own. Tier Two (about 7,000 word families) are the most promising and productive words to teach. The Tier Three words are quite low in word frequency and limited to specific domains of knowledge which means that they would not be worth teaching directly.

In his valuable review of research done in 2006, Biemiller reported the findings of different research projects that had experimented with vocabulary programs for elementary school students over the past 15 years. He notes that most of them consisted of having the teacher read stories to the students and then involve them in conversations about the words in the stories. Some of the scholars read the story once, others 4 or more times. Some gave explicit definitions of the words being covered and others concentrated on discussing the meaning of the words by their context in the story.

An important research question addressed in many of these studies is how many words will the students remember after instruction. In general they ranged from only 15% to 25% although Biemiller manages to reach a 40% retention level through fine tuning his approach. Other scholars such as Nation, Nagy, and Anderson have done seminal work in the effectiveness of various approaches in teaching older children as well as those who are learning English as a foreign language.

The problem that most scholars have in trying to introduce a more robust approach to vocabulary instruction for younger students is that they have never run a school and faced the frustrations of trying to fit all of the program requirements into a busy day. Generally, elementary school principals and teachers are willing to conduct an experiment that tests the efficacy of a particular vocabulary approach. This may require from 30 minutes to a full period from the daily schedule. All too frequently, however, once the experiment is over the participants don't adopt the technique as part of their daily curriculum. They often perceive that to do so would take too much time from their daily schedule and would require a great deal of preparation time to build curriculum from trade book stories and to purchase and maintain copies of books to provide the target vocabulary words in the early elementary classroom.

Although the scholars have shown us how to teach vocabulary, they have not solved the manual delivery system problem of trying to maintain an approach that is not overly work-intensive and time-intensive for the faculty. Biemiller has shown us how to run a vocabulary program that will enable the students to remember about 40% of the words taught to them, but his 30 minute segments will have to shrink to about 15 minutes before most schools would consider scheduling daily vocabulary instruction.

However, there appears to be a way to solve the vocabulary problem if technology is used to present the instruction from preschool through the 2nd or 3rd grade with a rich and robust curriculum that is carefully sequenced, intense, sustained, and explicit and does not demand too much time or effort from the overworked teachers.

Fortunately, technology taught on intelligent whiteboards or computers can present the necessary stories, words, context, and definitions in a shorter and interesting format that will encourage their daily usage. These stories will also be available on portable audio discs or interactive computer lessons that will enable the materials to be read or listened to multiple times, providing the redundancy necessary to insure mastery of the target words.

Given the importance of vocabulary and the preliminary research conducted by a number of scholars, I believe the next decade will see an exuberant outpouring of vocabulary programs involving technology.

Chapter Thirteen: Twenty-Three Times

Years ago, in 1964, when I was preparing for my PhD oral exams at NYU, I had to commute daily on the New York Central railroad from Garrison, New York, to Grand Central Station in New York City. At that time I was studying with obsessive fervor because I had just learned that the graduate English Faculty had failed 11 out of 14 graduate students in front of me in their graduate oral exams, and my attention was focused on trying to shore up my leaky memory in order to avoid a meltdown. After all, it is not a pleasant sight to see a 32 year old male crying in front of a committee.

Unfortunately just when I was "in the zone" and focused one morning on mastering the names of the major biographies on Emily Dickinson (a great American 19th century poet from Amherst, Massachusetts), having just concluded 2 hours of working on "old and middle English vocabulary" where I had courageously and ruthlessly wrestled verb forms to the ground on behalf of my quest to translate Geoffrey Chaucer with unerring accuracy, I looked out the train window and saw something unusual that I had never noticed before. There was a concrete marker a few feet high with a number on it which reappeared about every minute with a new marker with a number one less than the previous marker. After a decent interval I decided that these must be mile markers, and then on further reflection, came to the conclusion I should be able to compute the speed of the train. Here was an opportunity to justify all of those lonely hours

I had spent mastering math. Just like that, I was in the heroic position of a man thinking and demonstrating the power of using abstract symbol sets.

Using just my watch and the mile markers, I should be able to calculate the speed of the train I was in without even moving from my seat. I discovered that it took only 57 seconds to go from post to post. Using the formula D = RT (distance equals rate times time as remembered from my math and physics classes), I quickly set about calculating the speed of the train. I knew it had to be slightly over 60 miles per hour because it took only 57 seconds to travel a mile, but the problem was I could not come up with a recognizable number that clarified the miles per hour the train was travelling.

That night I asked my wife Nancy for help because she had received a perfect 800 on her math SAT scores, but she was unable to give me a simple and accurate answer, and neither was her brother who had graduated as an engineering major from Cornell. In the weeks ahead I created pockets of confusion wherever people gathered as I requested help. I kept coming up with the following equation as I filled in the traditional D = RT equation. I knew the distance was 1 mile and the time was 57 seconds. Since I was interested in the rate of speed, I modified the equation to read R = D/T, or the speed of the train should be the distance it has traveled (1 mile) divided by the time it took to go that distance (57 seconds). When you divide 1 by 57 you get .17543 as the speed of the train. This number confused me and others as we tried to make sense of this decimal when discussing the speed of the train. What I finally figured out was that, although it was true that the train was going .17543 miles per second, this had no meaning for me because I was used to discussing movement in terms of miles per hour. Accepting this, I converted the equation to miles per hour by multiplying the number by 60 which gave me miles per minute and then 60 again (a cumulative total of 3,600 times) to give me miles per hour which turned out to be 63.16 miles per hour. Who would have thought I had to multiply my answer by 3,600 to make sense of it? No wonder we feel uneasy about math.

I realize in retrospect that I had solved the equation many times but had failed to translate the solution into a format that I could recognize, i.e. into miles per hour. I was working in seconds and need-ed to translate the solution into miles per hour. Thus .17543 times 60 times 60 again (3,600) equals 63.16 miles per hour. At last I had an accurate figure of my original estimate of slightly more than 60 miles per hour.

This experience began to make me understand that my brain was a complex organ that helped me recognize variables (mile posts and the speed of the train) that would allow me to compute, calculate, and predict information, if I could only find the right equation or meta-phor to guide me. But I also sensed how difficult it was for our minds to fasten on an understandable image or metaphor that allows us to grasp the implications of the data streaming in through our senses.

In addition, I realized that much of my creative energy for decades had been taken up trying to fashion examples, or metaphorical ways of thinking (such as the Pony Express vs. the telegraph), to help others realize the importance of harnessing the power of the emerging tech-nologies to improve the educational delivery system. Our children's lives depend on it, as does the future of our civilization. I decided then that I would have to understand more about our brain, how it works, and what the best method is to help it (for me and others) to learn.

ZIPF'S LAW:

While doing research on vocabulary, I just this year had difficulty trying to understand the "J" shaped curve first discovered by Zipf (silent p), a Harvard linguist and mathematician who in 1935 noted that when he graphed the frequency that vocabulary words are used in a large body of prose, the graph assumes the shape of the letter "J." The letter J actually represents a series of dots that make up its shape. Each dot displays 2 variables, the number of words there are and how frequently they occur in the prose. They occur at an ever increasing frequency as the shape of the graph (in the form of the letter J) slowly drifts down and to the left and then back up at the far left.

I struggled with trying to find the proper metaphors for under-standing the implications of Zipf's Law and what it means. I found myself returning to it over and over in an attempt to understand the implications of the law. One day last summer, after a long walk over the dirt roads in northern Vermont and still obsessed with understanding the graph of Zipf's strange law, I called my Chief of Staff, Susan Dennin, in Utah and sailed into a discussion of my dilemma, noting that there was a confusing graph in the form of the capital letter "J" in an essay by Marilyn Adams on Zipf's Law in a book I was reading. She excused herself for a few minutes to search for a copy of the book in adjacent offices of the Institute. When she came back on the line she reported that her search had been fruitless, but then asked me to wait a few seconds. Shortly after this comment she said that she was looking at the graph. A bit stunned, I asked her how she could be looking at the graph when her search for a copy of the book had failed. She responded that once she realized it was not available locally, she downloaded it to her Kindle which had just taken a few seconds.

This was a stunning epiphany for me. I am always preaching about how technology can provide undreamed of access to instruction, but while orating fervently I carry a metaphor in my head contrasting the lack of portability of a book with the speed of light used by the Internet. This was the first time I saw the 2 forms merge. The next day I ordered a Kindle.

Never again will I allow a blocking metaphor like Zipf's Law to tyrannize me and surround me with comprehension barriers; instead, sitting in my chair, I can now not only figure out how fast the train is going without moving from my seat, but I can also better understand Zipf's Law with the help of Google and Kindle as I Google the world and Kindle its books. Instead of living in a perpetual state of exotic and enthusiastic confusion, I can continually launch new probes to breach the walls of ignorance that have been screening me from understanding. I realized that what was different about this new scenario was its ability to provide more "brain time" for me without having to travel to gain access to learning at discrete sites that were open only certain hours.

BRAIN TIME:

This idea of "brain time" began to intrigue me and impinge on my teaching. As I frequently contemplated the lessons learned in trying to teach the "who" and "whom" lecture that I outlined in chapter 1, I realized in 2000 that even after 40 years of teaching, I still had little understanding of what went on in the students' brains when they were learning, or not learning! I had extended my frustration beyond the "who" and "whom" experience to include all grammar, punctuation, writing, and knowledge in general, including my own.

I could see from my struggle with trying to calculate the speed of the train (1964) and to understand Zipf's Law (2010) that I had much to learn about the brain and the importance of providing appropriate metaphors and/or paradigms that could help organize the brain's capabilities. But figuring out how the brain works seemed daunting, so in the meantime my assistant Valynne Maetani and I decided to do some research of our own.

We designed a straightforward punctuation and grammar sequence to supplement the Honors American Literature class I taught at the Waterford School. To be scientific about our approach, we administered a pre-test in the fall before starting the formal instruction and then a post-test the following May. We kept track of how many times we paused to teach large segments of punctuation and grammar. In the end we calculated that we devoted all or part of 23 class periods to in-class instruction, or roughly one-sixth of our regular instruction days. We also required them to follow a weekly home assignment where they had to login to our computer database and take a grammar lesson which we monitored. With great excitement the following May we administered the post-test and discovered to our shock and horror that there had been no gain whatsoever. Not since the failure of Johnson's Great Society program has there been such incredulity from the participants about research results.

Here again I was facing some harsh data about the effectiveness of classroom instruction. To my mind, this ongoing saga screamed for an explanation of what exactly was going on in the students' minds. Frequently adults are the last to know. Think of how badly I judged what was going on in Judy's mind earlier. At best, teachers are on thin ice in their understanding of the students' thoughts in their classes. On one occasion I carefully rigged a test to check on cheating and found that over ⅔ of my students in a university English class were exchanging answers. This led me to research "cheating statistics" where I found that no matter how conservative or religious a school was, the cheating was pretty prevalent in all student populations at about the level I had witnessed in my class, which I never would have supposed.

On another occasion, when I had given midterm test questions ahead of time to my college English class, I expressed real anger when I discovered most of the students had not even bothered to study the questions they had been given ahead of time. I learned this when I graded their papers and found that the class average score on the exam was 37%. When I handed the papers back, I dismissed the students early and told them how disappointed I was with them. Two hours later I was called by the Health Center and told that my best student, the only one who had received an "A" in the exam, was contemplating suicide because she believed I was disappointed in her. Notice how generalizations about the state of mind that students are feeling are usually wrong.

Valynne and I were very confused when we realized that all of our work had apparently been for naught. After my students showed no gain, despite our 23 sessions, I decided that I would have to start studying the human brain to begin to understand what was happening in my students' minds.

I had learned some characteristics of the brain as I taught students English and writing over many decades. In particular I had become sensitive to a dual division in my and the students' brains that represented 2 different processes that in some ways warred with one another as we worked on our writing. There is an intuitive creative phase where ideas are spawned in a frenzy of partial thoughts where "Brainstorming" becomes the dominant mode, and all things seem possible. This is the planning phase and during this phase the mind (right side of the brain) avoids judging the merits of the ideas and enjoys the intuitive leaps from one insight to another without any logical sorting taking place. Any attempt to criticize or evaluate the value of the ideas turns the other part of the brain (the left) on and freezes the outpouring of the right side.

After the creative juices begin to wane, the writer then has to turn on the other side of the brain (the left). This side begins evaluating and organizing the creative insights. He or she has to establish what the paper will argue, and like attorneys aligning their arguments by citing precedents, they have to offer proof to validate their generalizations.

The paper must then be organized and structured. This leads the reader through an orderly process of discovery that transfers the insights of the writer to the reader. This means that there must be a clarifying title (as opposed to a confusing one), a logical description of the purpose of the paper as the prose gets underway, clear transitions between paragraphs to remind the reader of the purpose of the paper and how the new paragraph or topic relates to the overall theme, and then specific proof to illuminate the paragraph's thesis when needed.

What frequently destroys the integrity of a paper is a tendency, on the writer's part, to suddenly insert a great new creative insight (from the right side of the brain before it can be forgotten) into a paragraph that is arguing a different point. Novice writers insert this new insight into the mix while trying to organize the earlier insights, and this has the effect of confusing the reader who is trying to follow the logic of the existing arguments.

I found that I had to teach students that their brains had this dual capability and they had to keep these separate and not bounce back and forth mixing the processes. One was a positive outpouring, and the other a critical winnowing.

As I transitioned from being a college and high school English teacher to an executive managing a series of organizations including an English Department (Pine Manor), a private school (Spence), a nonprofit Institute (Waterford), and then a for-profit corporation (WICAT Systems), I continued to explore the dual nature of the brain. My intuitions were expanded in the late 1970s when I met Ned Herrmann who was manager of a facility for General Electric located in Croton, New York. There executives were sent to be trained in preparation for additional management responsibilities. He was intrigued by my organization's commitment to scaling instruction through the use of technology. We had just developed the first instructional videodisc in history under computer control for Mc-Graw Hill and were working on other materials for Smith Kline and various governmental organizations such as The Advanced Research Projects Agency (ARPA) and the armed services. After we visited the Croton facilities, our chief scientist C. Victor Bunderson invited Ned Herrmann to test his new 120 item "Herrmann Brain Dominance Instrument" (HBDI) on our fledgling organization where I had the most extraordinary experience further clarifying my minor insights about the dual nature of our brains.

After taking a 120 question test, my organization rented a large local theater where Ned seated us by name according to our test scores in the long curving front row of the movie theater. My wife, Nancy—who is an excellent executive—was assigned the farthest seat on the left side of the aisle while I was over on the far right, one seat from the end. Standing on the stage, Ned asked all those who agreed with the following statement to raise their hands: "I believe there is a place for everything, and everything has its place." I would have broken my right arm before raising it in agreement to such a narrow, unimaginative, small minded view, but I was quite surprised to see the entire left side of the aisle happily raise their arms in agreement. My wife's was first up and held the highest. Ned then asked those who agreed with the following statement, "I get my best ideas at midnight in the shower." I shot my right arm in the air nodding my head in agreement where once again I was surprised to see the entire right side of the aisle raising its arms joining my enthusiasm while the left side viewed us with suspicion as if we were involved in some unsavory act. I learned a great deal that day as he explained his instrument and findings. But as the next vignette illustrates, I had not learned enough.

A few months later, I was invited to address a leading accounting firm in Chicago to tell their executives about what was coming in educational technology, and particularly the use of the videodisc. The manager who called me asked me to be creative and to give them a glimpse of what his industry might be doing with technology in the future. Recognizing that I knew very little about accountants, I called Ned Herrmann and asked for his advice. He explained that accountants were ideal left brained subjects, and cautioned me that they would be responsive only to an argument that recommended how they go from "A" to "B" in a linear sequence, and I should avoid, at any cost, trying to excite them without specifying the "A" to "B" sequence. Somewhat confused, because the accountant that had called me seemed to want creative examples rather than a logical path, I called the accountant back and tried to sound more conservative and probed as to whether I should offer cold logic or an exciting view of the future. He was quick to laugh and requested that I give them an exciting glimpse of what the future would bring, and cautioned me not to hold anything back.

Still, heeding Herrmann's advice, I tried to be prudent in my presentation.

At the conclusion of the talk, the senior executive who had invited me, expressed a bit of disappointment with my comments. He stood up, walked to the long blackboard in front of the room. Whereupon he wrote an enormous capital letter A on the left side of the board followed by a line moving the length of the board to the far right where he wrote an enormous capital letter B saying emphatically, "While your comments have been interesting, you have not shown us how to go from A to B. That would have been far more useful!" As I flew home afterwards I decided that I would never again quarrel with brain research. In fact I would elevate it and give it priority no matter how counterintuitive it seemed.

Once back in Utah, I continued to experiment with students in order to see if I could learn more about what might help motivate their brains to increase their productivity. I had noticed the importance of motivation on learning productivity through some experiments I had made working on motivational strategies with my students. For example, one year I gave every student an "F" on his or her first paper no matter what the quality of the work, and this strategy produced the greatest growth in writing skills of any class I ever taught. But it seemed wrong to me, and I have never repeated the practice. But it certainly intrigued me and tempted me!

On other occasions during the past decades I have grown frustrated with a student's unwillingness to stop writing comma splices (the student forgets to put a period at the end of a sentence and just keeps splicing one sentence after another with commas). After 4 or 5 papers with a constant stream of comma splices despite my pleas to desist, I finally sent the students to the board and had them copy all of the comma splices from their papers and explain to the class why they were comma splices. After I did this, most students never wrote another comma splice, but I decided later that perhaps their dignity was worth more than publically correcting a comma splice. I have tried not to repeat the practice although at times I have been tempted. In any case it added to my knowledge about the human brain. I began to see the advantage of trials with feedback in a high stakes atmosphere.

About this time Valynne and I began a project with our research school (The Waterford School) in measuring how many of our 1,000 preschool through high school students needed tutoring. We had learned from Sally Shaywitz's 1983 Connecticut Longitudinal Study that about 1 child in 5 needed tutoring during their elementary years. We did not expect anything close to this in our student population at the Waterford School because of the strict admissions policies that include exams to screen out students who might have difficulty following the school's rigorous academic curriculum. We were quite surprised, however, to discover that even among the Waterford students, 1 child in 7 needed tutoring.

We decided that if that many students had disabilities, we should become experts in identifying and treating learning disabilities by developing software to help schools offer quality remediation inexpensively. As a result the Institute and the school hired a great many tutors who had been trained in one of the multi-sensory tutoring programs available in our country. These included those specializing in the Orton-Gillingham method, the Lindamood-Bell approach, the Slingerland Institute strategy, and the Wilson method, among others.

As the tutors worked with our students over a multi-year period we provided a development team to reverse engineer the strategies of the experienced tutors and the published research in the field (which, coincidentally, had begun with the publication of a paper in 1921 co-authored by Helen Keller and Grace Fernald, the founder of a reading laboratory at UCLA). After a number of years of effort, the Waterford development group produced "Camp Consonant" which is a multisensory tutoring program for tutors, schools, and families to use over the Internet. One of the fortunate byproducts of this research project was the knowledge the Institute gained about the brain processes involved in reading.

Sally Shaywitz, who conducts pediatric neurological research at the Yale University School of Medicine in partnership with her husband, is an acknowledged expert in learning disabilities, particularly dyslexia. Their lab is one of a number of research centers located throughout the United States funded by the National Institutes of Health (NIH). They specialize in studying brain processes involved in reading by imaging young children's brains with a machine called an fMRI (functional Magnetic Resonance Imaging device). The fMRI is capable of generating images of brain function while subjects read and respond to questions. This research has allowed scientists to identify the various areas of the brain that are involved in reading for both normal readers and dyslexics.

Beginning in the 1990s, Shaywitz and her husband published a series of articles on brain imaging which created quite a stir in the academic community. Along with other scholars, they discovered that 2 regions in the left rear of the brain activated by fluent reading remain dormant when the subject was dyslexic. It seemed that dyslexic students relied on other areas of the brain, including some on the right side, in a frantic effort to solve their reading problem. It turns out that these regions are associated with automaticity, or the process of making a correctly read word "automatic, and they just need to look at it and they automatically recognize it…. So this particular area on the left side of the brain, the word forming area, is the area that we and others believe serves the expertise in reading. That's very important because when you can read a word fluently it's read automatically. That means you don't have to devote conscious attention to it. And unless you can read words fluently, you're not going to enjoy reading."

As she continued her research with the children, Dr. Shaywitz developed the ability to articulate the problem and teach parents how best to deal with it. For example in an interview with *Parent & Child,* she notes that dyslexia "involves an inability to notice and manipulate the sounds in spoken words." Most people have learned that dyslexia is a visual problem where students reverse letters, but this is not the case. "Once a child develops an awareness of the sounds of spoken words, he can then link the letters to the sounds and go on to sound out new words." She also clarifies that, "Very often, children who are dyslexic also have terrible handwriting. Their mouths have trouble forming sounds and their hands have trouble forming letters."

In 2003 Shaywitz published an outstanding book called *Overcoming Dyslexia* which has been very helpful to parents and also to scholars interested in her fMRI research. I found her graphics and descriptive phrases extremely useful because she provides an excellent bridge to understanding the authentic scientific research on the reading brain. The before and after images, in particular, are powerful testaments for teachers about the effect of offering specific, intense, sustained, and explicit multi-sensory tutoring. Watching the optimal areas of the brain gradually come alive for students who have had reading difficulties and are now being retrained properly is very meaningful and exciting. Viewing these images was a "watershed" moment for me; there is nothing like hard data to convert the enthusiastic layman.

For the first time I found information that showed the brain can be "reorganized" or "rewired" to produce positive change for the desired educational tasks such as reading, and I found these data both helpful and hopeful. The idea of rewiring the brain is breathtaking. As Sally Shaywitz notes in an interview with David Boulton[1] "We are not hardwired for written language…reading has to be taught. It's artificial, it's required." Contrasting written with spoken language, Shaywitz notes, "Spoken language is instinctive and natural—you don't have to teach your baby to speak, you just expose that baby to a spoken language and that baby will learn, eventually, to speak." On the other hand, children who are not taught to read and write do not suddenly acquire those skills.

I found Shaywitz's work so inspiring that I bought some books on understanding the anatomy of the brain. But even *The Brain Color-*

---

[1] See David Boulton's wonderful web site called *Children of the Code* where he posts interviews with many of the world's leading reading scholars.

ing Book overwhelmed me. I thought a coloring book would be easy to digest, but I felt "sucker punched" because I had failed to notice that it was written by Dr. Marian Diamond who had a PhD from the University of California at Berkeley and also taught there as a professor. I was so curious about her that I purchased some books that she had written and did some research on her background and quickly understood that I had wandered into a "Berkeley buzz saw" who wrote when she was 14, "I, Marian Cleeves [maiden name], will go to the University of California Berkeley, because those who don't wish they did."

Marian received her A.B. at Berkeley in 1948 and her PhD in 1953. Her dissertation was on the hypothalamus. When asked at cocktail parties, "What do you do?" she answered that she studied the hypothalamus, noting that, "Inside your head there is a brain region that weighs just 4 grams, like a grape. Yet that part controls thirst, hunger, body temperature, sex, and emotions. Wow, what a remarkable piece of tissue."

After pursuing post-doctoral studies at Harvard, Diamond began a family with her husband, the nuclear physicist Dick Diamond. They moved to Cornell in upstate New York in 1954 with a young daughter, where her husband taught until 1958. While there, Marian Diamond talked a brain expert, Marcus Singer, into giving her a small research project in his department. Shortly after she began her research during the fall semester, Singer was indicted for contempt of Congress for attending Communist Party meetings, and this led to his dismissal from Cornell. He suggested that the department hire Diamond to take over his class of 250 undergraduates in human biology. This worked well, and during a subsequent semester she substituted for a course on comparative anatomy for a professor on sabbatical. In this way for 4 years she taught, kept up in her field, and unwittingly became the first woman science instructor at Cornell.

One day while reading the journal *Science,* Marian discovered an article by 3 Berkeley scientists who had been studying the brain chemistry of smart and dull rats from the original strain started in the 1920s at her beloved Berkeley. The Berkeley team had reported there was a higher degree of concentration of a chemical neurotransmitter (acetylcholine) in the smart brains. As Diamond notes, this "finding was significant: they showed, for the first time, a link between the physical makeup of an animal's brain and its behavior—in this case, its ability to learn."

At this point the Berkeley team discovered an article from a Canadian named Donald Hebb at McGill University who had let his children's pet rats run freely around their house. One day he took these pet rats to the university and discovered that these free-ranging rats ran a better maze than the rats living in laboratory cages. From this he speculated that rats that were confined to unstimulating cages "would develop brains worse at solving problems than animals growing up in a stimulating environment like a large house with hallways, staircases, and human playmates."

This gave the Berkeley group the idea of raising baby rats in 2 kinds of cages: an "enrichment cage" that was large and filled with toys housing 12 rats, and the other "impoverishment cage" that had only 1 rat and no toys. They found that the enriched rats ran better mazes than the impoverished ones. This key finding demonstrated that the intelligence of the rats was impacted not only by their genes, but also by how they were raised, an interesting addition to the classical "nature (genes) vs. nurture (cage environment)" debate.

The Berkeley scientists then checked to see if the rats who had a better environment in their cages (companionship, toys, space) also had more acetylcholine in their brains and found that they did, just as they found more in the brighter rats compared to the duller ones.

As her coauthor Janet Hopson wrote in their book, *Magic Trees of the Mind* (1998), the "remarkable, mind-expanding discovery that Diamond and her colleagues had made" was that "Given the appropriate mental, physical, and/or sensory stimulation, the brain's interconnected neurons sprout and branch." "The Magic Trees of the Mind" flourish and their connections are enhanced physically much as a tree grows deeper and more efficient roots and branches as it is nourished.

Hopson wrote that Diamond's work produced "an igniting of ideas surrounding the simple but profound notion that the brain grows with deliberate stimulation. Diamond's was a life-transforming idea: enrich your own experiences and enlarge your cerebral cortex; deprive yourself of stimulation and the brain will shrink from disuse."

As I pondered her remarkable findings I began to wonder if this would help me understand why my students had not learned their punctuation and grammar even though they had been exposed to it 23 times. I wondered if in my teaching, the stimulation had mostly been mine and not the students who were, after all, trapped in a class with little direct interactive stimulation. But I sensed there was more to learn.

JAPAN, 1958: Dusty Heuston on shore leave while serving on the U.S.S. Shangri-la as an Air Intelligence officer in the U.S. Navy

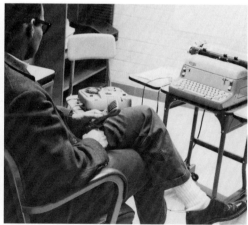

PROVO, UT, 1962: Dusty Heuston as an instructor at Brigham Young University

PROVO, UT, 1965: Dusty Heuston writing in the faculty library at Brigham Young University

NEW HAMPSHIRE, 1960:
Dusty Heuston and his wife, Nancy,
vacationing in the White Mountains

GARRISON, NY, EASTER 1967:
The Heuston family (from left to right)
Kimberley, Nancy, Heather (in hand),
Kelley, and Kary

VERMONT, 1974: The Heuston family (from left to right) Kimberley, Benjamin
(in hand), Hilary, Kary, Heather, and Kelley

VERMONT, 1990: The Heuston family (from left to right) Kary, Jenny, Nancy, Kimberley, Alex (in hand), and Benjamin

SALT LAKE CITY, UT, DECEMBER 1997: The Heuston grandchildren at their home, from left to right: Alex, Sage (in hand), Mark, Jenny, Elijah (in hand), Leo, Isabel, Andrew, Nathaniel, and Max

PROVO, UT, 1986: WICAT Systems

NEW YORK, 1990: Dr. Dustin Heuston presenting to a foundation for the New York City Project

NEW YORK, 1992: Dusty and Nancy Heuston, New York City Project

NEW YORK, 1992: Nancy Heuston, New York City Project

SALT LAKE CITY, UT, 2010: Dr. Dustin Heuston shaking hands with His Excellency Abdoulaye Wade, President of the Republic of Senegal, at a convention held at the Grand America Hotel

SALT LAKE CITY, UT, 2009:
Dr. Dustin Heuston teaching an Honors English class at Waterford School

SALT LAKE CITY, UT, 2010:
Dr. Benjamin Heuston, President/COO, with his father Dr. Dustin Heuston, Chairman/CEO of Waterford Institute™

SALT LAKE CITY, UT, 2011: Dr. Dustin Heuston on Waterford Institute™ Sandy Campus

SALT LAKE CITY, UT, 2011: Dr. Dustin Heuston with Dr. Marilyn J. Adams at inaugural Early Education and Technology for Children (EETC) Conference held at Little America Hotel

SALT LAKE CITY, UT, 2011: Dr. Dustin Heuston presenting at inaugural EETC

SALT LAKE CITY, UT, 2011: Inaugural EETC keynote and featured speakers (from left to right) Dr. John Dexter Fletcher, Dr. Marilyn J. Adams, and Dr. Warren Buckleitner, with Nancy and Dusty Heuston

Chapter Fourteen: First Quantity! Then Quality!

In the 1830s Alexis de Tocqueville and a friend sailed for America in order to study the young country's penal system. De Tocqueville's fascination with the way democracy influenced aspects of American culture soon transcended his interest in prisons. He published his classic, *Democracy in America,* shortly after his return to France. One of his insights was that, because Americans were born believing that all people were equal, this put a lot of pressure on individuals to compete and become successful. As a result, this new democratic approach tended to release enormous amounts of energy. Opportunity bred a competitive atmosphere. Thus, although he disdained the lack of taste and respect for tradition he found in America, de Tocqueville stood in awe of the political and economic systems that encouraged all to participate and work to their capacity.

Also in the 1830s, James Fenimore Cooper, another author, returned from Europe where he had lived with his family for a few years and wrote a series of scathing novels about the crude taste of this burgeoning democracy (e.g. *Home as Found*). Both Cooper and de Tocqueville sensed that this new nation had the resources and political structure to allow its citizens access to unbelievable options and opportunities, but both were concerned about the lack of tradition and taste that they valued and had observed in aristocratic societies. They valued "quality" over "quantity"!

Most Americans take the opposite position. They believe that quantity is more important than quality because it establishes the ultimate potential available in any delivery system and sets the boundaries of what is possible for its citizens. By enlisting the efforts of all its citizens, America believes that the nation will reach its maximum potential. A democracy, they argue, can produce more focused energy and useful work than restrictive political systems like aristocracies that limits intellectual learning and growth to a privileged minority, or a dictatorship that benefits a few, or a socialist government that dampens the entrepreneurial spirit and substitutes governmental control by a bureaucratic class destroying the economic potential of the nation. A democracy holds that the most important ingredient is an unfettered citizenry provided with the opportunity to develop his or her talents in service of both self and nation.

If the individual potential of all citizens is nurtured and harnessed, those who favor democracy believe the cumulative energy generated through this strength of numbers will create the maximum potential possible for the nation. Think of a tug of war pitting strong and knowledgeable faculty (akin to aristocracy or dictatorship) against the student body (think a democracy which harnesses the efforts of all including preschoolers and elementary children of little heft or girth). It's obvious that the students will win every time because quantity almost always trumps quality. In this sense, equity (the inclusion of all) is more important than the excellence of a few (aristocracy), and fairness (encouraging all to participate) trumps efficiency by generating much more useful work through harnessing the efforts of all of the citizens who will work the hardest when given the opportunity to develop their own limitless talents and interests.

During the latter part of the 19th century the United States bet on quantity, equity, and fairness as its citizens fought a bloody civil war to establish equality for all citizens and destroy an aristocratic class system where slavery was permissible and teaching slaves to read was a crime. On July 2, 1862 Abraham Lincoln signed the Morrill Act which ultimately granted, in the decades ahead, 17,400,000 acres of land for land grant colleges and universities to teach agriculture, military tactics, and engineering. In 1890 there was a second Morrill Act for the Confederate states that provided funds instead of land. Some of the great African American colleges and universities are a result of this second Morrill Act. Altogether the Morrill Acts created about 70 colleges or universities.

The creation of the "land grant" colleges demonstrated America's commitment to educating its citizens so that children from every state and location had a chance to receive a postsecondary educational experience. Then, during the 20th century, this trend was further accelerated as Americans built "community" colleges to provide local access for students to encourage higher education for all. Many cities (such as Dallas) have ringed the outskirts of their city with community colleges for students and adults who are interested in improving their skills and may have fallen outside the standard college bound track.

America's real temples are not its soaring business empires, but its colleges and universities. The business empires come and go but colleges and universities continue to grow because knowledge is their product, and knowledge has a patent on the future. Visiting our great campuses is almost a spiritual experience (if one can find parking! UCLA, for example, has 24,000 parking spaces for 37,000 students).

Following the Civil War, the nation decided to back public elementary and secondary school systems in lieu of funding private education. Our public school systems have been developed to insure that all children have an equal educational opportunity. As a nation we have bet on the melting pot approach which integrates all children into a common system that imbues the students with our democratic ideals. I am a product of this system. I was raised in the Bronx in New York City where I attended public schools (PS 81 and PS 7), the Bronx High School of Science, and years later finished my PhD at New York University commuting 60 miles a day each way to take evening courses. Along the way I graduated from a New England boarding school (Mount Hermon), a small liberal arts college in Upstate New York (Hamilton), took a few courses at schools in San Diego and San Jose State while in the Navy, and earned a master's degree from a West Coast university (Stanford). I have Norwegian, German,

English and Irish genes that I know about, but truly, as a breed, I am an American mutt.

I have been particularly impressed by the cycle that these new schools experience as they start, with democratic enthusiasm and marginal quality, to serve a local population and then morph into effective colleges or universities. What drives the growth to quality is the quantity of students showing interest. Legislators are impressed by numbers rather than by an elitist approach which limits education to just a few. This sounds counterintuitive, but it represents an important insight that many people miss. Initially the quantity (amount or capacity) metric is more important than the quality metric.

In my lifetime, starting in the 1950s, I have had the exciting privilege of watching many marginal colleges and universities grow from mediocre to quality institutions. I remember as a young faculty member at Brigham Young University in the late 1950s noticing a small local vocational school that had a modest presence. Over time the combination of student interest as well as support from the parents, the local business leaders, and the state legislature allowed this modest vocational school to expand until now it is a full university (Utah Valley University) with a student body of approximately 30,000 students and a number of embryonic satellite campuses underway. During these growth spurts the numbers not only grow, but so does the quality.

When I first taught at Brigham Young University, I found the students marginally prepared for college; in other words, anybody that was warm and semi-functioning had a good chance of being admitted. The same was true of the faculty. Over time all this has changed and 50 years later BYU only accepts students who have excellent records and high test scores.

The quantity might be barely discernable or modest at first, but starting with enough quantity in a delivery system improves the chances of people having access to it, and access to something is more important than having nothing at all, particularly if it is convenient and costs little. Thus access, convenience and low cost make possible the growth of delivery systems, not only in education, but also in transportation. A bicycle is better than walking, and as a country improves economically, motorbikes, scooters, and motorcycles are replaced by buses, trains and cars. Then at some point airplanes and airports become available.

In education, community colleges first appear and then evolve into universities. In 1881 the California State Legislature opened a southern branch of the California State Normal School that was located in San Jose (now San Jose State University) in downtown Los Angeles as a 2-year teacher training institution. In 1887 the school was renamed the Los Angeles State Normal School. In 1914 the school moved to a 25 acre site on Vermont Avenue. Then in 1919, the college was transferred into the Southern Branch of the University of California and added a College of Letters and Science to the teacher training program. The undergraduate program was still limited to 2 years, and in 1919 there were 250 students enrolled in the letters and science program and 1,250 students in the teacher's college. During the 1920s the college changed its name to the University of California, Los Angeles, (UCLA) and became a 4 year institution, and by 1929 a new 400 acre campus was opened in the Westwood area of Los Angeles the same year the Spence School expanded to a 9 story building for 500 students in NYC. By 1933 the university awarded its first master's degrees and in 1936 its first doctoral degrees. Currently UCLA has 163 buildings located on 419 acres offering over 300 undergraduate and graduate degrees to 37,000 students and has more applications to its undergraduate programs than any school in the United States (55,676 in 2009). Meanwhile Spence has grown from 500 students to 650. Democracy outpaces aristocracy every time.

THE EDUCATIONAL DELIVERY SYSTEM:

As mentioned in previous chapters, we organize in society into delivery systems that offer goods and services to those around us. The limits of these delivery systems are determined by the quantity of work that they can deliver, and each delivery system has a natural maturation level that is hard to overcome once reasonable efficiencies are reached. Traditionally we invent new sources of labor and technologies to overcome delivery system limitations. For example we harness wind to sail ships or horses to ride, race, and pull.

A problem that many individuals working within these delivery systems face is that sometimes they neither recognize that they are part of a delivery system nor that, in most cases, the technology of the delivery system determines the capacity of that delivery system. This leaves them vulnerable because it never occurs to them that their delivery system can be replaced or modified by a new one, almost overnight, if their institution can harness a new technology that can accomplish exponentially more work for less money in a shorter time. If we understand that we are part of delivery systems, then we can remain flexible and look for new sources of work to improve the delivery system we work in and even become experts in using new technologies to help us rather than being obliterated by them.

On the other hand, if we do not realize that we are involved in a delivery system, then we tend to resist all change and try to become more efficient with only what we know and understand. The Pony Express riders were hand-picked talented riders who had to be small, lightweight, and capable of riding under extraordinary conditions. Knowing they were the best, they were not afraid of competition, but it never occurred to them that their business would close in 2 days because a new delivery system could accomplish their responsibilities 67 million times faster by using telegraph clerks who only had to exercise their brains and fingers to complete their tasks. Not knowing we are part of a delivery system can leave us vulnerable to being displaced by a new delivery system.

As I write this chapter in August of 2010, the Department of Education has just announced its first round of awards for innovative new reforms to improve public education. This was an eagerly awaited announcement because, for the first time, universities and other nonprofits were invited to recommend truly innovative projects. Unfortunately, since there is no one in Washington with authority who understands delivery systems and the potential of the new technologies, the awards went mostly to the old warhorses. Solemn declarations were made that the choices had been guided by panels of experts who offered objective "peer reviews" of the proposals. Huge grants (up to $50,000,000 each) were given to 2 programs so they could be scaled, even though they have already been scaled and dropped numerous times over a 20 year period by many districts. Both involve expensive manual supplementary programs where more teachers are added and trained to follow a carefully prescribed program that can provoke short term gains that tend to wash out over time. Although they are well-run programs and can help some children, they are too expensive and fragile to scale rapidly. Also an additional 25 million was awarded to the Smithsonian, and 5 million to the teachers' union, neither of which is known for its educational innovations despite the alleged objective judgment of the peer reviewers.

Waterford submitted 3 proposals and was turned down for each despite the fact that it had outstanding results in precisely some of the areas that the proposals called for. Moreover, there was not a single grant given to an educational technology project that would use the new delivery system work to individualize instruction for the students. Now that is what I call real innovation! Not a single grant for the projects that will dominate the future of education! Not a single leader who comprehends what is coming like an express train! I have become accustomed to being turned down for educational grants by various government agencies such as NSF or IES, but I am appalled when a program is developed and sold to the public as a paragon of innovation and ends up betting on yesteryear. This experience does have hints of rearranging the deck chairs on the Titanic while sailing into difficult waters.

What is clear about this is that the leadership in Washington appears to lack an understanding of delivery systems, technology and educational innovation. Innovation usually starts with a small group of people who have new ideas; it does not consist of polishing up the old chestnuts and pretending they are fresh corn. Corn pone perhaps, but not fresh corn.

The government defends its decisions by arguing that it follows the recommendations of "peer reviewers" who objectively analyze the proposals offered in a process called "peer review," but this screens out new innovations because there is no one present who understands the potential of the new delivery systems. The purveyors of the current delivery system (e.g. the horse) have no clue about the new delivery system (i.e. the telegraph) coming on stream, and when quizzed about the most useful ways to improve delivering the mail would suggest titanium horse shoes or a new lightweight stirrup that would at best provide some minute improvement that would allow the riders to average 10.0001 miles per hour instead of 10.00. They cannot imagine that their jobs will be eliminated in 2 days because there is a new delivery system coming on stream that uses technologies that are 67 million times faster because they harness the speed of light. The "peers of yesteryear" are no help in choosing those who will become the "peers of tomorrow."

Unfortunately, as Max Planck explained to Einstein at the beginning of the 20th century, they would have to wait until their senior professors (peers) died off before the discoveries they had made in quantum theory and relativity would be allowed into the universities. We need some leadership that understands the speed of light rather than excitedly stalking new algorithms for feeding and training horses. We need "guiding intelligence" not "ignorant guiding." We certainly do not need the Smithsonian or the unions or 20 year old programs to receive huge awards for their path finding leadership in educational innovation.

For a nation obsessed with "educational accountability" it is time for us to hold our educational leaders accountable for designing a delivery system that will guarantee that our children will have access to both excellence and equity. Mediocre equity is not enough. Educational leaders are always demanding that the children live up to standards and faithfully do their homework even if it is difficult and takes hard work. It is time for our leaders to do their homework and learn about the speed of light and what is coming even if they have to stay up late after a long day at work. Just as I am tired of listening to student complaints about homework, I am upset by government leaders and educational scholars who are too lazy to do their homework, no matter how tired and busy they are. I am tempted to tell them (Just as the teachers preach in the charter schools that follow the "no excuse" approach) STOP YOUR WHINING! SUCK IT UP AND DO YOUR HOMEWORK! NO EXCUSES! Learn about delivery systems and the speed of light. Stop sponsoring your pet reform for improving the horse and learn about the telegraph (or if you are giddy with excitement, you might even study the wireless or the Internet).

Drop your rationalizations and excuses that claim that "educational technology" does not work; that studies run by the government show it produces no substantial results. No one ever did a formal randomized study to prove that the printing press was more effective than hand written papyrus. The most quoted government study[1] about the failure of educational technology is one that is full of holes because it declares its results as definitive without acknowledging that the results are invalid because the programs measured were used only a fraction of the scheduled days. Furthermore, we do not need a 30 year randomized double blind study to prove that technology can teach effectively. Once we proved (which we have) that young children in their homes can have access to individualized learning 365 days a year on interactive software attached to the Internet, that they will use it, and they learn from it, and the costs are far less than any alternative, then the excuses are over. Get used to it; it works!

Definitive studies are for static delivery systems where one is trying to tease out data that is not very obvious. The introduction of technology into any delivery system usually creates so much of a difference that the studies soon concentrate on comparing the subtle difference between using various technologies rather than measuring whether the telegraph is better than the horse for communicating messages. There has never been a valid study to prove that cars are better than horses in transporting us, that telephones are better than carrier pigeons or smoke signals for communicating, or that calculators work faster and more accurately than paper and pencil options.

If our mission is to help children learn, then let us use the best tools available to help them. What distinguishes human beings from the lower animals is the humans' capability to develop and use tools.

---

[1]See the report by the IES National Center for Educational Evaluation and Regional Assistance published as NCEE 2009–4041 by the Department of Education entitled *Effectiveness of Reading and Mathematics Software Products* (February, 2009).

For those that believe in evolution, scholars start defining the beginning of civilization in terms of the tools that humans developed.

In other words, rather than spending infinitely more capital with diminishing returns trying to improve the efficiency of the manual educational workers (and/or hiring more of them), it is time to provide technological support to the students, parents and teachers who are the workers in the current delivery system.

THE COMING COST SQUEEZE:

As we shall see, there are emerging financial problems surfacing that will begin to limit and degrade the educational boom and accelerate the acceptance of technology either with government support or through new channels developing in parallel and independent of the government and its traditional institutions. These problems all stem from the same phenomenon: Zero does not inflate! But any number above zero will inflate over time and ultimately reach a level that restricts its delivery system attractiveness. Public education fits this category. From the standpoint of the consumer, there is no cost for the child, but there is to the taxpayer.

Services that cost a few pennies a day will inflate to a few dollars a day which will inflate to a few thousand dollars a day etc. Instructors at some universities are being paid 15 times as much as I was when I started teaching in a university about 50 years ago. There is a question as to whether our schools and universities will be able to afford another 15 times factor in the decades ahead. When I first took over the Spence School the tuition was a few hundred dollars a year, and now it is $35,000 some 40 years later. The apartment the school bought to house the head was $120,000 and it now is worth many millions. Waterford believes that the teaching profession will start to implement technologies in order to improve services and lower costs to provide greater access because that is what technologies are best at.

One scholar, Clayton Christensen, who has studied the ongoing 8% rise in school budgets, noted that the rise was not going to be sustainable because the public tax base could not afford it. Clayton Christensen is a businessman-scholar who has a clear vision concerning the implications of technology when it comes to changing and improving traditional delivery systems. He has an interesting background that has prepared him to understand the disruptive impact of new technologies on what appear to be large, mature, and impregnable organizations such as big corporations or schools.

Christensen graduated from Brigham Young University after serving a 2 year mission for his church (Mormon) in Korea. Then, as a Rhodes Scholar, he studied at Oxford before returning to the U.S. to study at the Harvard Business School where he received his MBA. Then he served as a consultant and product manager with the Boston Consulting Group for 5 years before cofounding some businesses. Approaching the age of 40, he decided he would rather become a teaching scholar and joined the Harvard Business School faculty after receiving his doctorate from Harvard in 1992.

In 1997 he published an award-winning book entitled *The Innovator's Dilemma* which brilliantly details the organizational pressures that the use of new technologies generates in traditional delivery systems. In his analysis he has worked out the underlying laws unleashed when new technologies are introduced that are simple, convenient, and inexpensive enough to create new markets for users who benefit from them even though initially they offer only limited capabilities. He labels these as "disruptive technologies" which undermine the traditional "sustaining businesses" that dominate the markets. They accomplish this by offering people a product or service that they never would have contemplated having because it was beyond their expertise, budget, or available time to implement such as simple transistor radios for teenagers or home computers, cell phones, iPods, Sony Walkman, and printers for home use.

Christensen's educational thesis is that the traditional school system, as we know it, will be impacted by the new disruptive computer and Internet technologies which will offer inexpensive alternatives to a school system that is inflating at a cost which cannot be maintained. Under the inevitable financial pressure generated by inflation, districts are being forced to drop out some of their traditional courses such as foreign languages and advanced placement classes and will begin to offer them electronically as an inexpensive alternative. Over time, school districts, following a prolonged economic downturn in their neighborhoods, will start to offer a full curriculum over the Internet to students whose local schools are closed because the population has grown too thin to support their cost.

But in addition to cost considerations, Christensen believes that the new technologies will be needed to individualize instruction and hold the attention of an emerging generation of students who are being raised in rather opulent settings and are not seriously interested in pursuing the rigors of a science or math curriculum. John Adams noted that he had to study law and politics so his children could study engineering and architecture so their children could study the arts. Christensen notes that, when a culture is struggling to succeed economically, the children are pressured to major in science and mathematics and to work hard as a way out of poverty, as in the cases of Japan, India, and China. But, once they become successful, their children no longer want to work that hard and seek easier college majors than science or engineering. Or in some cases, they will prefer just to live off the family's capital and forget schooling.

Thus he argues that we now need to individualize instruction so that our students will be motivated to stay connected to the educational system. Once given the economic option to drift in their schooling because they are bored by the approximation inherent in the public school system where only some of the class commentary is appropriate to their individual needs and interests, the newer generations are blind to the importance of schooling. They do not understand that they will be competing for jobs with children who start attending preschools in foreign nations at 2 or 3 years old at 7:00 AM that go until 6:00 PM because their parents understand how important education is to their future. For many it will be the only way out.

Summing up this critical point, Christensen writes that only software can individualize instruction to the degree required to insure the successful education of American students whose prosperity has reduced their extrinsic motivation for academic achievement. By catering to their intrinsic motivation and addressing their individual interests and talents, those offering software will provide a "promising educational path" that will enable America to remain competitive on an international stage where access to an education is a life and death issue for many of the players

Christensen is one of the few scholars who recognizes that the key to our educational future will be the development of the finest software possible in order to attract the interest of a new generation of Americans who might not realize the importance of education until it is too late. Unfortunately, the development and support of educational software is an expensive enterprise that has no logical base of support in America. This is because the markets are too small to support the financial requirements of developing and supporting world-class educational software. The single most important investments for philanthropists and government leaders interested in education should be in developing the new generations of software. The hardware and networking portion of the system is developing naturally and does not need funding. We must help realize that once they help develop excellent software that this contribution can scale over time and offer direct world-class education to billions of children. Talk about leverage!

As Thomas Friedman has shown in his perceptive book, *The World is Flat* (2005), the successful harnessing of the speed of light is allowing nations and populations to communicate and transfer information inexpensively and to demolish many traditional trade barriers which will cause severe labor problems to nations that are unable to educate their citizens. His thoughtful analysis suggests there are 10 forces that have been unleashed between 1989 and 2000 by the new technologies that are flattening the world's traditional barriers between nations. One of the byproducts of harnessing the speed of light is that 3 billion new competitive workers were suddenly produced from India, China, Eastern Europe, Latin America, Central Asia, and Russia at about the year 2000, and the existence of these workers has changed forever the rules that will govern commerce and education. In a world of flattened barriers, we compete at a distance with unseen opponents.

In a column in the *New York Times* on August 3, 2005, entitled "Calling All Luddites," Friedman succinctly sums up our technological challenge:

The world is moving to an Internet-based platform for commerce, education, innovation, and entertainment. Wealth and productivity will go to those companies or countries that get more of their innovators, educators, students, workers and suppliers connected to this platform via computers, phones and PDA's.

SOME OTHER BARRIERS TO HARNESSING "QUANTITY":

Paul David, a Stanford economist, who has written many excellent articles on economics and technology, argues for the existence of a 40 year gap between technological breakthroughs and their general acceptance. His article on "The Dynamo and the Computer" (1990) is very helpful in clarifying the long time delay in the United States between the time new technology is introduced and when gains in productivity follow. For example, although the light bulb was invented in 1879 and the first power station for generating electricity was built in 1881, there were no substantial productivity gains in the factories using electricity and electric motors until 40 years later in the 1920s. He suggests that we note "the existence of special difficulties in the commercialization of novel (information) technologies that need to be overcome before the mass of information-users can benefit in their roles as producers." In other words it takes about 40 years before the current guardians of a traditional delivery system die off and allow a new generation to use the newer technologies far more productively.

In 1990, when David published his article on the dynamo and the computer in *The American Economic Review*, almost 40 years had passed since the computer's commercial introduction in the early 1950s. David's paper was in response to the economists' concerns that, despite massive investments in computer technologies in America, there seemed to be a lack of discernible productivity gains. Economists were discussing the "productivity paradox" with great gusto. As Robert Solow, a Nobel Laureate from MIT in economics, noted wryly, "We see the computers everywhere but in the productivity statistics." The point of David's paper was to inform other economists that "many features of the so-called productivity paradox will be found to be neither so unprecedented nor so puzzling as they might otherwise appear" when approached from the perspective of economic history. In other words, just wait! It took 40 years for electricity to have a productivity impact; productivity gains from computers are coming.

Just as David predicted, within 2 years, sudden gains began appearing in productivity indexes. In a discussion paper he coauthored with Moses Abramovitz, David summed up the stunning productivity gains that were being realized. In fact, the gains from the information and communications technologies (ICT) sector were so substantial that economists began to talk about "The New Economy." Typical of the commentary was an "Economic Letter" from the Federal Reserve Bank of San Francisco:

> The increase in productivity growth rates beginning in the mid-1990s has helped boost economic growth and speed the rate at which living standards rise in the United States. Between 1995 and 2000, productivity growth averaged 2.8%—almost double the rate during the preceding 22 years! This increase in productivity growth is thought by many observers to be associated with the increased importance of information technology (IT), a hypotheses often referred to as the "New Economy" view (FRBSF Economic Letter 2001–14; May 11, 2001).

Another economist, Paul Krugman of Princeton, after reading the economic report in February 2000 issued by the President's economists, noted the same trend, and he commented in his February 20th column in the *New York Times* called "Dynamo and Microchip" that their conclusion "that technology, not policy, is the main source of good news" is "surely right."

> A technology-driven surge in worker productivity is directly responsible for about two-thirds of the acceleration in our economic growth from the 2.5 percent norm of the 70's and 80's to the 4 percent of recent years. The report plausibly argues that our unexpected ability to get unemployment down to 30-year lows without inflation is also an indirect result of the productivity boom. So there is no mystery about why we are doing so well: the microchip did it.

He notes that in trying to understand why it took the micro-processor revolution so long to have an impact, he remembered the Paul David article from a decade earlier that had impressed him and predicted this type of delay. So he dusted it off and read it again and decided it "makes even better reading today."

Thus we learn an important lesson from David: introducing technology takes time, but once it clicks in, it has an astonishing impact. This will be important to understand in tracking the potential of technology to help schools in America that have been struggling with the introduction of computers for about 30 years and should begin seeing productivity gains and success in schools in about 10 years if David's assumptions hold true.

THE DEMOCRACY TAX:

In a perverse twist of fate, America's democratic obsession with harnessing the energy of all of its citizens by educating them in public and secondary schools insures that its elementary and secondary schools are not as efficient as other countries even though the U.S. spends more per student than most others. We also pride ourselves on our competitive capitalistic economic system that we believe almost mystically permeates the schools' atmosphere. Paradoxically America has the finest university system in the world and is the envy of other nations, but its elementary and secondary systems are definitely not the envy of other countries.

A key reason is what I call the Democracy Tax, which is not a literal tax, but an indirect drain on the efficiency, capacity and excellence of our public K-12 schools. We accept this liability because we value democracy as our guiding national principle, even if it reduces school efficiency, just as we accept sacrificing efficiency in the government when we balance power between the executive, legislative, and judicial branches. The causes of this inefficiency include:

(1) No matter the cost, all children through high school have the right to a public education paid from the public tax base regardless of

their physical and mental circumstances. Thus a considerable amount of our educational funds are used for special education.

(2) Funds from the public tax base are primarily restricted to public schools. This makes the public schools a quasi-monopoly, i.e. most of the funds are not available to competing private schools, and this will slowly reduce efficiency, innovation, and accountability. In general, socialistic monopolies do not increase in efficiency over time. They run down and become less efficient.

(3) Congress will continually pass costly new laws extending public school services, and the courts will also intrude on school policies and drive up the costs of services as a result of lawsuits over various school services. These lawsuits further bureaucratize the system, drive up costs, and reduce the core instructional efficiency in favor of special interest groups that now have the protection of legislation and the law.

(4) Because of its traditions and economic pressures, American schools are open 180 days or less for about 6 hours a day which means the instructional services are available for less than half the days in the calendar year.

(5) America believes in diversity and encourages immigration policies that require public schools to accommodate many non-English speaking students and their cultural traditions. Some schools are flooded with a plethora of languages far beyond their capacity to understand or deal with, and many others have such a great turnover from migrant families that the children have difficulty studying a coherent curriculum in the face of constant moves and school changes.

(6) Unionization is allowed and encouraged, depending on state laws, and the accompanying seniority and job security will dampen teacher accountability and system efficiency in favor of protecting the rights of the teachers and school workers. Generous retirement policies will also add significant costs to the system over time which reduces capital available for current operations.

THE IMPLICATIONS OF THE DEMOCRACY TAX AND A POTENTIAL REMEDY:

(1) The democratic tax on school efficiency represents a conscious decision by Americans to value democracy over efficiency. This is a deliberate and positive policy that must be respected even though it reduces the quality of the K-12 schools. People trust a democratic political system more than they trust educational efficiency.

(2) Americans are often frustrated by the quality of some of the schools so there is a great hunger for reforms to fix what many view is a flawed system. Given the built-in inefficiencies of the system, this is not financially possible unless technology is utilized in place of investing in more people and time. Technology can add more capacity (quantity) to the system, not just use what is available more efficiently (quality). Unfortunately, our "successful" reforms fail because they are too expensive to scale.

(3) The only solution that makes sense is to utilize technology to add capacity (quantity) to help our workers (the teachers, students, and parents) who are penalized by the democracy tax. Adding capacity to support workers is what technology always has done best, and in the educational delivery system technology is inexpensive, scalable, and very effective. We do not need to add more people or costly ineffective reforms; we need the new technologies to add capacity to compensate for the inefficiencies of our democratic tax.

Our first task is to provide instructional software in homes and preschools to insure that all children are academically prepared for kindergarten no matter what their family background. Lacking a level playing field in kindergarten, most children will simply play out their family circumstances. Ironically, this is precisely why America built public schools: to insure that all children could overcome any family circumstances that might keep them from receiving an excellent education as a gateway to a productive and rich life.

Chapter Fifteen: The New Frontier in Education: Using Technology in the Home for Preschoolers

By 2005 we at the Waterford Institute realized that, just as Paul David had predicted, public schools would probably need another decade or so before they would be far enough along in the 40-year-cycle for the successful introduction of a new technology. Only then would the schools be willing to introduce serious software in the early grades, make sure the materials were used daily by the students for at least 15 minutes a day, and reorganize the curriculum around the strengths of the new technologies.

In the meantime, the Institute believes that while these new technology traditions are developing in the schools, a parallel new frontier will emerge which uses the resources of the homes. This third source will be supported by the new software and technologies that can be scaled overnight without institutional barriers. By concentrating the use of the new technologies in homes during the preschool years, the nation will take a critical step forward in helping to solve an important educational problem that is caused by an increase in the number of homes where more and more families are having children out of wedlock.

The family unit in America is under siege and crumbling. According to the National Center for Health Statistics, the number of unwed mothers in America has increased over the past 70 years from 3.8%

to 40%, expanding over 10 times. In the past 5 years this number has increased 25%. Many of the children from these families are impacted by stress and show up for school so poorly prepared that there is little chance they will be successful and stay in the system. In America, there appears to be a correlation between out of wedlock births, race, and future academic success. Those states or cities that have the highest out of wedlock birth rates have dismal academic scores.

This trend is frightening and suggests that we are allowing our family units to destruct without understanding the full educational implications of this national problem. Notice how we have become desensitized to the data: In 1965 the Moynihan Report noted almost 25% of the African American families were having their children out of wedlock (up from 18% in 1950) and created a sensational firestorm of comment and criticism.[1] Now we are not upset when we learn that the white families are up to 28% from the 3% reported in 1965, the Hispanics up to 51%, and the African Americans have reached over 72% without disturbing the national conscience. The lack of married-couple families takes a toll on children, and not just in areas of illiteracy. Ron Haskins and Isabel Sawhill are scholars at the Brookings Institution who have reported that married-couple families have ⅕ of the poverty rate of female-headed families with children.

In order to insure the success of these single-parent families, new technologies will have to be developed to provide interactive and proactive services using the Internet and telephone to train and support the children and parents in these homes. The state and federal government will ultimately pay for these services for all families (no matter what their financial status) because the return on this investment, which is less than 10% of the cost of preschools and will ultimately drop to less than 5%, will guarantee government support once experimental trials establish the efficacy of the technology home-based model. This program will not replace the universal preschool movement

---

[1]"The Negro Family: The Case for National Action," Office of Planning and Research, United States Department of Labor (March 1965), www.dol.gov/asp/programs/history/webidmeynihan.htm.

which is already underway in over 80% of the states; instead, it will supplement and support existing pre-K programs while providing a cost-effective option to states without pre-K programs.

America's schools are facing the increasingly unsolvable problem of having too many uneducable children entering kindergarten. These children are uneducable because they have received too little preliteracy training at home because of family circumstances (including language barriers). As a result, teachers are overwhelmed by student needs.

The students are uneducable not because they lack basic intelligence, but because; (1) their environments have restricted their exposure to rich language and vocabularies, particularly academic English; and (2) they have failed to receive critical skill training in both cognitive (e.g. alphabet, numbers), and noncognitive subjects (e.g. patience, deferred gratification, sharing) during their critical early-learning years at home.

We make a dreadful error if we think this is simply a problem of preparation that can be rectified with a little support and attention from parents or by adopting a new school reform. Once they enter 1st grade many of these children are statistically uneducable. Many of them from difficult environments have received less than 7% of the preliteracy training that their fellow students have received, and they have been spoken to as much as 32,000,000 fewer words than some of their peers by the age of 4. This group of children live uneasily in the system until the end of the elementary years when they begin to drop out in droves (between a quarter and a third of all students drop out of school from the 8th through the 12th grade-or fail to graduate) leaving them in a precarious position to succeed in a knowledge-based society. Their inability to perform successfully economically also negatively impacts the nation's productivity and hence hurts all citizens.

THE NEW LEARNING ENVIRONMENT: THE HOME PORTAL:

Generally we assume we know what constitutes a learning environment and believe that it includes only teachers, books, and schools. Going one level deeper, however, we can see that people and technologies (books, paper, pens, pencils, audio, TV, computers) are used to produce, store, and organize information for students to master. Teachers have traditionally been the preferred primary source of instruction, but they come with 2 drawbacks: (1) They are the most expensive of the available options for student learning, and (2) their availability to the children is limited by school schedules.

To gain access to a teacher's instruction, children have to leave home and travel to a school where teachers are available for less than half the days in a year for only 6 hours a day. And once in school the students find they must share access to the teacher with 20 to 30 other students which means that at best they can expect to receive an average of about 1 minute a day of individual instruction from the teacher, a condition which insures they will have difficulty ever making up their preliteracy training limitations.

Fortunately, there is a new learning environment emerging: the home portal. This will be available for all waking hours every day of the year for young children at home before they enter kindergarten and will give them access to new technologies and software. This home portal will consist of a computer with powerful educational software connected to the Internet and a special support organization that also is connected to the families and their children. If the children access this portal for just 15 minutes a day, they will be provided with over 90 hours of individualized instruction a year compared to the 3 hours they currently receive in any formal school setting. This is a 30 times improvement. Even if we cut the time to 15 minutes a day for only 5 days a week with a 2 week vacation in the summer, the students will have an improvement of over 22 times what would normally be expected. The depth of this learning experience will be of inestimable value in securing a successful set of learning habits and skills for each child in literacy, numeracy, and science, with the possibility of training children in additional areas, including languages, as a future option. The potential of this approach is so profoundly powerful that those societies that ignore it will find it difficult to compete economically because those that implement it will enjoy a number of advantages:

(1) **Access to quality instruction:** Most young children have little access to knowledgeable instruction in their preschool years because most of their parents or teachers lack the time and knowledge to deliver outstanding curriculum to them. There are many national organizations and university scholars dedicated to teaching parents or caregivers how to teach their children, but because of the prohibitive cost involved, they are unable to travel to homes or preschools and actually teach the children themselves.

By contrast, the software will be available in the home to give parents a ready-made curriculum for preschool use in an attractive artistic format individualized for each child every day of the year any time of the day the children are awake and at home.

Only software will be able to deliver affordable individualized, interactive instruction to our increasingly dysfunctional homes. This new access to inexpensive instruction is what will define the context and setting of the new educational frontier. And, although this frontier will likely emerge first in the United States, it will impact the new instructional paradigms and spread globally. The only limiting factor will be the speed of software development.

(2) **Access to diagnostic information on the status of the child:** Having actual knowledge of a child's learning status is a critically motivating variable for all parties involved in the learning process. This pertains particularly to children who are at either end of the learning curve and are either bored or terrified by the pace of learning. This knowledge will be very motivating to parents and encourage them to use the new technologies, software, and services, including the training available to them to support the child's ideal learning path.

(3) **Access to a multisensory tutoring program for the 20% of children who need tutoring:** The latest research suggests that at least 1 child in 5 needs tutoring because he or she is having difficulty learning in schools. If this difficulty can be identified and remediated when the child is young, a great deal of anguish and future trouble is averted. One of the true strengths of the home program will be its ability to offer a new multisensory tutoring program to a child who

is struggling and has no idea why he or she cannot "get" it. Research has shown that a good multisensory program can help rewire a child's brain in order to foster learning instead of leaving the child frustrated and consumed by shame because of the failure of the traditional teaching approach.

(4) **Training for parents and caregivers:** Having a portal available to provide instruction to the adults in the child's life is extremely important. This can help harness the resources that adults can provide in a nurturing family setting and will be a valuable channel for scholars and heads of organizations who want to reach parents and teach them how best to work with the children. The curriculum will ultimately contain a broad spectrum of options that go beyond reading, math and science to also include such subjects as nutrition, how to read a book interactively to a child, and how to use the Internet. Experts will develop a broad array of useful information for parents and learn how to motivate them and hold their attention.

(5) **Access to ongoing motivation:** Because a network portal can communicate in both directions, there will be new types of organizations constructed to interact frequently with the homes in order to provide strong motivation for the users to use the instructional materials on a regular basis. For example, a state program could provide free materials and support as long as the parents or caregivers schedule the children to use the materials for at least 15 to 20 minutes a day. These organizations will also help the parents understand the importance of education for the future success of their child. The challenge of using the portal optimally and successfully will be to learn how to provide compelling motivational strategies that retain the children's and caregivers' attention and commitment.

(6) **Provide a portal to other organizations and resources:** Other organizations will be encouraged to use the home portal in order to help support their programs. Schools, colleges, parent organizations, researchers, social services, public service nonprofits, and state agencies will find value in providing information, training, help, and a

myriad of other services to this audience of users. Other community organizations such as libraries, churches, and community centers will also find this portal useful in helping to make people aware of and dispense their services.

(7) **Provide a portal to social networking:** One of the most powerful forces unleashed by the new technologies is the potential for social networking on sites such as Facebook for families who are often socially isolated because of financial constraints and the stress of living in single parent families. This social networking will spread to other activities such as blogging and sharing information with other parents who have similar interests in providing a successful academic preparation for their children. This portal will also serve as an excellent forum for parents who want to have specific questions answered by other parents who may have had similar issues with their children. The portal will actually form an educational network with a broad array of services including a Q & A section answering the most frequently asked questions and a training component with movie clips which will provide important advice on how to use the full potential of the software. There will also be research alerts broadcast throughout the entire social network of users whenever new findings are published by the scholars that would be of value to the parent users.

(8) **Cost effectiveness of delivering superior services:** The portal has the primary advantage of being able to provide services for a fraction of the cost of any alternative that only uses people to deliver goods and services. The portal will use fewer people but will support them with technology. Typically a strategy mixing technology with people will cost less than 10% of a strategy using just people as the delivery mechanism, and over time this will drop to less than 5%.

(9) **Ability to scale educational excellence:** In addition to the primary cost advantage of using technology, there is a secondary advantage in that under certain circumstances, it can scale excellence far better than people can. Once a well-designed

instructional sequence is developed in software, every student has access to it, as compared to only the few who have access to excellent instruction in a typical home or school setting. The lack of technological scaling also invokes a social cost because only those with financial means, political influence, or talent can obtain access to this scarce excellence.

(10) **Access without constraints:** The issue of educational access is a profound one. In the past few centuries most nations have been able to provide schools for their children, but there are still many populations such as India and Africa where the expense is too great and upwards of half the children are unable to attend school. As these nations strengthen economically they will be able to provide schooling for most of their young. But then they will discover the same educational problems that America is facing where optimal access turns out to be limited to those with wealth or unusual intelligence.

Technology and its ability to scale excellence will extend access to educational excellence and equity for all populations. This suggests that those who are interested in furthering educational excellence should begin to transition their educational efforts to include software development, new educational models such as the construction of home portals for the young, and the architecture of a new type of support organization that is proactive.

During their preschool years, the neediest young students tend to move frequently because their parents are having financial difficulties. Often these moves interrupt a solid instructional sequence, and the early instructional effort is wasted because of the instructional interruption. Once the home portal model is fully developed and the families issued technology and access to the Internet that is continuously available as their family moves, the home portal will avoid this educational disruption problem brought on by frequent moves. The children will be able to sustain their educational involvement as the technology travels with them (as well as their records), which will be stored on file servers that can be accessed from any location.

NEW PARTNERSHIPS WITH THE HOME PORTAL PROVIDER:

The original portal will be funded and constructed to insure that the children's educational success will be significantly enhanced; however, as other groups realize that there is an operating portal in position to help facilitate the delivery of their specialty services, a series of unique partnerships will appear which will be the hallmark of this new frontier.

To begin with, however, the organization running the educational portal will have to build a new type of learning environment which is interactive and proactive in its relationship with the families it serves. Waterford calls this the "third source" which provides technology and support to supplement the other 2 traditional areas that foster learning, the home, and the school.

This 2 way interaction will help facilitate user motivation and training for young children and their families. Unlike a typical Internet support organization, which is passive in relation to users except when there are problems and questions to be solved, this educational portal will maintain frequent contact through written materials, DVD and online training, emails and telephone calls. The strategy will be to provide the families with a steady stream of data on the children's usage, performance, and needs as well as introduce other motivational strategies to maintain parent and student interest. New users' groups will form to recruit, motivate, and train members to benefit from the technological portals being constructed.

**A GROWING NATIONAL CONSENSUS SUPPORTING
A PRESCHOOL PORTAL:**

While this book is the product of the Waterford Institute's thinking, a survey of scholars and social commentators suggests that this initiative could offer a collective model that utilizes the best of many insights and responds to many needs.

NIH (the National Institutes of Health) has analyzed the available data and concluded that more than a third of children in fourth grade are unable to read at a basic level, more than two thirds cannot read at a proficient level, and very few are capable of reading at an advanced level. A solution to this problem is a high priority for our nation's future. NIH also concluded that at least 1 child in 5 requires tutoring, a much higher percent than had been previously understood.

Eaton Conant has demonstrated that a typical elementary school setting is hard pressed to offer more than a minute a day of individual instruction for each child. This eliminates the possibility of offering adequate individual support in schools for the children who are hopelessly behind their peers and heightens the importance of using the home to supplement school efforts.

Betty Hart and **Todd Risley**, 2 experienced researchers, show in their research that the children from the families living in poverty are spoken to using 32,000,000 fewer words by the age of 4 than children whose parents work in the professions, and that ⅔ of the words spoken to the children in poverty are negative in tone as contrasted with only one-sixth for those from professional families. Their data clarify the problem and suggest that if it is not solved, schools will continue to fail many students from impoverished backgrounds. The only viable and affordable solution appears to be the home preschool portal. The Waterford Institute is also developing a new generation of educational software specializing in vocabulary training for the youngest children in the early preschool and elementary years in order to address Hart and Risley's vocabulary shortfall problem.

Jeanne Chall and **Andrew Biemiller** have documented the specific needs and potential strategies to develop a vocabulary of sufficient strength so that the children coming from impoverished backgrounds do not face the dreaded 3rd and 4th grade reading slump which destroys their ability to stay up with their class because of their insufficient vocabularies even if they have appeared proficient in the K-2 years while learning to decode.

Marilyn Adams, a leading reading scholar, suggests that children raised in poverty have less than 7% of the preliteracy training in reading from their families than the professional class. Along with Hart and Risley's data, Adams stresses the need for early intervention for preliteracy training and believes that technology can help solve the dilemma.

Robert Sampson, the former chairman of Harvard's sociology department, with his colleagues from other universities, has shown that children in isolated and dangerous neighborhoods lose as much as 4% of their IQ because their vocabularies are limited by the mandatory isolation required for their safety. Having a portal to the home with a direct link to instruction and support is an ideal solution because it offers a bridge out of verbal and educational isolation to a safe and interesting working space for the child to explore, interact, and learn in.

James Heckman, the economist and Nobel Laureate, has demonstrated the importance of concentrating financial investments on the youngest preschool children where the return on investment is greatest. As a consequence of Heckman's research about 80% of the states have introduced some version of a universal preschool approach. Since the home portal will offer superior training in reading, math, and science, its introduction will provide an even greater cost-effective approach for the remaining states as well as supplement and improve the existing preschool efforts.

Susanna Loeb, a Stanford scholar, writes in a PACE (Policy Analysis for California Education) report that about two-thirds of children in America attend a preschool, and their attendance generates modest intellectual gains with some mixed data on the behavioral impact of the preschool on the children. The implications of the research on preschools (including Head Start) are that while they can contribute modestly to the children's improvement, they will not solve the "uneducable" problem and the variables causing it. Her work heightens the importance of finding other solutions.

Herb Walberg, the noted scholar and evaluation expert, notes that the home has a great potential for influencing the child because from birth until graduation from high school, only about 13% of the waking hours of children are spent in schools. This suggests that an inexpensive program that could use the time and resources available at home might be the wisest investment for addressing the problem.

Clayton Christensen, the successful Rhodes Scholar, entrepreneur, prize-winning author, and professor at the Harvard Business School, believes that only software can individualize instruction to the degree required to insure the successful education of American students whose prosperity has reduced their extrinsic motivation for academic achievement. By catering to their intrinsic motivation and addressing their individual interests and talents, those offering software will provide a "promising educational path" that will enable America to remain competitive on an international stage where access to an education is a life and death issue for many of the players. Because of his outstanding reputation, Christensen will have a strong impact on educational policy in the years ahead. He has just published an important book entitled *Disrupting Class* that will contribute to an acceleration of the understanding of the importance of the new technologies and software for educational success.

The Organization for Economic Co-operative Development (OECD) is a respected international organization that collects data that compares the practical educational abilities of the students from different nations every few years in different categories. Its latest report rates the United States as 14th of 34 countries in reading, 17th in science, and 25th in math. In overall academic achievement, the United States is rated as 23rd. However critics might disagree about the meaning of the statistics, there appears to be a discernable need for the United States to improve its educational delivery system, particularly when one considers that it spends more per pupil than almost any nation.

Paul David, a Stanford economist, has suggested that it takes about 40 years for a new technological invention to penetrate an existing mature delivery system. Schools are probably still a decade away from integrating technology wisely and well and, given the importance of starting children on an equal playing field, Waterford believes the most fertile approach for the foreseeable future will be the use of the new technologies and the Internet to give the children at home a huge resource bonus to supplement the efforts of their parents and any preschools that they attend. However, as David points out, once the multiple variables required to engineer, design, install, support, and train a work force to use the new potential is in position, then there is a rapid adoption of the new technology and explosive improvements in productivity for the delivery system. David is very helpful in explaining why technology has not yet had a strong impact in schools, but also useful in alerting us to the stunning improvements it can offer once it is in position.

Alvin and **Heidi Toffler**, futurists, whose book *Revolutionary Wealth* makes 2 important relevant points: (1) On a scale of 1 to 100, with 100 being the fastest, schools change at the maximum rate of 10. Businesses must change and adjust at 100 in order to survive. Hence both David and the Tofflers are suggesting we cannot look short term at making fundamental changes in schools. (2) Fortunately the capability to provide a new source of energy and work to the home (the computer) and connect it to the world (the Internet) will empower the home to again become a source of production and useful work just as it was before the industrial revolution. The Tofflers note that schools mimic and were formed to serve industries, and both were built to share their expensive resources which required daily commuting to gain access. The cost of technologies forced families to commute to them and obsoleted the home as a source of productive work. But now this will change!

Ray Kurzweil, our greatest technology futurist, in his book *The Singularity is Near* has drawn on the ideas of John von Neumann to note that human technological progress is exponential, not sequential, and that as it doubles it is exponentiating the amount of energy and work available to help man. He also notes that these increases start slowly, but suddenly become "explosive and profoundly transformative." He estimates that during the 100 years of the 20th century we accelerated our rate of technological progress and averaged a doubling every 10 years. A constant doubling actually accelerates the rate of change. During the 100 years of the 21st century "we won't experience 100 years of progress—it will be more like 20,000 years of progress (at today's rate"). This means that while people are debating the efficacy of using educational technology based on past experiences, they are missing the inevitable conclusion that what is available and improving will become "explosive and profoundly transformative."

The Waterford Institute: The advantage of the use of technology in the home has been elaborated by researchers at the Waterford Institute who have been at the forefront of software development for over 34 years. Having access to the home provides a multitude of educational benefits that are not available in the standard school or preschool environments. As part of its research Waterford has built a proactive interactive support team testing the home portal approach with a program called UPSTART funded in Utah for a few thousand families by the Utah Legislature. This program has demonstrated the universal efficacy of this approach using diverse populations from isolated rural areas to inner cities. Waterford has the expertise, the software, the experience, and the dedication to help lead the development of this new frontier. Waterford also believes that offering a nonprofit approach to its customers insures that the organization can concentrate on serving the customers without distorting its efforts in order to please its investors by offering a higher return each quarter.

The most important lesson Waterford has learned is that a new type of support organization has to be constructed as part of the "third source," which is both proactive and interactive as it initiates an ongoing dialogue with the families. Waterford discovered that it must hold the participants' attention, train them, provide constant ongoing feedback through the telephone and the Internet, and offer encouraging motivational strategies for the parents, caregivers, and children. The Institute calls these tasks the 3 "M"s: The new support organization has to Monitor, Motivate, and Measure the program and share the information with the families.

The Hardware Providers: Without doubt one of the most exciting aspects of providing a home portal will be the possibility of introducing parents to the potential of the new technologies using the microprocessor, lasers, and the Internet. Once they become acquainted with the standard computer and monitor used for the project, they will then be ready to take on the new devices that are appearing rapidly.

Think of the cell phone which has morphed from a telephone into a still camera, a photo album, a movie camera, a source of songs and music, a calendar, a list of contacts, a texting device, a calculator, and a personal portal to the World Wide Web with all of its services including email and access to newspapers and video clips as well as Facebook, YouTube, athletic events and a myriad of other services that are just being invented. These devices are starting to become replete with games that have educational value and ultimately will be part of the new delivery system available to the home that can handily complement the standard educational training the children can receive at school. Waterford will fashion these devices to serve a total educational solution.

What the nonprofit Waterford Institute has learned, after 35 years of research, is the joyous news (yes "joyous news") that in using the third source approach we are able to teach children to read or calculate as fast as the software can be installed, (thousands of children per week), and students start learning within a few minutes without training once the software is attached to the network. And to our delight they learn with equal success whether we are working with students from the poorest villages in remote areas or from the wealthiest families in great and spacious buildings in the cities or suburbs. We have also discovered that children develop their cognitive skills far better in this setting than in traditional nursery schools or preschool settings. This news is exciting because it suggests that whether or not students have access to a quality preschool, they will be able to begin to master their cognitive skills in their homes as a matter of course.

The success of the Waterford UPSTART project, with its attendant third source support approach, has brought hope to those involved who previously have seen reform after reform fail. Many have spent a lifetime watching good people introduce a beloved reform only to discover that, when the reform is replicated far away from the presence of the enthusiastic founder, the results inevitably show little or no significant difference. Sadly there are many scholars who have worked on a succession of reforms every few years for decades without achieving any replicable (scalable) success beyond their own locality.

THE IMPACT OF ENHANCED SOFTWARE SUPPORTED BY THE THIRD SOURCE:

The new ingredient that makes this possible is the software package that individualizes instruction embedded in artistically stunning packaging that is carefully designed to represent the latest scholarly research including the emerging science of the brain. What drives our sense of hope is that it is possible to make a huge difference educationally for children if they are exposed to these new educational packages for just a few minutes a day. As one outstanding brain researcher from France, Stanislas Dehaene, notes in his book *Reading in the Brain* (2009), when cutting through all the theoretical distracters, one clean, core issue remains: What is the "appropriate stimulation strategy for optimal daily enrichment" of the child's brain?

Brain research has revealed that, for optimal learning, a daily, highly specific, intense, carefully sequenced and sustained explicit learning trial is ideal. We see this in action in other areas where we practice daily to habituate a talent, be it practicing the piano or some athletic sport, for the acquisition of some desired skill. As outlined later in this book in a chapter on the brain, the reader will see how we actually build much of the capacity of our own brain through developing the neuronal networks that are constructed and strengthened through these daily exercises.

Fortunately, the availability of the new technologies and networks will allow us optimal daily access to these specific and highly precise instructional exercises. In fact the very act of having these available in the home and not just in school immediately doubles instructional access for the student because schools are open for instruction less than half the days in the year. The new "enhanced instruction" accomplishes this by offering levels of individualization that go far beyond a normal school setting.

The new mantra is becoming "brush your teeth every day, take your vitamins, and practice your learning for 15 minutes." This is a healthy prescription for the child who has access to the third source.

PRESCHOOL VS. THE THIRD SOURCE:

Recently (2007) scientists have been studying the impact of preschool on children. Two thirds of the students in the United States are in preschools, and those preschools usually have an effect size of only .10 on the students' educational growth. An effect size of .20 is considered the minimum, .50 is considered sound or good, and .80 is high or excellent. The Waterford effect size in their home-based program is between .71 and 1.67 depending on whether usage is medium or high. These surprising data on the impact of preschools on children were unearthed by the PACE study in California led by scholars from Stanford, Berkeley and UCLA digesting the rigorous ECLS study of 21,000 children nationally funded by the federal government. PACE is an acronym for the respected Policy Analysis for California Education.

The third source has a number of advantages over a typical preschool as well as a few disadvantages. The primary disadvantage is that an electronic curriculum is not very efficient in teaching the noncognitive skills. Some of the advantages are: (1) Less cost; (2) More effective cognitive instruction individualized for each child patterned after the latest brain research with a much higher academic effect size. These first 2 points produce a dramatic price/performance advantage that makes any alternative pale by comparison; (3) The quality of the new enhanced software is more apt to interest the typical American students who are facing a problem they do not understand in their economic prosperity which has enticed them more toward entertainment and games than is good for their academic careers. Many of the students do not sense the pressure of the emerging international financial competition and are more interested in pleasure than productivity.

The new enhanced software enriches the presentation by making the materials artistically pleasing, individualized for each user, and fortified with a design using the latest findings from brain research. The artistic beauty enhances the instruction by energizing multisensory areas of the brain and helps motivate the student as music, 2D and 3D graphics, stories, games, photography and beautifully illustrated books are presented for appeal and clarity.

But beyond the artistic beauty is a software kernel in the enhanced software called a sequencer that controls the sequence of instruction for each user. This level of individualization is critical to the success of enhanced instruction and insures that, in the shortest possible time, the student is provided explicit learning trials with feedback appropriate for his or her needs. Hence, we can understand why there is such a strong instructional impact even when only 1% of the day is available for instruction on technology. Thus through the emerging new communication networks, world class instruction will soon be available requiring a minimal commitment of time and money to all children.

The Cost Benefit Ratio: The new software and technologies will provide such a stunning cost/benefit ratio that the programs will scale rapidly in the years ahead. As I write this book we (the nonprofit Waterford Research Institute and its companion research school, the Waterford School), have just finished calculating the implications of the research that the Institute has conducted for the past 34 years and have concluded that the emerging cost/benefit ratio will propel usage of the new enhanced software into the public arena no matter what the current attitude that people have toward educational technology.

We project that in the decades ahead, while the public cost per pupil in the United States will grow to over $25,000 a student per year (New York City is already close to $23,000), the cost to deliver a superb curriculum to a home or school in high volumes will be less than 5% of this. In the future the technological approach will increase its capabilities and lower its cost while the traditional school cost per pupil will continue to rise in cost. As the United States and other nations struggle to fund education for the emerging knowledge-based societies of the future, the cost issue will drive the expansion of technology to supplement and strengthen the traditional schooling, not replace it.

For example, within a few years, a state legislature might make the software available to all families by merely adding a 3–5% increase in cost per pupil to their legislation. The home software would help the legislature financially in 2 ways: (1) They would save money on remedial services in the K-12 years as well as the second round of investment required as they enter community and regular colleges and again need remediation and; (2) They would also avoid the enormous expense of trying to add more manual workers (teachers) to the payroll to improve a mediocre system. Recall that, in an effort to improve our K-12 educational delivery system we have already tripled our per pupil expenditure in constant dollars without demonstrating any significant gains in the United States over the past 30 years.

Another way to address the Cost/Benefit Ratio is to cast it as a Price/Performance Advantage: The price performance measure consists of 2 separate components: the price of the service and the effectiveness of the intervention it offers. Occasionally some new technological breakthrough is developed that gives a powerful advantage to a delivery system. (For example, the steam engine triggered the Industrial Revolution by providing machinery for many delivery systems such as mining (pumps for mines), manufacturing (textile factories) and transportation (railway trains with locomotives to pull the passenger and freight cars, and steamships without sails.) Similarly the invention of the internal combustion gasoline engine led to cars, trucks, and airplanes, and the invention of the vacuum tube and transistor led to radio, television, computers, and the cell phone.

Each of these technological breakthroughs is successful because it provides a stunning price performance advantage over any alternative. Education has not experienced many price performance breakthroughs (the last large one was the invention of the book which replaced the hand written manuscript over 550 years ago), but this is about to change. As detailed in this book, our latest research findings are that a well-run technology program for young children gives a price performance advantage of somewhere between 7 and 17 times, depending on the amount of usage. For example, in comparing the effect size of preschools (.10) with the effect size of our software (.71 to 1.67), the software has a 7 to 17 times advantage depending on usage. But in addition, if our software is installed on a statewide basis to all 4 year old children, then our costs will ultimately drop to a quarter, then a tenth, and ultimately in another decade to about 5% of the school option, or about $\frac{1}{20}$ of their cost. Combining these 2 price/performance advantages, we can see that no matter how entrenched a traditional organization such as a school might be, the new technologies will have a strong impact on educational reform in the decades ahead.

What is left unnoticed is that, increasingly, technology provides still another advantage over traditional delivery systems: sometimes it not only improves a price performance option, but also technology opens up possibilities that have not existed at any price. Think of travelling to the moon, imaging the insides of the human body, or sequencing DNA.

Chapter Sixteen: UPSTART, A Third Source

Over the past 3 decades the Waterford Institute slowly came to understand some important research issues: (1) we needed to reach children much earlier than kindergarten or 1st grade, (2) we needed to use the time available at home to offer direct instruction to the children to empower and support the family unit which was currently unreachable, and (3) we needed to build a new model that supported technology at home from a distance even though there was not yet a traditional funding source available.

As we contemplated how to go about translating our knowledge of how to help children learn into a concrete initiative, we realized that what we had learned really did not fit into any of the existing educational models. While it is true that many thoughtful educators and policy makers had read and absorbed the same research we had and were looking for ways to impact early childhood learning, their solutions were inevitably limited by their inability to find a new source of work for their endeavor.

Congress seemed to favor Head Start (age 4) and Early Head Start (age 3), which were wildly popular with their constituencies. There was also a national movement underway, with state legislators, to provide universal preschool for all children. About 80% of the states have already committed to various stages of a universal preschool program for their young children, although most are still sparsely funded. As a result, there was no logical source of funding for a new program that was expensive to set up but would drop dramatically in cost when distributed in high volumes. In an attempt to remedy this problem, the Institute took 2 years to educate legislative leadership in Utah about the value of such a technology-based program for 4 year old children at home.

We also had to come to terms with an image problem that caused us considerable anxiety: combining early childhood education with technology often triggers fury from critics who hate the thought of children in bondage to technology. They have seen what mindless TV does to the young (although parents trust Sesame Street) as well as the deleterious impact of the gaming industry that swallows up their children's attention. Or, even worse, parents and critics are aware that children may use the technology of the Internet to access pornography or to chat with strangers who may turn out to be predators. Or they may gain access to cell phones where they talk endlessly in lieu of studying, practicing musical instruments, or developing social skills with other people. They may also text friends during family dinner, family prayer, or during school or church classes, and even disseminate shocking photos instantaneously to a whole community. And sooner or later many of them make themselves publicly available to the entire world by baring their photos and dreams on Facebook.

There is also another problem Waterford faced which is less volatile but just as real. The preschool community is sensitive to the needs of young children and does not want adult or grown-up values to be prematurely impressed on young children's minds. Many of these critics believe that young children learn best through "play" and "discovery learning." This community is fiercely protective of what its members consider "age appropriate" learning activities for young preschool children. They do not want childhood violated by aggressively ambitious parents and teachers who will set their children up for blighted futures like so many humorless programmed and emotionless robots. Thus a conflict potentially exists between some of the core values of early childhood advocates and those who are equally sensitive to the research data which suggest that certain vocabulary and preliteracy skills need to be mastered during the early childhood years to avoid future academic catastrophe and inequality of opportunity, particularly for children from at-risk homes.

Frequently this opposition does not recognize that there are 2 necessary groups of skills that children have to master: cognitive skills and noncognitive skills. The cognitive skills have been the subject of this book, and by now the reader understands that these skills must be carefully trained through carefully crafted stimulation events because although the human brain is wired for speech and handling simple numbers, it is not wired to "read" or to handle advanced mathematics. These must be explicitly taught and the brain provided specific stimulation until it has these new capabilities.

Just as importantly, the noncognitive skills must also be taught and are the traditional values that the preschool community is comfortable sponsoring. These include learning how to share, how to be a friend, how to delay gratification, how to listen and take directions, how to control a bad temper, how to be responsible for assignments, how to play, how to put things away, wash hands, etc. These noncognitive skills are just as important, and sometimes even more important, than the cognitive skills.

A technology based curriculum will provide better cognitive instructional results, but it is not as effective as schools in teaching the children noncognitive skills. For example schools excel in teaching children many noncognitive skills such as how to delay gratification, to learn to get along with others, to compete in sports, to learn to study, to pay attention to nutritional issues, to avoid obesity, drugs, and cigarettes, to learn to adjust to difficulties without the presence of parents, to learn how to relate with the opposite sex, to develop organizational skills, and to provide adult models for student imitation, among others.

For these and other reasons schools will never be replaced by technology! But the technology will help solidify the cognitive skills component that is critical to the future success of the students. Ultimately the cost of providing curriculum to the home will drop to the point where for a small percentage of the per pupil cost in a standard school setting, software in the home coordinated by the third source team will become part of the per student cost allocation by state legislatures to insure the academic component of a school's mission is successful.

This struggle between the noncognitive and cognitive camps is reminiscent of the reading wars when whole language fought with phonics for primacy, and to some extent the solution will probably be the same. Research indicates that, although brighter children from vocabulary rich environments can usually learn in a whole language environment, it is a fatal environment for those from families with lean vocabularies. The proper protocol for these children is that they be taught a phonics approach with enriched vocabulary. The same appears to be true in the preschool years where children from stressed families or with language difficulties need specific instruction in the cognitive skills involved in reading and mathematics if they are to succeed.

I believe that the 2 camps will ultimately come together in a partnership where the technology will handle much of the cognitive skill assignment and the preschools the noncognitive training. They will form this partnership because the technology will provide additional work to support the teachers' tasks (what technology always does best), which will free the teacher to handle the tasks that humans do best, relating to other humans, providing models, hope, love, support, inspiration, guidance, encouragement, motivation, and a profound understanding of what the child's needs are at any given moment. The teacher also has to serve a "real time" function where she is constantly tracking the mood and conduct of her charges and intervening when appropriate such as when 2 children start fighting, or a child suddenly gets sick. She also has to give advice on relationships, dating (when the students are older), drugs, bullying, careers, sports, etc.

Although, to some, the thought of offering direct, sequenced, sustained, explicit, and intense instruction in place of allowing the child to play and utilize discovery learning is distasteful, scholars have found that sometimes it is far more efficient and effective to provide it directly to most children. Having spent over $135 million during the past 20 years, the Waterford Institute has developed a treasure trove of explicit instructional software in reading, math, and science as well as copious activities that allow children to play various games and activities and replay songs and nursery rhymes.

Still, even though we had the materials there were 2 difficult questions still to be answered: (1) could we receive funding for a home project? and (2) would this project work for the children in all homes no matter what the socioeconomic status of the families?

We realized that educational services for preschool children at home were the assigned domain for no known organization, so we could not latch onto any funding sources that were already in place. By state charter in Utah the public schools are limited to the K-12 years which does not include preschool children. Therefore, we decided that the state might be interested in this area because legislators were concerned with providing a positive educational environment to insure that their students could compete in and enjoy the fruits of a knowledge-based world that would, in turn, attract knowledge-based industries to the state.

We then engaged in a 3 year effort to convince the Utah State legislature to fund and sign a contract with the Waterford Institute to test a pilot project on a representative sample of the Utah preschool population including Native American, African American, Hispanic, Pacific Islanders, Asian and Caucasian populations. The pilot program was to be administered in inner-city, suburban, rural and reservation areas.

As we met individually with the legislators they expressed many concerns including the following:

- How could a single mother with minimal or no command of English understand how to install and use a sophisticated computer attached to the Internet?

- How would we fix the machine when it broke down?

- How would we prevent parents on drugs from selling the computers?

- How could we prevent the families from using the machine and the Internet to access pornography?

- How could we be sure that 4 year old children would have the discipline to work on the machines for the required 5 days a week for 15 minutes a day?

- How would we install the Internet technology everywhere including reservations and isolated rural areas? How would we provide it to the few where it is commercially not feasible?

- How could we be sure that the disadvantaged and poorest families would hear about the program and be interested in signing up? How could we recruit the suspicious and those who did not understand English?

- How could technology really teach a 4 year old child who knows nothing about using a computer? How could we teach the youngest users to use a mouse when some of them might have inadequate control over their hand muscles?

- How do we know enough families already own computers and are connected to the Internet so that the program only has to buy computers and the Internet for less than 30% of the students who are within the 200% of poverty range defined and mandated by the legislature?

After we successfully addressed each of these issues—and more— we finally negotiated a contract with the state that allowed us to start the project in the latter part of April in 2009.

We named the program Utah Preparing Students Today for A Rewarding Tomorrow (UPSTART). Our first concern was to ascertain whether enough children would register. We had been allocated funds for about 1,300 students and had divided the state by school districts with the goal of including children from every school district in the state in order to satisfy legislative intent. We had formed an advisory board, distributed thousands of flyers in both English and Spanish, advertised, been on TV interviews, contacted influential providers of children's services, built and trained a support center, signed contracts with hardware and Internet providers, preloaded disk drives and computers.

Finally, it was 8:00 AM on the designated day, and I was standing by the banks of terminals and telephones waiting to see what would happen. The first call came precisely at 8:00 AM from a city in the southern part of the state that had alerted its parents to the program through an automated telephone call system. Most of our early calls came from that district but then, slowly, they started coming in from all areas. Within a few weeks we had registered 1,347 students with our desired goals of ethnic and geographic diversity. In order to insure that the necessary background information was collected properly for future research purposes, we had our support personnel speaking both English and Spanish as they entered the data from the parents calling in.

Another concern was that we would lose many of the 4 year olds to kindergarten in August and therefore would be unable to get enough of them registered, provide the hardware and Internet where needed and get the families running before they had to leave the program (the legislation required that the students leave the program when they started kindergarten). However, if the families already had a computer and the Internet, then we sent them a disk drive with 70 gigabytes of software preloaded with reading, math, and science which they connected to their computers through the USB port. There was a problem almost immediately. We got a frantic call and email with pictures showing that one of the first disk drive parcels sent out was intercepted and eaten by the dog of the house while it was still in the package. We have a lovely photograph in our archives of a tooth-punctured disk drive by a jealous and anti-intellectual dog who did not want the child he was assigned to protect contaminated by exposure to a world of learning that would give his charge "airs."

For those families who did not have a computer or access to the Internet—and qualified economically for support—we installed computers with the preloaded software, contacted the Internet providers and scheduled Internet installation, trained the families on how to use them, and started the children on the program. We also provided bilingual training videos for these families. The majority of the initial program installation problems came from trying to overcome firewalls for those families that owned their own computers, but the staff soon worked out solutions for them and the program was underway.

Once we were operating, my real concern was whether or not we could successfully maintain a healthy daily usage of at least 15 minutes a day, 5 days a week. We had already learned that students would not show very much of an educational effect until they had been on the program for about 1,100 minutes. After this they would start to pull away from a comparison control group at a steady rate that keeps climbing without slowing down. Using 75 minutes a week (5 days at 15 minutes a day) as a standard, I knew that students would not show very much growth for about 3½ months. This meant if we were unable to get most of the students started early enough because of installation difficulties or problems, that many could be leaving the program in late August without reaching enough minutes to provide a critical instructional impact.

But even if we succeeded in starting enough families in a timely fashion, there was the larger problem of whether we could count on the 4 year old children reaching the 15 minute a day quota and sustaining it in the months ahead after the initial thrill wore off. Usage had become my private hell because time and again I had seen Waterford introduce the program into a school, have it produce outstanding results, and then drift and die out as the traditional school culture failed to understand the positive impact of the program just as Paul David had prophesied in his 40 year rule. David understands how difficult it is to change any traditional culture when introducing new technologies because the leadership has been trained to trust and manipulate the variables of the earlier delivery system. With this in mind, some critics believe that schools will try all sorts of options, but they will not commit to technology's potential and generate productivity gains until the current leadership dies off.

I spent an anxious summer constantly muttering, "all I need is 15 minutes a day; it's like brushing teeth; it has to be done every day without arguments and discussions; it's only 1% of a day." Seeing me coming, parents fled and vaulted over hedges to get away before I could again button hole them with my 15 minute a day mantra. Finally in September I had all the data collected and graphed. I believe the following is one of the most important graphs in educational history.

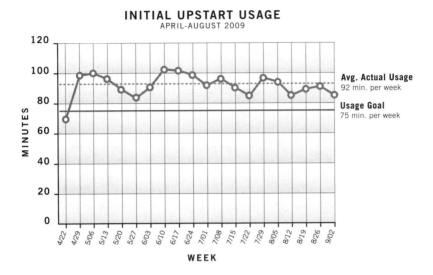

INITIAL UPSTART USAGE
APRIL-AUGUST 2009

Avg. Actual Usage
92 min. per week

Usage Goal
75 min. per week

The reason this is such an important graph is that it demonstrates that it is possible to have children learn in their homes (or other off-school environments) every day of the year (not just the 180 days in the traditional school system) no matter how difficult the family situation might be. I had learned that, when using technology to teach children, "Usage is King!" I recognized that the available software and our support framework for it might not be fully effective, but that these could improve over time. What I was looking at was incontrovertible evidence that even in the first attempt we had succeeded more than 20% beyond our ambitious goals, and it would be possible someday in the future to give all children an ideal start in their homes all over the world, no matter where they were located or what their economic circumstances might be.

There was a Santa Claus! There was a third source to reach families directly with only a support center and the technologies. We had the first glimpse of the future of education, and it looked good.

At this I burst into tears for the second time in my life while examining experimental data. This time, however, they were quiet tears of joy and hope. I would not have to wait a decade for schools to begin to use the technology effectively. With this new flexible model I could just as easily substitute homes or willing school sites in

Africa, Mississippi or California. The projects could begin within a few weeks of commitment. No buildings or campuses would need to be built or faculties trained. Here was a way to democratize and scale educational excellence and equity for all children. I could, after all, offer a Spence or a Waterford School experience—or its academic equivalent—to every child at some point in the future when the software has been fully developed for older children. I realized that if the student usage was this positive on our first efforts, then it would be possible to improve them still further in the future when we had learned more about our customers and how to best serve them. By then we will have also improved our knowledge of how to motivate the children while assuring they accomplish their academic goals.

Months later as we continued to track the usage we noticed two changes: (1) the vacations such as Thanksgiving and Christmas distracted the children and dramatically lowered their usage so that it dropped below the 75 min. line. (2) then as the year progressed, usage slowly began dropping as we approached the summer months. The results from year 1 can be seen in the graph below.

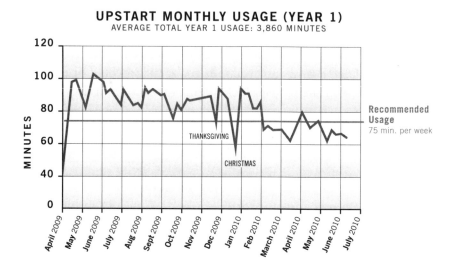

UPSTART MONTHLY USAGE (YEAR 1)
AVERAGE TOTAL YEAR 1 USAGE: 3,860 MINUTES

But as I anticipated, as we learned how to interact with the families from our support center more effectively, the next year we were able to improve the usage. In the graph below, notice that neither at Thanksgiving or Christmas during 2010 that usage drops below the minimum. And furthermore, by March of 2011 we were maintaining our improvement above the previous year's usage. This is encouraging because it suggests that over time we will be able to continually improve the parent's and child's motivation which will lead to more impressive student learning. The 2011 data ends in March as this manuscript went to press.

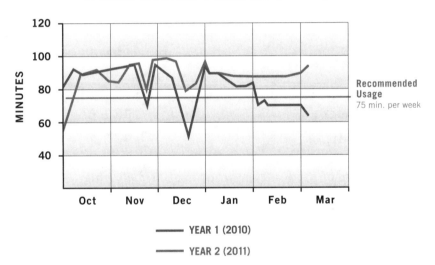

Having passed the "usage test," we began parsing the data to make certain that children from the lower SES homes or non-English speaking families used the materials as frequently and learned as rapidly as their more affluent peers. The following table includes all the sites and the mixed demographic populations. One of them, for example, was an Native American reservation on the Nevada-Utah border that required our people to drive in from a road in Nevada to gain access to the families and install the technology required so that they could gain access to the Internet. The site is 2 hours from the nearest preschool. We had hoped the students would work at least 300 minutes over an initial arbitrary period, and to our great delight they used the materials for over 500 minutes during this assigned period. What a relief!

USAGE ANALYSIS AMONG ETHNIC GROUPS

ETHNICITY	MEAN USAGE
American Indian/ Alaskan Native	2121.72
African American	2647.46*
Caucasian	1932.66
Hispanic	1930.23

*number of students in group statistically small

A preliminary study of the data indicated that all of the groups advanced at about the same speed, and the legendary ambitious white suburban mother actually had her child use the materials about the same as the poor Hispanic families. Over 70% of the Hispanic families shared their equipment with others.

The cost savings using technology will accelerate over the alternatives in the decades ahead and will insure a heavy commitment to the use of technology. We then developed a graph comparing projected costs of the program to standard school options, and found the following positive data:

COMPARISON OF PROGRAMS: ANNUAL COST PER CHILD

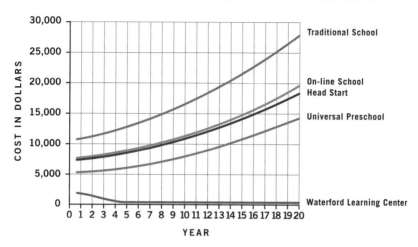

Traditional School: 2009 projected cost per student at traditional school ($10,844), National Center for Education Statistics, September 2008. 5% year-over-year growth.

On-line School: BellSouth Foundation: *20/20 Costs and Funding of Virtual Schools*, 2006. 5% year-over-year growth.

Head Start: Average Head Start cost as reported on the Health and Human Services Website at http://www.acf.hhs.gov/programs.hsb.research/2006.htm. 5% year-over-year growth.

Universal Preschool: Children's Defense Fund, 2008. 5% year-over-year growth.

Waterford Learning Center: Waterford Learning Center cost utilizing a scaling of both student volume and technology efficiencies. Cost is based on 2009 UPSTART program costs.

THE LONGTIME COST IMPLICATIONS:

As the graph above indicates, in many public school systems costs for instruction will grow over the next 20 years to over $25,000 per pupil. New York City is already approaching $23,000 a child. During this period the cost of a pure technology approach in the home will flatten and ultimately should reach less than 5% of the cost of a standard school enrollment. Note that the home product will be available every day of the year. This combination of offering an excellent education at home for less than 5% of the cost of the standard school tuition suggests that there will be a huge market for quality software in the years ahead. In all probability state legislatures and school leadership will begin to subsidize a parallel track of home-based software in order to insure that their students achieve competence and high scores because this insurance will only cost them less than 5% over their current expense commitment.

Along with the usage data, the speed of learning, the advantages for the minority students, and the cost benefits, the findings on the effect size of the software are extraordinarily hopeful and impressive. Scholars rate research projects by their "effect sizes," a single figure that suggests the effectiveness of an experimental approach being evaluated.

- An effect size of .20 is considered small, but authentic. For example in trying to decide how important SES (Socio-Economic Status) is, scholars found it makes a modest to small difference of .25.

- An effect size of .50 is considered medium. A .50 effect size means the experimental approach is having a definite impact. For example scholars studying the impact of the family home environment found an effect size of (.37); and others studying the amount of instructional time found the effect size to be (.38); and others found the effect size of tutoring to be (.40). Other significant effect sizes are those for personalized instruction (.57) and IQ (.71).

- An effect size of .80 is large.

- An effect size of 1.00 or above is considered unusually effective and rare.

- The effect size for the first few months of the Waterford UP-START program range from .71 up to 1.67 depending on how the data are analyzed. These data are rather extraordinary and suggest that the program has unusual potential even if the effect size lessens over time.

CONFIRMING THE THIRD SOURCE:

Reviewing these data, I am convinced that we now have clear proof of the efficacy of the 3rd way to provide all children with an outstanding and inexpensive education with undreamed of access. This diagram below illustrates the Third Source, which uses distance learning centers to empower the home by providing limitless access to instruction year-round for their children.

A THIRD SOURCE: THE DISTANCE LEARNING MODEL

The schools benefit by having 2 other organizations help to insure that their instructional goals are met as they supplement what has become an impossible burden for them to fulfill.

There is ample evidence available that, in a knowledge-based society, the schools alone can rarely salvage the students from families who have failed to provide the necessary preliteracy training and vocabulary required for their children to succeed in school. This is a serious problem that is generally unsolvable and contributes to the 50% dropout rate of so many urban schools no matter how hard the school tries or what new reforms it sponsors. For it is, when all is said and done, a delivery system problem, not a school problem. The implementation of the third source will offer a number of benefits as it adds new workers and components to the delivery system. Although the expense for the support teams and their technologies will seem to make education even more expensive, in the long run they will enable costs to plummet as many of the supplemental costs of poorly educated children will dwindle away.

Chapter Seventeen: The New Science of Education

There is a new science of education emerging that we will have the pleasure of observing even though there will be considerable stress and delays occurring as we struggle to implement this wonderful scientific opportunity. There are 5 variables emerging that will coalesce into a new science of education:

(1) TECHNOLOGY, (2) INSTRUCTION, (3) ACCESS, (4) MOTIVATION, AND (5) RESEARCH

Their combined strengths will allow them to revolutionize education because the traditional educational delivery system has matured and will have difficulty improving; whereas, these new areas are in their infancy and still blessed with accelerating capabilities and declining costs which will insure universal access in all settings for all children in all nations.

(1) TECHNOLOGY:

Although the instructional technologies such as computers, storage, and the Internet are thought of as mature technologies, they are not. Computers continue to improve in speed and storage at almost 1% a week (doubling about every 2 years) without any increase in cost. This doubling phenomenon takes a while to become visible, but the further along the curve, the greater the impact of the doubling. The difficult concept for most people to understand is that we are entering an era where almost unlimited power will be available to an individual in his or her home or school to receive interactive individualized instruction of undreamed of quality.

(2) INSTRUCTION:

Educational Software is Approaching Usable Maturity: Software is the variable that allows the new increasing power of the computer to become useful in any human endeavor. Bill Gate's great contribution was in developing inexpensive software at Microsoft that allowed this new power to be useable for a host of business and personal applications: It has taken educational developers longer, but after about 40 years of development, educational software is emerging that is powerful enough to begin to offer advantages that a standard classroom alone cannot match. Some of these advantages are:

- **Individualized Instruction:** The average elementary classroom is fortunate if it can give each child 1 minute of individualized instruction a day. In a typical reading program on a computer in the classroom, the child can easily have 15 to 30 times the individualization in a given day. Using sequencing techniques, the computer software can craft a unique instructional sequence for each child based on real time need.

- **Interactivity instead of Passivity:** The computer software forces the student to become an active agent. The computer requires interactivity and the student's attention, and it does not allow gaps and lapses in student learning because the software is tracking the student's progress and adjusting the program to insure understanding.

- **Immediate Feedback:** Every learning trial receives immediate feedback, an optimal strategy in mastering new materials and cementing old ones that are shaky. The computer also has infinite patience and allows constant repetition without comment or judgment.

- **Undiluted Curriculum:** Most children are exposed to, or learn, only a diluted and partial curriculum because of attendance issues involving either the teacher or the students, or the lack of student attention during class time, or because of poor teaching. Technology is not immune to attention issues, but it has 3 unequivocal advantages. It can insure that the entire curriculum is available and taught in a proper sequence, that it is mastered before moving on, and that it can be buttressed by spectacular artistic presentations with music, graphics, and animation to insure student interest and willingness to use the materials over and over.

- **Minimizing Disconnects from the Ideal Curriculum:** The common denominator in many of the problems of school failure is that the students disconnect from the sources of work (teachers, books as stored work, audiovisual devices, etc.) available to them. Most disconnects come from a myriad of student reasons (e.g. cutting class, daydreaming, peer pressure, chasing social myths, dating, boredom, fear, anxiety, athletics, etc.), although some are induced by poor teaching.

  One of the little noticed disconnects is the disparity of what may be available in instruction to the student compared to what the latest research is showing to be effective. Most teachers will update their expertise sporadically, at best, and many simply teach what they are familiar with and have been trained to believe is effective. Some will teach out of date materials for decades! Here technology has a clear advantage in avoiding a disconnect with the latest research because it increasingly is becoming updatable overnight. Research will go from the laboratory to the product very quickly compared with the decades (if ever) that it takes currently to reach either the textbooks or many of the teachers.

(3) ACCESS:
Inexpensive Convenient Access: From Scarcity to Abundance:
The hallmark of the new technologies is their ability to provide inexpensive, convenient, access to outstanding education anywhere at

any time because the newly connected hardware will be ubiquitous in nature. Thus sources of instructional work will morph from scarcity to abundance. As the noted futurist, Alvin Toffler, has stated, these new sources of energy connected by the Internet and wireless technology will allow us access to work on instruction at home, or wherever we might be, instead of requiring us to travel to gain access at offices or schools. These new instructional capabilities will also be scalable without requiring the construction of a new physical plant or hiring new personnel to staff it. We will continue to have offices and schools, but the work they sponsor will also be available elsewhere where it will be inexpensive, convenient, and more effective. As the field of Economics has discovered, scarcity is synonymous with high cost, and abundance with low cost. As millions of homes are served, the price will drop to pennies an hour for instruction.

(4) MOTIVATION:

Motivation at a Distance: Usage as King: This new science will require extensive research in motivational strategies because many of the traditional motivators such as school teachers and administrators, or well-trained and motivated parents, will not always be present. Instead, the materials themselves and a new supporting organization built by the providers will have to provide motivation for the children (and adults) using them. After decades of research, we now realize that usage is the critical variable, and unfortunately there is little tradition or understanding of its importance.

When not part of the daily routine, the lack of usage is the ultimate disconnect. The goal of new motivational research will be to "institutionalize usage" so that children and parents assume that 15 minutes usage a day, for example, is a standard norm, like brushing teeth or practicing the piano. 15 minutes a day is only 1% of a day, so I suspect that in the future we will try to habituate the usage at somewhere between 1% and 4% of a day. This way there can be little criticism that the children are being forced to leave their play behind and becoming obsessed with sitting in front of computer monitors.

(5) RESEARCH:

Brains and Databases: From Approximation to Precision: The new technologies will soon make outstanding individualized interactive instruction available inexpensively in every conceivable setting. I sense that most people have no idea of the spectacular instruction that will be emerging as the software industry matures. The new instructional materials will be presented in dazzling artistic settings and supported by superb motivational strategies. Perhaps even more significantly, 2 relatively new areas of research will help inform our instructional strategies as they utilize the new technologies: (1) the study of the human brain and (2) the construction of powerful new student databases on enormous file servers which will be linked together over the Internet. As John T. Bruer has cautioned us in his well-timed book reviewing the literature on the brain, *The Myth of the First Three Years,* we must be careful about over generalizing as the new brain data becomes available; however, as this science matures it will help clarify what the most effective strategies are for teaching specific disciplines, when they should be taught, and most importantly, what is the individual learning profile of each child? The learner profile will, in turn, guide the instructional strategies for every student.

These databases will ultimately contain the real time records of millions of children and allow software providers to transition from being approximate in their instructional approach to offering a more precise knowledge of what the child actually knows and how best to teach him or her. For example, ultimately we will have detailed records available on how millions of children have learned the letter "A." Gradually we will build learner profiles that categorize how specific children have learned this letter, what confuses them, and what instructional approach will best serve them given their unique learner profile. We will also be able to experiment overnight on testing different instructional approaches for different learner profiles by assigning millions of children tasks that can be completed and compared in days instead of months or years.

Testing will gradually be built into the instructional program so that student progress can be monitored in real time and not only at the end of a grade or term. Real time testing is a function of being able to track the status of every item the child is working on. We will be able to know precisely what the child knows because the test item will be the same one taught to the child during the instruction. Thus we already have a record of what the child knows and does not know. Over time we will also measure the learning decay rate for every child in every area of his or her learning so we can tell when the item needs to be refreshed before it falls below a retrievable status.

The coming great breakthrough is a function of the amount of work that will be provided to help educate children. New energy sources will now be utilized to provide more instructional resources (work), and the addition of work to any task has the felicitous effect of allowing humans to substitute precision for approximation, be it in brain scans, teasing data out of giant databases, or offering children the precise instruction they need whenever and wherever they might need it. We also have the gratifying thought that energy sources will be continuing to double every 2 years and, therefore, will be constantly adding to our ability to become more precise and knowledgeable in our instructional sciences. This, of course, means that soon we may be entering the realm we all seek: The possibility of offering both equity and excellence in education to all the children on our planet.

Chapter Eighteen: Waterford on the Brain

The proper training of the human brain, particularly for younger children, is one of our most important responsibilities as adults. Many of the functions that are regulated by the brain, such as breathing, hearing, seeing, speaking, walking, and eating, are automatic, but others that humans have invented, such as music, reading, writing, and mathematics, require specific instruction and training through regular and explicit stimulation of the brain's neuronal cells.

At birth the brain has billions of brain cells (neurons) ready to be trained that are located in specialized areas appropriate to their functions. Depending on the level of stimulation that these various brain cells receive, they can grow and strengthen, lie dormant, or gradually lose their functionality altogether. The only way to train and physically enhance the neurons is by providing external stimulation collected and transmitted by our senses to the neurons in the brain. We believe that children learn naturally as they are raised in families, and we do not tend to think of brain growth being only a function of stimulation because this sounds abstract and cold. However, we have learned that in some areas we need to initiate regular periods of scheduled stimulation in a child's life when we want to develop explicit skills such as playing the piano, practicing ballet, shooting a basketball, or working on a golf or tennis swing. Also, humans have invented schools to provide a training/practice/

stimulation schedule where regular instructional periods are provided during the day to practice different disciplines. Unlike speech or sight that occurs without specific training, most of the disciplines that we have invented require specific training through regularly scheduled periods of brain stimulation.

As neurons are stimulated and trained, they change physically. We are used to this in athletics where physical exercise builds up the muscles, but we usually do not think of physical change as part of developing our reading skills in the brain. Nevertheless, the regular stimulation of a neuron causes profound physical changes in it. As mentioned earlier, this was first discovered by Marian Diamond in 1964 who directed research teams at Berkeley working on the anatomical changes of the brain caused by the stimulation from enriched environments. In her first experiment she discovered that in a group of 9 rats "the enriched rats had a thicker cerebral cortex than the impoverished rats," and "this was the first time anyone had ever seen a structural change in an animal's brain based on different kinds of early life experiences." The implications of her findings are extraordinary and suggest that our experiences physically change the neural networks in our brain and hence our capabilities for future success. No one can predict the future and what might happen to us as humans, but we now know that our brains can be enriched positively through patterns of stimulation that literally change the physical nature of our mental networks (our wiring), or conversely, limit them if there is inadequate stimulation to allow the potential to develop.

The basic brain cell, illustrated on the following page, is called a neuron and consists of a cell body called the soma and a long thin axon which is covered by a myelin sheath. Also attached to the cell body are dendrites that receive signals from other neurons and deliver them to the cell body.

At the end of the axon is a bulbous terminal that releases transmitter substances into a gap called the synaptic cleft which is between the terminals and the dendrites of the next neuron. The stimulated brain does not grow more neurons, or brain cells (the number is fixed at birth), but it helps the neuronal cell grow more branches that can collect incoming signals (through dendrites) with robust connection points on its branches (spines) to facilitate the collection of the signal being sent from another cell.

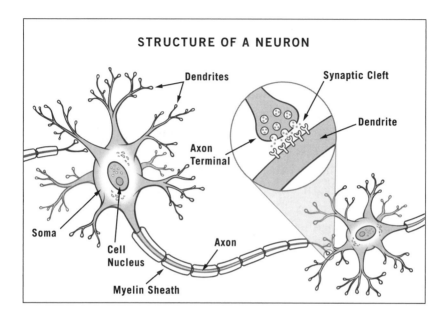

The neuron's cell has an output and an input side. The collecting input side (the thread-like dendrites) receives their electrical signal from another cell's output (an axon) across a junction called a synapse, and the synapse connection also grows larger and more efficient as a result of its use and stimulation.

In addition to its 100 billion neural cells, the brain also has 1 trillion of a second type of cell called a glial cell that appears to offer support to help the neurons become more efficient. For example it will form a myelin sheath that looks like a string of sausages around the neural cell's axon which is the long thread-like extension from the cell nucleus that transmits signals to connect with other cells. The myelin sheath acts like insulation around a wire which helps improve the quality of the electrical impulse the cell is transmitting to other cells. The amount of myelin also grows thicker as the cell is stimulated.

On the threadlike dendrite filaments that expand like tree roots, little spines grow that are shaped and changed by the organism's exposure to its environment. Diamond notes that a scholar at the University of California at Davis, Richard Coss, studied the dendritic spines from young honeybees that had never left the hive, then compared them to the spines of bees that had made just one single flight out into the meadows near the university and back. They also looked at dendritic spines in forager bees that made repeated forays in search of pollen and nectar, and at spines in nursing bees that remain in the hive permanently and tend the larvae. The Coss team found a number of different spine shapes depending on the bees' level of stimulation from the outside world: young bees that had never flown had lollipop spines, with small heads on tall stalks. In bees that had made a single flight many of these lollipops had grown bigger heads! In the forager bees, with their extensive real-world navigating experience, the spines had very large heads and very short stalks. Experience—even just an hour or two's worth of flying through the meadow—obviously had a dramatic enlarging effect on the bees' dendritic spines.

At the end of her book entitled *Enriching Heredity*, Diamond summarizes her findings after almost 30 years of laboratory research. Notice how a lack of stimulation can have as great a physical impact as extra stimulation. With stimulation the nerves grow larger and without stimulation they literally become smaller.

> We have learned that every part of the nerve cell from Soma [cell body] to synapse alters its dimensions in response to the environment. The enlarged nerve cells with their more numerous glial support cells are apparently utilized by the rat to solve maze problems more effectively than rats without such modified cells…just as the cortical neurons become larger in a stimulating environment, they decrease in size when there is less input from the millions of sensory receptors reporting from the body surface and the internal organs. It is just as important to stress the fact that a decrease in stimulation will diminish a nerve cell's dendrites as it is to stress that increases stimulation will enlarge the dendritic tree. We have seen how readily the cortical thickness diminishes within impoverished environments, and at times, the effects of impoverishment

are greater than those brought about by a comparable period of enrichment.... Perhaps the single most valuable piece of information learned from all our studies is that structural differences can be detected in the cerebral cortex of animals exposed at any age to different levels of stimulation in the environment...in fact at every age studied, we have shown anatomical effects due to enrichment or impoverishment. The results from enriched animals provide a degree of optimism about the potential of the brain in the elderly human beings, just as the effects of impoverishment warn us of the deleterious consequences of inactivity.

As Daniel Coyle notes in his book *The Talent Code*, myelin "plays a key role in the way our brains function, particularly when it comes to acquiring skills." He adds that myelin is helpful because of "3 simple facts. (1) Every human movement, thought, or feeling is a precisely timed electrical signal traveling through a chain of neurons—a circuit of nerve fibers. (2) Myelin is the insulation that wraps these nerve fibers and increases signal strength, speed, and accuracy. (3) The more we fire a particular circuit, the more myelin optimizes that circuit, and the stronger, faster, and more fluent our movements and thoughts become." Quoting Dr. George Bartzokis who is a professor of neurology at UCLA, he writes that "myelin is 'the key to talking, reading, learning skills, and being human.'" Coyle explains that "*Skill is myelin insulation that wraps neural circuits and that grows according to certain signals.* The story of skill and talent is the story of myelin."

In a brief review of the history of research on myelin, Coyle notes that, in the 1980s, Bill Greenough discovered at the University of Illinois that rats raised in a stimulating environment increased both their number of synapses and the amount of myelin they generated by 25% over a control group. Then fortunately, after the year 2000, there were technical developments that enabled scientists to measure and map myelin inside living subjects. In 2000 Torkel Klingberg linked the development of reading skills with increases in myelin, and in 2006 Jesus Pujol discovered similar increases from vocabulary development.

Coyle notes that "other researchers, like Dr. Fields, uncovered the mechanism by which these myelin increases happened. As he described in a 2006 paper in the journal *Neuron*:

> Supporter cells...sense the nerve firing and respond by wrapping more myelin on the fiber that fires. The more the nerve fires, the more myelin wraps around it. The more myelin wraps around it, the faster the signals travel, increasing velocities up to 100 times over signals sent through an uninsulated fiber.... Myelin quietly transforms narrow alleys into broad, lightning-fast superhighways. Neural traffic that once struggled along at 2 miles an hour can, with myelin's help, accelerate to 200 miles an hour. The refractory time (the wait required between one signal and the next) decreases by a factor of 30. **The increased speed and decreased refractory time combine to boost overall information-processing capability by 3000 times.**

What's more," Coyle notes, "myelin has the capacity to regulate velocity, speeding, or occasionally even slowing signals so they hit synapses at the optimal time." Coyle also quotes Fields as saying "your brain has so many connections and possibilities that your genes can't code the neurons to time things so precisely [in few milliseconds], but you can build myelin to do it."

Stimulation also affects the terminal end of the axon which grows much larger and improves its capabilities to pass on the electric signal as it connects to a dendrite across the synapse space. When there is a great deal of traffic, the number of dendrites collecting signals connected to a single cell nucleus increases as much as roots spread out in the ground to provide nutrients for a single tree. All of this physical change is a function of the level of stimulation the brain receives as it builds up its capacity to function more effectively and efficiently.

Of all the skills that need specific stimulation, reading is one of the most important because it can provide access to information (a type of stimulation for the brain) without requiring the recipient of the information to travel or be present at the original source of the stimulation. With reading, knowledge can be portable and inexpensive. With the invention of the Internet, worldwide searches for information can be completed in a fraction of a second, and information can be shared in real time with people all over the globe. For those who have not yet learned to read, the Internet can offer reading instruction any place at any time. The Internet enables parents to import well-designed and highly motivating software instruction that can teach their children to read at home if the children are carefully scheduled for brief daily instructional periods.

In the words of Stanislas Dehaene who has just completed a definitive book on brain research and reading,[1] what is important in teaching students to read is to initiate "an appropriate stimulation strategy" that will provide "optimal daily enrichment" for the brain cells that insures children learn to read properly. With the help of technology, software, and the Internet, access to reading will become much less expensive and more available. And for those children with learning difficulties there will be excellent remediation available carefully designed to provide multisensory stimulation to fit the brain's architecture.

Most parents are not sufficiently knowledgeable to be able to teach their children how to read or how to play a musical instrument, but they can provide an environment where there are daily moments of scheduled stimulation that are ideal from the standpoint of developing the brain cells for areas of interest that humans have invented. Remember, these invented areas require daily stimulation and will not happen automatically even in a loving family setting where the parents read to the children. Fifteen minutes a day (1% of a day) on a computer with outstanding reading software can have a profound impact on a child's reading skills because it provides a minimal stimulation strategy individualized for each child given the design of the brain. Time and sleep then weaves their magic after the cell has received its daily stimulation which helps improve the reading apparatus as myelin clothes the axon for more efficient performance, the terminal connections are enlarged, and dendrites spring up to add to their information gathering possibilities for each cell.

---

[1] Stanislas Dehaene, *Reading in the Brain* (New York: Penguin, 2009).

The preschool years are an ideal time to schedule this daily stimulation package because children are less mobile and tend to be available at home most days of the year. Whereas a school is usually open less than half the days in a year, a young child is apt to be home every day of the year. Parents need only to help develop a habit pattern where the children are expected to work on the reading software for 15 minutes a day 5 days a week for about 75 minutes a week. This habit needs to be developed as firmly as the daily brushing of teeth. If a 4 year old preparing for kindergarten spends 15 minutes a day for an average of 5 days a week for 50 weeks a year, he or she will have access to 3,750 minutes (62.5 hours) of age appropriate individualized instructional materials in reading during his or her fourth year.

This means every child exposed to the program will have experienced about 62½ hours of individualized instruction during the year on exciting and artistically pleasing materials designed by leading scholars in reading. What is truly stunning is that when the child attends a full day kindergarten the following year when she is 5 in her first year of formal schooling, she will receive only about 3 hours of individualized instruction which is less than ¹⁄₂₀ of what she received at home using the computer software when she was 4.

Note that each individual trial that is appropriate to the child's need at that time helps to strengthen the neurons being stimulated and helps the myelin sheath grow stronger and become a better insulator. All that is required for this to succeed is that the parents' insure that the children spend 15 minutes a day using the reading software. The parents need not be present for the daily instructional period. In order to help the parents succeed, Waterford has learned the value of building a Waterford Learning Support Center to provide monitoring, motivation, and measurement of the child's performance for the parents or schools using the materials.

A formal stimulation package such as UPSTART also addresses a serious SES (socioeconomic status) problem. Beginning in 1965, scholars began to discover that the impact of the family on reading skills was greater than that of schools, and in fact contrary to popular and scholarly lore, schools were relatively equal in resources (Coleman). Trying to improve the schools directly failed to address the real source of the problem which is that low SES families have an environment that offers a diminished stimulation level for their children, particularly in vocabulary (Hart and Risley). Introducing preschools (such as Head Start or state universal preschool movements) to attempt to offer a more stimulating academic environment for the children is too diffuse a solution. What the brain needs is a rich daily exposure to a carefully designed specific stimulation package that systematically trains the neural networks and prepares them for academic tasks such as reading, mathematics, and science.

The value of the daily stimulation period is that it provides training for the neurons and sensitizes them so they are able to recognize what a given signal represents. For example, in learning to read, neurons have to be stimulated to recognize each letter of the alphabet, both upper and lower case, so that when an incoming stimulus of photons reflected off a page of text enter the brain through the eye, there are neurons trained to recognize the stimulus of the incoming letter. But the graphical image of the letter must also stimulate another group of trained neurons that are sensitized to recognize the sounds associated with the shape of the letter. Then this second group of neurons will have to pass the signal on to another group that recognizes what the word means. The more the neurons are stimulated through appropriate daily instruction, the more the neural networks strengthen, speed up, and improve their efficiency for recognizing the incoming signal, and the more the nerve cells change physically and build their capacity for the task at hand. This process can take years to perfect and is dependent on the daily stimulation strategy available to the learner.

As Daniel Coyle notes in his excellent book *The Talent Code*,[2] to achieve world-class competence and "genius" status in areas such as dance, chess, math, tennis, etc., experts estimate that a human needs as much as 10,000 hours of practice over a 10 year period to train the brain to its capacity. People who are labeled as "geniuses" usually have spent considerable practice time polishing their skills. While Bobby Fisher became a grandmaster at chess by age 17, he had already spent

---

[2]Daniel Coyle, *The Talent Code,* (New York: Bantam, 2009), pp. 52–53.

9 years working hard to master his craft. Mozart had studied music under his father's strict tutelage for 3,500 hours before his 6th birthday. Describing this phenomenon, Coyle has written an equation: *Deep Practice x 10,000 hours = World-Class Skill.*

Brain research is showing us that we should be concentrating on a daily stimulation package in order to offset the stimulation shortfall in many of our low SES families. Unfortunately, most current reforms continue to concentrate on improving the school environment and extending the academic day to increase academic learning time (ALT) using the same delivery system for many more hours. This approach lengthens the school day with "after school" programs, include weekends, and also assumes summer school. Such an approach can be successful, but it is very expensive and exhausting for the personnel (e.g. Harlem Children's Zone or KIPP).

A better solution for our nation as a whole is not to concentrate on increasing the standard diffuse approach with average stimulation and little individualization, and instead to turn to technology with its ability to generate ideal stimulation packets for home and school settings. This approach will offer a carefully designed daily brain stimulation package to complement the low stimulation atmosphere of many low-income families and immigrants and their schools. We must remember that all children deserve the finest education possible so they can develop their full potential for not only their economic and social success, but also for their nations as well. In order to achieve academic success in reading, we now know what neuronal stimulation is needed for optimal daily enrichment of the brain, and it requires a carefully sequenced, explicit, intense, and sustained daily enrichment package that is not available in many diffuse family and school settings.

This stimulation package for young children needs to train the brain in 2 important areas: first, the ability to decode rapidly and accurately, and second, the ability to build a deep and rich vocabulary that can be rapidly accessed when decoding. The past few decades of scholarly research have helped clarify the advantages of a phonics-based decoding strategy given the design of the brain (Adams, Dehaene) and also outlined the approximate vocabulary sequence that children need to follow if they are to stay afloat academically. What comes as a huge surprise is the emerging importance of vocabulary training for the children. Vocabulary appears to be the fuel of the reading engine. Traditionally we have masked its importance and not noticed how fundamental it is to academic and economic success.

Children who have learned 8,000 words by the end of the 2nd grade in homes with strong verbal traditions generally begin reading at an accelerating rate that initiates a spectacular academic flourishing. On the other hand, those children from less verbal homes usually know only 4,000 words and have great difficulty staying up with the class which, of course, then leads many of them to drop out of school before high school graduation. The message is clear: one group was exposed to a daily stimulation experience that built their brains into a formidable reading machine, and the other lacked access to meaningful stimulation and floundered.

The presence of a good vocabulary often impresses people, but it also can irritate them and seem beside the point. During our elementary and high school years we learn about 1,000 root words a year automatically, so it seems silly to some to be taught and drilled on a few words during our 180-day school years. What scholars missed was that, if children know too few words by the end of the 2nd grade, they will be unable to read successfully in the 3rd and 4th grade as the new books will have too many words they are unfamiliar with. When this occurs, they begin a psychologically devastating dropout spiral which takes them out of formal schooling somewhere between the 8th grade and graduation. Some districts lose over half their students during this period.

The impact of a poor vocabulary on children's academic success has become clear through some brilliant scholarship over the past few decades. Hart and Risley (Kansas City) taught us why all of the Great Society reforms were failing (vocabulary); Chall (Harvard) showed us why the 4th grade slump for the children from low income families suddenly emerged and started an academic dropout death spiral (vocabulary); Sampson (Chicago & Harvard) clarified why inner city African American children in Chicago were losing four IQ points in the early elementary years (vocabulary); Alexander and Entwisle

(Johns Hopkins) taught us about the "summer slide" where children from low income families lose up to a third of what they have learned during the school year over the summer vacation (lack of vocabulary stimulation); and a number of scholars have clarified how to teach vocabulary to young children (e.g. Beck, McKeown, Adams, Scarborough, Biemiller, Stahl, and Nation).

Now that we know how to teach decoding and vocabulary to young children, the new issue will be how to develop appropriate stimulus packages for these tasks and learn how to implement them in traditional home, school, and business settings. Another task will be to define the role of vocabulary in adult lives. We have crystal clear proof of its importance for young children, and the question will be "Is this just as important for adults, and if so, how can vocabulary instruction be implemented for an older population?" There is a reasonable chance that many adults are being damaged by their lack of vocabulary and the flexibility it provides for both new careers and personal growth in interesting new domains of knowledge with their accompanying skills. The ability of the brain to develop new theses, innovations, and concepts depends on the depth of its training and vocabulary because the brain can only create from knowledge and insights it already has as it collects information from all its neurons to serve its decisions.

The new tools that are evolving will include even more powerful computers and Internets which will eventually provide a private home portal for everyone. Hardware will keep doubling in potential (without additional cost) every 2 years, so this portal will gradually evolve into a command and control center for every family that can provide undreamed of educational opportunities for all family members. In the future, Waterford will be developing (1) the rationale and strategic metaphors to clarify this new emerging educational world; (2) the educational, testing, and administrative software for the users optimized to fit the brain's design; and (3) a new type of service and support center to provide monitoring, motivation, and measurement for its clients. As previously mentioned, the Waterford Learning Support Center is being designed to serve a broad range of clients including schools, school districts, state and federal legislatures, foundations, the federal government, preschools, and families. Gradually new generations of instructional units will be developed with the goal of offering measurable and precise instruction optimized for the human brain supported by the Waterford Learning Support Center to provide monitoring, motivation and measurement for the users.

An understanding of the latest brain research as it applies to reading is an important component in developing and deploying the educational software successfully. For example, although accomplished readers suggest that reading seems like an effortless process, in reality it requires a great deal of practice to achieve automaticity and the ability to break the processes into tiny discrete bits of data that later have to be refabricated into a recognizable whole. Chunks of letters are routinely broken into small components and then reassembled into a recognizable form. At the same time, other skills must be mastered. Reading requires harnessing motor skills to direct eye movements that move in small jerky steps called saccades 4 to 5 times a second focusing on reflected photons from the page of text through the central part of the retina called the fovea (15 degrees in the center of the visual field). Each saccade or gaze advances the reader about 7–9 letters. Notice the inherent biological constraints in the brain's design. These rule out attempts to circumvent the rigorous, detailed, and explicit processes that are required to train the neurons to recognize the nature of the stimulation. The brain will not allow for speed reading or other holistic processes that try to ignore or bypass the discrete, detailed, and granular nature of brain input circuitry through the jerky saccades of the eyes.

In Dehaene's words, "The peculiar characteristics of the primate visual system explain why reading does not operate like a fast and efficient scanner. As we move our eyes across a page, each word is slowly brought into the central region of our retina, only to be exploded into a myriad of fragments that our brain later pieces back together. It is only because these processes have become automatic and unconscious, thanks to years of practice, that we are under the illusion that reading is simple and effortless." He concludes that, "there are not many ways to convert a primate brain into that of an expert reader." In fact, there is only one "development trajectory that appears to exist.

Schools might be well-advised to exploit this knowledge to optimize the teaching of reading and mitigate the dramatic effects of illiteracy and dyslexia."

Again in Dehaene's words, "The general architecture of the visual system is tightly constrained and is identical to all of us, but the detail of how much each neuron responds depends on the particular visual events to which we are exposed. Sophisticated statistical learning techniques detect irregularities of the outside world. Our brain is built so that non-accidental properties, like the near line of several bars on the retina, the presence of T-or L-junctions, or a repeated succession of 2 images, are quickly extracted and stored in our cortical connections."

Our ancestral scribes developed the alphabet using many preprogrammed discrete shapes that the brain had learned to recognize in nature such as shapes formed like Y, T, X, L, V, U, M, and O. This small "letterbox" area has neurons that can be trained to recognize letters and are located in an area of the brain (occipito-temporal) between neurons that are sensitive to large units such as houses and faces off to one side, and neurons that can recognize small objects such as a toaster on the other. The "letterbox" neurons are the ones co-opted or recycled to recognize discrete letters. In Dehaene's words,

> The infant brain, like a young naturalist or statistician, systematically extracts, sorts, and classifies segments of speech.... At the end of the second year, a child's vocabulary grows at the amazing rate of 10 to 20 new words per day. At the same time, he establishes the basic grammatical rules of his language. At the age of 5 or 6, when children are exposed to their first reading lessons, they already have an expert knowledge of phonology. They also possess a vocabulary of several thousand words, and have mastered the basic grammatical structures of their languages. These 'rules and representations' are implicit. The child is not aware of his expertise and cannot account for it. Nonetheless, this knowledge no doubt exists in an organized set of speech circuits that are on standby for the written word.... In their second year, babies recognize stripped down versions of objects, thus indicating that they are capable of abstracting the essential elements of shape from an image.

Starting at the back of the brain, where the eye circuitry provides input, the neural networks for letters grow more and more sensitive as each stimulus moves forward toward the front part of the brain. At first the neurons detect only "local contrasts and oriented bars." Then, the scenes in progressing and moving forward in the temporal lobe, they can be trained to detect individual letters, and farther on, significant pairs of letters (bigrams) that speed up recognition, morphemes (prefixes, suffixes, plurality etc.), and even small words. The recognition grows more abstract and begins to ignore size, place, meaning, and capital or lower case so the letter can be recognized amidst a confusing background of noise. This phenomenon is called "invariability" and is at its core a trainable skill that allows us to extract the shape of the letter and recognize it in everything from handwriting to carefully constructed fonts.

Dehaene likens the timing sequence of an incoming stimulus to a "tidal bore" which happens twice a day when the inrushing tide floods river systems and tributaries and rushes up-stream in a wave. He notes this as a beautiful phenomenon to observe from an airplane where,

For a few minutes, a whole network of streams is simultaneously swollen by a powerful surge of water, simply because they all flow into the same sea.... A written or spoken word probably activates fragments of meaning in the brain in much the same way that a tidal bore invades a whole riverbed. If you compare a word like 'cheese' with a non-word like 'croil,' the only difference lies in the size of the cortical tidal wave that they can bring on. A known word resonates in the temporal lobe networks and produces a massive wave of synchronized oscillations that rolls through millions of neurons. This tidal bore goes even as far as more distant regions of the cortex as it successively contacts the many assemblies of neurons that each encodes a fragment of the word's meaning. An unknown word, however, even if it gets through the first stages of visual analysis, finds no echo in the cortex and the wave it triggers is quickly broken down into inarticulate cerebral foam.

Notice the importance of training the brain to recognize letters, words, sounds, and domains of knowledge. Unless the brain has neurons that are trained to be sensitive to incoming stimuli, it has no means of understanding the stimuli, no matter how important or significant it is, and it will simply treat it as "inarticulate cerebral foam," or a type of noise. This is why training the brain with vocabulary offers enormous and priceless dividends to humans. It allows that brain access to worlds of information that otherwise might be unrecognizable, and hence, unavailable.

VOCABULARY WORD STORAGE:

In order to "recognize thousands of familiar words, a...massive store is needed. Cognitive psychologists compare it to a dictionary or 'mental lexicon.'" In fact, Dehaene believes that we should think in terms of many mental dictionaries in our heads, each carrying "around a number of different types of information about words. As proficient readers, we all possess a (1) lexicon of English spelling that lists the written forms of all the words we know from the past, and these orthographic memories are probably stored in the form of hierarchical trees of letters, graphemes, syllables, and morphemes." In addition to the orthographic dictionary or lexicon, we also have a (2) phonological lexicon, a mental dictionary of the pronunciation of words. We also have another mental dictionary for "dozens of semantic features that specify its (3) meaning" and another where we store the (4) grammar of given words. "These mental dictionaries open up, one after the other, as our brain retrieves the corresponding information. This metaphor holds that our mind houses a reference library in several volumes, from a spelling guide to a pronunciation manual and an encyclopedic dictionary. The number of entries in our mental dictionaries is gigantic."

Dehaene concludes, "each of our lexicons probably contains between 50,000 and 100,000 entries. These estimates are further proof of the impressive capacities of our brain. Any reader easily retrieves a single meaning out of at least 50,000 candidate words, in the space of a few tenths of a second, based on nothing more than a few strokes of light on the retina."

Connections: Dehaene stresses that important sections of the brain are all connected together to enable us to make sense of the constant barrage of stimuli. When measuring the brain's response to a stimulus,

> we begin to see massive synchrony across distant regions. What that means is that initially, prior to conscious ignition, processing is essentially modular, with several simultaneous activations occurring independently and in parallel. However, at the point where we begin to see conscious access, our records show a synchronization of many areas that begin to work together in a global neuronal workspace.
>
> If you look at the associative brain areas,…what you find is that these areas are tightly intertwined with long distance connections, not just within a hemisphere, but also across the 2 hemispheres through what is called the corpus callosum. Given the existence of this dense network of long-distance connections, linking so many regions, here is our very simple idea: these distant connections are involved in propagating messages from one area to the next, and at this very high level where areas are strongly interconnected, the density of exchanges imposes a convergence to a single mental object out of what are initially multiple dispersed representations. So this is where the synchronization comes about.

Synchronization is achieved as a signal for agreement among different areas of the brain. When the areas begin to agree with each other, they converge onto a single mental object. In this picture, each area has its own code. Broca's area has an articulatory record and, slightly more anterior to it, there is a word code. In the posterior temporal regions, we have an acoustic code, a phonological code, or an orthographic code. The idea is that when you become aware of a word, these codes begin to synchronize together, and then converge into a single integrated mental concept.

According to this picture, consciousness is not accomplished by one area alone. There would be no sense in trying to pinpoint consciousness in a single brain area, or in computing the intersection of all the images that exist in the literature on consciousness, in order to find the area for consciousness. Consciousness is a state that involves long distance synchrony between many brain regions. During this state, it's not just higher association areas that are activated, because these areas also amplify, in a top-down manner, the lower brain areas that received the sensory message in the first place.

"It seems that the visual brain does that in a massively parallel manner, and is able to compute an optimal...interpretation of the incoming image, thus coming up with what is essentially the posterior distribution of all the possible interpretations of the incoming image. This operation seems to occur completely non-consciously in the brain. What the conscious brain seems to be doing is amplify and select one of the interpretations, which is relevant to the current goals of the organism." In fact, "under it all there is a very simple process underway that has each neuron 'checking to what extent the stimulus letters match its target word.'" Summarizing this point, Dehaene notes that "composed of close to 100 billion cells, the human brain is the archetype of a massively parallel system where all neurons compute simultaneously. The connections that link them, called synapses, bring them evidence from the external sensory stimulus.... A fierce competition between lexical units finally identifies a dominant word that represents the networks preferred hypothesis about the incoming string." This means that

> Letter and word identification result from an active top-down decoding process whereby the brain adds information to the visual signal.... It is noteworthy that most of these conflicts are resolved automatically, without our conscious intervention. When our nervous system is confronted with ambiguity, its fundamental strategy is to leave all possibilities open— something that is only feasible in a massively parallel system where multiple interpretations can be simultaneously entertained.... Our reading processes are so efficient that we are hardly ever aware of the ambiguities.

Fortunately Dehaene not only understands the brain research on mathematics and reading, but he also has helped create it. And, even more significantly, he comprehends the importance and potential of developing and using educational software both for basic instruction and also for helping to offer remediation for those with learning difficulties. He has studied the favorable impact on the brain of such software and believes it is an ideal remediation strategy for children who have dyslexia and other learning difficulties. Perhaps the best way to understand Dehaene's findings is to read his final summary at the end of the book where he writes, "our growing understanding of how reading develops in young children, the emergence of reading software based on solid cognitive foundations, and its adjustment to each child's brain should bring renewed hope to all of those for whom reading is an ordeal." In other words, he not only is well-versed in the brain research, but he also understands the importance of educational software. His major points are:

- Software is an ideal approach to insure that the optimal daily stimulation of the brain takes place, with time for sleep every evening between practice (neural stimulation) sessions that help improve and stabilize the brain's educational capacity.

- Compared to any other alternative the cost is a fraction of the usual instructional or remediation efforts.

- Software allows sophisticated games to be added to attract and hold student interest.

- The instruction can be interactive individualized for every student.

Individualization is particularly valuable because it allows the student to work precisely in the area that he or she is ready to learn. It avoids needless repetition of skills that have already been mastered or wasting time teaching materials that the child is not ready to learn. Scholars like to use Vygotsky's phrase the "zone of proximal development" to describe the task of teaching the child the appropriate cognitive skills he is ready to learn with the help of a teacher whose role is to provide "scaffolding" for the child. Here the computer can be very helpful because it knows what the student knows and also what should be studied next. Additionally, it can measure learning decay and help refresh the child's learning with a minimal effort when appropriate. Thus it can be used to both offer daily doses of stimulation in the shortest possible time and also offer patterns of refreshment and review to help solidify vocabulary, concepts, and domains of knowledge.

Scholars like Dehaene have begun to understand the contribution and potential of developing new generations of software in order to help us harness the constantly evolving power of new generations of machines. Parallel scholarship has also evolved which has clarified for us how the educational software should be designed to fit the architecture of the brain. Soon there will exist rich new packages of educational stimulation that will be designed for short and intensive periods of usage based on the 1% rule, i.e. 15-minute blocks that represent 1% of the time in a day. The UPSTART program has already shown the stunning results available from following this method. The transition will be away from diffuse learning situations that do not always support the needs and interests of students at home or school, to a more organized individual instruction approach directed by programs with embedded sequencers that keep track of the learner's status and provide carefully sequenced explicit and intense instruction (stimulation) sustained for short periods of time. The sequencer will also provide regular review periods to solidify the instruction. In Dehaene's words, the task is to find the "appropriate stimulation package for optimal daily enrichment."

Summarizing the lessons learned in our review of brain research, I would note:

- We now know that parents at home and teachers at schools can educate their young children far more effectively by utilizing sophisticated software that has been built to run on micro-computers and connected to the Internet. For maximum effect software must be designed to fit the architecture of the brain's neural functions and should be supported by a Learning Support Center using both the Internet and the telephone to monitor, motivate, and measure the students' performance.

- Scientists have demonstrated how important it is to: (1) teach children to decode and (2) to build a powerful vocabulary with increasing domains of knowledge. The available vocabulary and the domains of knowledge set the limits on what the brain can recognize and speculate about.

- The reading brain and its neural circuits can be trained to become an efficient decoding engine that, after taking years to train, ultimately runs flawlessly with little effort. Then the secondary task of developing a richer vocabulary that includes many new domains of knowledge becomes paramount. The vocabulary and its domains of knowledge then determine the ongoing capacity of the reading machine. The initial task is to insure that low income families have their children learn an additional 2,000 words over their normal annual vocabulary growth during their first 4 years of school so they know an average of 6,000 words (as their classmates know who have not been raised in low-income homes) instead of their 4,000 words which many of them are currently limited to.

- The neural circuits must be trained with carefully sequenced, explicit, intense, and sustained stimulation that fits the discrete units the brain is organized to recognize.

- The task becomes finding the appropriate stimulus strategy to optimize the daily enrichment of the neurons and their circuits.

- Appropriate stimulation produces a physical change in the neurons and their networks that improve their ability to function. There is no other way to improve their function than to offer regular and explicit stimulation to myelinate the axons, enlarge their terminals, and build up the number of dendrites and the size of their connections.

- A new educational option, The third source, in addition to the home and the school, is coming online to support both home and school with hardware, software, the Internet, and a support center. Here are some of the advantages of the new system using The Third Source:

  - Over twice the number of days of access compared to a school.

  - At a fraction of the cost.

  - The ability to increase individualization more than 20 times.

- The ability to offer quality instruction to preschool children in the safety of their homes.

- The ability to offer an ideal instructionally stimulating package daily to train the brain optimally requiring only 1% of the day!

- Ability to identify early learning problems and dyslexia in the preschool years and start intervention 3 to 5 years sooner than most schools can.

- The ability to offer a multisensory tutoring package at home or school that research has identified as the most efficient way to remediate learning difficulties.

- The ability to offer a computer adaptive test to children who have not yet learned to read without requiring an adult to test and score each student individually.

Finally, we must understand that we are offering a brand new concept in education: the delivery of a very specific and compact daily lesson that is designed to stimulate the brain to grow in educational capacity while monitoring the users, motivating them, and measuring their performance. The instructional units are very explicit and intense and lack the diffusiveness of an average classroom presentation because the instruction is individualized for each child and carefully sequenced and sustained for optimal daily enrichment of the neuronal brain.

This is truly a revolution. Waterford is providing an alternative to the informal learning available in the home, or the generalized curriculum of a school with its limited access and individualization, by offering a third source with (1) new individualized interactive educational software designed to stimulate and enrich the brain optimally and (2) a support team to maintain the system and motivate the users that is available every day of the year. Just as we earlier followed the research and transitioned from whole language to phonics, so we are following the research and transitioning from diffuse generic lectures to truly individualized learning designed for the brain's neurons; in the words of our familiar motto, we will be harnessing the speed of light to help us move our instruction from approximation to precision. We will also be offering a third source to provide support and instruction at a distance where we will monitor, motivate, and measure the user usage.

Chapter Nineteen: Two Equations & The Heuston Test

In 2004 when a trustee of the Waterford Institute from New York City was visiting our Utah sites, he interrupted my oratory excesses about the power of understanding delivery systems and suggested "strongly" I come up with a simple equation that would cut through all the malarkey and allow the listener to have a simple mnemonic (memory aid) to be held in the head so that the essence of the message could be reconstructed without the "presence of my passionate arm-waving carcass." For the next few hours I tried various metaphors, phrases, and even equations on the blackboard before presenting my simple equation which he accepted: $W = PE$. Despite my multitudinous shortcomings, the equation has been helpful in explaining the extraordinary power that technology can bring to a delivery system.

$$W = P\,E$$

W stands for the amount of work available in order to educate students in a school. This book assumes that the key to educating children successfully is the ability for people such as parents, caretakers, relatives, siblings, and teachers in combination with technologies, such as books, chalkboards, interactive whiteboards, radio, television, overhead projectors, slideshows, movies, wireless, the Internet and computers to generate enough work on behalf of children to insure that they master the curriculum. Given this assumption about the importance of having enough work available to insure their success, then we can assume that having a lot of W available is a good thing. This equation suggests that the amount of W available is the result of 2 other variables, the potential that is available from the teachers and technologies, and the efficiency with which the work potential is utilized by the school or home community.

In terms of the equation, we represent the potential by the letter P and the efficiency with which the potential is being utilized by the letter E. While both these terms are important, they differ in one important aspect. One is a positive variable suggesting how much useful potential the system contains (or how much work is theoretically available to help educate each child) and the other is a negative variable that measures how much of the original potential is being lost through inefficiencies. One giveth and the other taketh away.

P represents the theoretical potential in the school of all the possible sources of work in the community before inefficiencies reduce this potential. E represents the level of efficiency under which the school is operating in terms of utilizing its full potential. Since efficiency is incapable of adding new work to a school and is only a measure of how well the school is using the potential available, it can never be represented by a number larger than 1. And since no school is run perfectly, this number is usually somewhere between a .3 and a .7. A well-run school is probably running in the range of 70% efficiency (.7), and a poorly run one is likely to be running at about 30% efficiency, or at (.3).

In other words, the amount of work that a school can bring to bear in educating its children depends on 2 issues: how much potential work there is available from a combination of the teachers and the technologies supporting them, and how well this available work is utilized. Hence W (the amount of work the school actually produces) = (is equal to) P (the potential work available from the teachers and the technology) × (multiplied) E (the efficiency with which it is administered), or $W = P \times E$, or $W = PE$ in its simplest form.

Understanding this simple equation's implications can be of great value for professional educators, policy makers, and interested parents because it can help clarify the fundamental variables at play in education and how they work, much as another simple equation such as D = RT might help us to think about travel. If we want to know how far our vehicle will travel in distance on a trip, (D) we have only 2 variables that we can adjust, (R) the rate or speed we are traveling and, (T) the time we travel at that speed. Hence I will travel 100 miles if I average 50 miles an hour in my car for 2 hours.

Notice that no matter how much I might care about time and distance issues on my trip, if I have 2 hours available and want to travel as far as I can, my only choice is to increase the speed of my driving. Similarly, if I want to increase the amount of work available in a school to improve the caliber of instruction, my only choice, assuming that the teachers are reasonably efficient and the school has the usual consignments of books and other simple technologies, is to add components to the delivery system that increase the potential work available at the school. Generally speaking, this means that I have the choice to add more people to supplement the teacher's efforts or to add new technologies, such as the computer, that can produce exponentially more work to help teach the child more effectively. As salaries rise and the cost of computers continues to fall, the addition of extra people will become far more expensive than the addition of technology.

But even better, the technology will carry with it the additional advantage of doubling its capabilities every 2 years at no additional cost. This produces such an advantage for students and teachers that inevitably the addition of technology and its software will become a major component of school reform. Restating this generalization in terms of the equation, a variable that will engage educators in the years to come will be P, or the amount of potential or capacity that is available in the system to increase student learning and support the teacher's efforts.

This will be a very difficult adjustment for educators to make because without realizing it they have been working with a static delivery system for centuries. When the amount of available work in a system is fixed over a long period of time, then workers and leaders fixate on efficiency strategies to help them utilize the available work in the system more effectively instead of developing new strategies that entail increasing the amount of work in the system. Sadly since the last significant technological breakthrough that added work to the educational delivery system occurred sometime in the mid-fifteenth century with the invention of the printing press, educators tend to toil mindlessly on polishing up efficiency strategies (E) because such an approach is all that has been possible for about 550 years. Hence it will be important for policy makers to help encourage the educators to adopt strategies involving technology that can generate huge gains in the total potential work available in the system (P). In other words, the question is whether or not a .4 improvement is adequate because these are the limits suggested by the equation for the traditional approach!

Offering an example involving actual numerical data will help clarify the full implications of this equation. We can assume that a teacher will each be worth 1, otherwise known as 1 person power, in the manner of measuring the power of engines in "horsepower." And we will assume that the available technology in the classroom, such as books, chalk, blackboards, overhead projectors etc. will be worth some fraction of a person in that they have value, particularly in storing work that others have already performed, so that it can be retrieved and studied in a useful format such as a book or a blackboard. Let us then suppose that the technological contribution is about one-fifth of a person, or .2. Hence, W = PE becomes W = 1.2 × E when we add .2 (the technology bonus) to the person doing the work in the classroom which is 1. Thus we have 1.2 totaling the 1 (the person power) and the .2 (the technology power).

E in the equation represents the efficiency of the school, and we will assign 2 values here, one for a good school and one for a poor one. The good school we will assume is running at 70% efficiency and hence will be rated as a .7, while the poor one will be running at 30% and be assigned a .3 for its efficiency rating.

Thus E = .3 in one case and .7 in another, and W changes accordingly to 1.2 × .3 in a poor school, or W = 1.2 × .7 in a good one. The poor school equation for W = 1.2 × .3 provides a total delivery system capability of .36 for a poor school.

On the other hand, a good school will provide a W of 1.2 × .7 which will deliver a total delivery system capability of .84. Notice that there are 2 interesting implications from these results. First, a good school is over 2 times as effective as a poor school. But the second point is even more important and suggests that, as impressive as this difference is, that there are severe limits in educational reforms that concentrate on improving the efficiency component of the equation. The difference between .3 (a poor school) and .7 (a well-run school) is a total of .4.

What this means in practical terms is that the billions of dollars being spent to improve educational efficiency (almost all reforms are attempts to increase efficiency) are limited to struggling for a maximum gain of approximately .4. Unfortunately these reforms have a ceiling which restricts the potential work improvement to a rather modest .4 which is forever frozen at that limit no matter how generous the financial investment might be. Hence our question in our heading, "Is .4 enough?" Because, as long as we follow the manual solutions of the traditional reform movements, we will be restricted to an approximate .4 limit; whereas, an investment in P involving the use of technology has no fixed limit and will continue to improve at an ever accelerating rate for the foreseeable future. It may skyrocket from an estimated .2 where the technology is only ⅕ as valuable as a human teacher to a value that is more valuable than a teacher under certain circumstances, much as there are times when technology dwarfs what a human could accomplish in various delivery systems such as transportation (cars, trains, airplanes, rockets), communications (radio, telephone, TV), the military (tanks, rockets, artillery, atomic bomb,) or medicine (x-rays, MRIs, blood tests). In education, for example, the technology used in our UP-START project dramatically improved the quality of education for a few thousand 4 year old children who might otherwise not have had access to such instruction.

I would estimate that within 10 years those families and schools using the latest technology and software will have a significantly higher P value than 1.2 because, in addition to the person power of 1, the technology value will probably grow from .2 to at least 2.0 giving P a higher potential total of 3.0. Thus the new equations would look like this for a marginal and a good school.

$$W = PE$$
$$W = 3.0 \times .3 \text{ or } .9 \text{ for a marginal school}$$
$$W = 3.0 \times .7 \text{ or } 2.1 \text{ for a well-run school}$$

Notice that although there will still be a significant difference between a good and a poor school, a poor school with appropriate software will soon be performing at .9, or slightly above the .84 that a good school achieves with only the rudimentary technology of books and writing instruments. In other words, children who have access to the newer software will be able to master their basic skills and achieve a strong foundation for future academic success. The brighter children will also gain considerable benefit from the improved instruction. Critics may argue that we will be unwittingly expanding the gulf between the slow and the brighter students, but since the purpose of technology is to help all students achieve their maximum potential (Spence), what will really be happening is that the slower students will be brought up to a level of performance that will keep them academically on track for the economic opportunities that are available and help them to contribute to the economies of their countries. And for those who are averse to tying the benefits of education merely to commercial gain, we can see that the richer instructional environment is more apt to produce stronger, more independent, and more interesting citizens that will not only contribute to their societies, but also appreciate the full spectrum of life's possibilities.

Because of Moore's Law, the improvement multipliers will no longer be restricted to fractional numbers such as .3 or .4, and will become ever increasing amounts such as 1 or 2. These will gradually evolve to 10, and possibly even 100 before the doubling phenomenon loses its edge. This means that those who introduce technology-based reforms to schools in the decades ahead will have such staggering advantages that they will begin to dominate the reform efforts. For example, when the technology component of P reaches 10, which is inevitable someday in the future, notice the new values in the equation when .2 expands to 10.

W = PE

P is now 1 person power + 10 (technology factors) for a total of 11.

Thus, in comparing the impact of the new equation on a poorly run school, we can see that W = 11 × .3 = 3.3, is a considerable improvement over the earlier total of .36. In fact, what this equation makes clear is that sometime in the future a well-run technology initiative will have over 9 times the impact on any school compared to any alternative reform. Such an impact will guarantee that the reforms of the future will concentrate on wringing out as much of the potential of technology as possible. But what adds to the sense of hope that this potential generates is the knowledge that, unlike the efficiency component that must remain within fairly static boundaries, the technology component will continue to improve upwards. Thus someday the 9 times advantage may soar again to 90.

The reader might question the analogy by noting how the technology component may reach such a high number that it would be absurd to argue that the additional work being added by technology may be useable beyond a certain point that a child can handle. In other words should we really believe that a machine interacting with a student could be 90 times as effective as a teacher someday? The short answer is a "definite maybe!" As the reader will discover, the power of the future hardware in conjunction with enormously sophisticated software that will encapsulate the knowledge and instructional skills of thousands of the world's greatest teachers will offer students instructional sequences tailored to their individual learner profiles that will someday supersede the capabilities of any single teacher. The contribution of such software will also offer a steadiness of quality in the instructional process that the average teacher would have trouble matching.

RECOGNIZING SOME NECESSARY LIMITATIONS OF TECHNOLOGY:

But here we must offer some cautions that must be faced by rabid technologists as they wax positive on how technology will replace teachers and use my W = PE equation as proof that the technology will ultimately dwarf any effort that a teacher can produce. While the mathematics of the equation might suggest this, we must retain some humility and recognize that we are entering a new domain where our parade can be rained on rather brutally and unexpectedly at any time. Here are some of the problems:

(1) There is more to education than just learning how to handle abstract symbol sets. Children have a series of needs and dependencies that can only be addressed by adult humans who can provide a model for children to emulate as well as become a source of motivation and inspiration to encourage them to attempt to achieve growth in a myriad of important areas.

(2) For many of the children the severest challenges will come from social issues involving their relationships with other children and adults, and they will need emotional support from their communities at home and school. James Comer has argued in his book *School Power* that there is little sense in trying to teach children until their psychological needs are addressed by the entire school community, including the parents. He makes a compelling point in an interview when he notes that "what low-income children particularly need is socialization and preparation to participate in mainstream institutions."[1] Certainly any ideal technological model will have to take into account Comer's perceptive cautions about addressing the total needs of the child and not just the academic ones. Furthermore, his comment presupposes that we already know what a child should learn and how to teach it.

Frankly we do not know enough yet to decide what an ideal teaching strategy is to assure successful learning for all children. We do know that someday we will be able to guarantee a powerful and effective instructional sequence for most children, but there is still the question of whether this will be enough for them to learn successfully if their other social and psychological needs are not being satisfied. We are, after all, just human!

---

[1]James Comer, interview on Public Agenda Online, (accessed 14 May 2004) http:www.Publicagenda.org/specials/learning/experts1.htm.

Perhaps this point can best be expressed by recounting an incident that occurred during a speech I was giving almost 40 years ago to a large audience of engineers at a national convention. Just as I was finishing my talk, which had predicted how helpful their engineering work in the development of computers would be for the schoolchildren of future generations, there was a sudden commotion in the audience as a gentleman leaped to his feet, pushed his way into the aisle and began ranting and screaming at me with a rage-filled face bellowing, among other things, that he "would be damned if" he "would allow" his children "to get up in the morning and come to school to report to a computer." We must acknowledge his very human concern about the primacy of honoring the elemental sanctity of his child's human nature and note that there will be many uneasy moments with man-made machines in future educational environments, just as there have been in the past.

Plato was not keen on the use of written manuscripts to preserve and transfer knowledge. He said that, among their other sins, they allowed people to avoid exercising their memories. And just as the computer has been criticized for isolating children in a lonely inhuman environment devoid of human contact and relationships, so were books criticized with the same fervor after the printing press began making them available in school settings. Suffice it to say that there will be much passion, uncertainty, and confusion in the decades ahead as we gradually learn the strengths and limitations of this spectacular new instructional tool. And during the passionate moments in future debates, we must avoid demonizing inanimate tools that are being used to generate additional work on behalf of humans. I suspect that it never occurred to the gentleman who attacked me that to be consistent in his view of machines that he would have to protect his child from "reporting to" a bathtub, a thermostat, an electrical light switch, an elevator, a library, or a school bus on the way to school.

(3) Even if we learn how to present almost perfect instructional sequences on an individual basis to each child, at some point we will reach a limit where the child will not be helped by having more instruction because he or she cannot or will not want to process

additional information. For this reason, while there may be the theoretical possibility of having a computer present an ideal instructional sequence based on the latest research with spectacular graphics, animation, photography, movies, music, and instructional audio all tuned to fit the individual learner profile of the student, we cannot count on having technology continue to improve instruction beyond a certain limit for each child. Thus at some point the size of the technology portion of P will cease to have meaning after crossing the threshold that the child can use.

But until that happens, we will have a wonderful journey where undreamed of educational possibilities will roll out in a stunning succession of new product breakthroughs that will dramatically improve the individualized interactive instruction for all children. Or stated another way, when it comes to teaching certain types of subject matter, the computer will gradually begin to move ahead of human capabilities, but it will be fruitless to argue how many times more (9, 90, 900, 9000, etc.) the computer can accomplish a limited set of teaching tasks better than a human. Hence there will be limitations to pushing the mathematical implications of the $W = PE$ equation beyond a reasonable limit which we will be incapable of understanding until we can gain experience with the new capabilities.

But there will be limits because at some point we will discover that more power is not always an improvement providing there is as much power available as the delivery system can handle. More of something is not always desirable. A child may need a glass of water on a regular basis, but designing technology to deliver a gallon, a barrel, a lake, a river, or an ocean on demand has marginal value. We must not suppose that just because we can design a hose that can deliver a thousand gallons of water a minute that this will help the child get a drink in the school hall more efficiently than a drinking fountain that is already in position.

In acknowledging the ultimate limits of educational technology, we must not underestimate its future potential either. This book is about the beginnings, and not the end. We still have generations of new capabilities to uncover as we break the manual log jam and provide new hope and excitement to an educational system that has too many limited resources to handle the stresses of our modern society.

In addition to the extraordinary gift of extra work, technology provides other advantages. For example it is usually able to replicate and scale up with greater accuracy. Manual efforts usually waver in accuracy when we try to replicate them. Each new hand copied version of a manuscript usually introduces errors, while every copy from a printing press is identical. Information is usually distorted by humans as they process the information and transmit it to others. Every person of the millions who view a TV program will see (thanks to the contribution of technology) an identical program as everyone else, even though each will describe it differently to others.

They will have only picked up part of the stream of information being presented because of distractions. They may be so taken by a scene that they miss part of the next scene; or they may fall asleep for a few moments, be interrupted by a question from someone, take a telephone call, or start an argument either with someone present or even with the TV program, particularly if they do not like a referee's call.

Being human, teachers are not always accurate and dependable transmitters of information. They rarely teach a topic the same way to students over time, and questions and crises can pull them off topic without their remembering that they may have failed to teach an important point. Student or teacher absences can leave significant gaps in instructional presentations. Lost information in a school setting can be tragic for a child, particularly in the early elementary years when the basic skills are being taught that will allow the child to become an independent learner in the future.

During the 4-year New York City project when we were studying 1 of the 20 computer labs we were working with, we noticed that one section of 1st graders had extraordinarily low scores. As we pored over the data, we discovered that the section with the lowest scores had had 4 different homeroom teachers from the start of school through the December holidays. Because this happened during their 1st grade year, this almost assured that a number of the students from that school would never become successful readers.

Some 50 years earlier, when I was in the 7th grade in the same NYC public school system, my homeroom teacher—who was close to retirement—"fainted" 2 or 3 days a week, after which she would be helped to the faculty room, and we would be admonished as a class to settle down and work on homework or other activities without supervision. Obviously my class missed some critical materials of educational value during her frequent collapses, but our loss was insignificant compared to what happened to the 1st grade class I described above because by the 7th grade we had already learned to read and had lost only some knowledge of science and math. We had not been left behind and failed to learn to read with all of the social tensions that this failure generated which could lead to "print flight" and a silent but deadly sense of shame.

Here we see one of the strengths of technology in comparison with a system that only depends on human teachers to teach the materials to the students. In such a setting the children are not always provided with consistent instruction because teachers are human and have human shortcomings and cannot be counted on to always teach in an exemplary manner; whereas, technology has the advantage of consistency, which assures that each child is provided an accurate presentation of materials in an appropriate sequence that provides all students with sound instructional content free of human foibles and distortions.

OUR SECOND EQUATION:

There is another important equation we need to consider. This has to do with the cost of software development and is $C=V+I+M+S$.

What the equation shows is that the cost (C) is equal to the total cost of the sum of 4 separate variables. These variables constitute a staggering drain on the resources of any organization developing serious software for education because the market is too small to support the high cost of developing high quality educational software.

In essence the cost to support the product grows so large that there is almost no money left for new improvements. The first cost variable is (V) which stands for the particular version of software that vendors have sold the developer in order to operate their hardware and develop new software products. For example, Microsoft or Adobe might change a new version of their product to improve it, but their changes might render inoperable whatever version of their software is being used at that time. Yesterday I literally had to shut a product line down because the vendor that supplies us with an important software graphics package changed its software on successive Fridays and this rendered our program inoperable.

The (M) in the equation stands for the maintenance cost of running our own different versions of the software that we are developing for others. As we find bugs in our software or introduce desired changes at the recommendation of our clients, an additional expense we incur represented by the cost (I), we will inadvertently, but certainly, introduce a new series of bugs in our new versions. The variable (S) in the equation represents the size of the code that must be tested after each code change is written and introduced to the total code base. The larger the size of the code, the greater the cost. Some of our code has reached over 70 billion bytes of code. The practical consequences of maintaining all of the different versions are this: what costs an organization just a few hundred thousand dollars to build may ultimately require $5–$10 million a year in maintenance costs. The implications of this cost support problem are that unless you have a sudden "hit" with your new product, over time your support costs will soar and take so much of your revenue that you will be unable to improve the product. This leaves the educational software developers with a series of products that are slowly becoming obsolete.

My conviction is that the industry will not progress until a way is found to introduce substantial capital streams into new product development. The real difficulty in building a world-class program using the latest graphics and animation techniques is that its development combines the cost of writing many books, filming a movie, writing comic books, building 3D characters, and writing computer code for a large sophisticated program.

But no matter how stressful the investment might be, the upside potential for changing the lives of billions of children continues to motivate the best and the brightest to find the funds for the necessary software development.

THE HEUSTON TEST:

The Heuston Test is to be applied like litmus paper in a chemical experiment to see whether or not the educational reform you are planning to support will really help the children who need the most help. As an educational "thought experiment," it simply asks you to consider the extent to which a given reform is actually capable of solving problems in the classroom. I will use the youngest children as the target audience, but the principles apply to all children at any age.

Imagine that you are observing a typical inner city kindergarten class of 23 that has the following composition: Six of the students do not speak English very well, 20 of them have had very little pre-literacy training from their families, 12 are average in intelligence, 3 are above average, and 2 are bright. Three are also below average, and 2 are slow learners. Finally, 1 child has a behavior problem that requires a great deal of attention from the teacher's aide assigned to help the teacher. Aside from noting the difficulty the teacher faces in trying to talk with 6 children who are unable to understand most of what she is saying, you realize the following about the teacher's responsibilities and dilemma:

(1) Only 26% of the school day will be instructional because almost three-quarters of the teacher's time will be spent managing and looking after the children, not teaching them.

(2) The teacher will be limited to 1 minute a day of individualized instruction per child. This is a natural delivery system limit that cannot be circumvented because the teacher only has the children for 6 hours a school day, or a total of 360 minutes, and 26% of this is approximately 93 minutes.

(3) In coming to terms with the needs of each child there are 3 general considerations:

- **The child's basic talent for learning such disciplines as reading, mathematics, art, foreign languages, or science.** Children differ considerably not only in their ability to handle abstract symbol sets such as the alphabet, mathematics, scientific equations, etc., but also they may have talent in one area and not another. For example Howard Gardner of Harvard has noted that he believes children have 7 or 8 areas of intelligence or potential talent that can be trained.

- **The pace and level of instruction that is required for each child given his or her intelligence and preparation.** Here is where the manual model breaks down because the teacher will be unable to teach each child individually for more than a minute a day even if the child's talents require more time. Most of the work available to teach the children comes from the teachers' labor without serious support from technology. This necessary limitation of the manual delivery system will inevitably force the teacher into adopting a "teaching by approximation" strategy where her lessons are designed on the assumption that they target the middle range of students but will be inappropriate for the extremes represented by the slower and faster learners. This approximation strategy has the disadvantage of terrifying the slower students who cannot keep up with the classroom pace and boring the faster learners who want more of a challenge.

- **The history of the child's academic preparation.** When thinking about teaching a young child, we tend to concentrate on sorting children in terms of their general intelligence without paying enough attention to the importance of their preparation, preparation that involves a significant amount of work from both supporting adults as well as the child. For example, recall that Marilyn Adams estimates that knowledgeable parents make certain that their children are given approximately 3,000 hours of preliteracy training from birth until the 1st grade when they are taught to read in school. Adams also estimates that inner city children and rural poor children receive only 20 to 200 hours of preliteracy training from their families during the same years, or less than 7% of their more fortunate classmates.

- **The child's emotional landscape.** As any thoughtful observer can tell you, survival trumps learning. Children will not—in fact, cannot—attend to academic tasks when they are preoccupied by volatile or dangerous family or social situations. Although this would seem to lie outside the purview of educational technology, anecdotal evidence suggests that it does not. Teachers and lab supervisors frequently comment on 3 ways in which they feel UPSTART and other programs are helpful to children and adults in crisis. First, it provides a safe and engaging refuge. Single parents often report that when their children are sent to visit an estranged parent, they use the world created by the Waterford materials as a kind of safety blanket. Second, teachers and lab managers frequently point out individuals who blossom as a result of the privacy of computer-based instruction. One particularly poignant example is the drill sergeant who had spent his whole life hiding his reading disabilities. Once he could address them in private, however, with carefully sequenced and effective programming, he discovered that they could be overcome. Which brings us to the third source in which educational technology helps heal damaged or fearful students. It shows them that they can and do learn. One mother told us that she had believed that her autistic child did not know his own name. But when UPSTART asked him to point out the letters of his name, he did so immediately. Because he knew he had been able to do the other things it asked, he felt safe enough to display knowledge he had previously hidden.

We can see why trying to solve this problem with a standard reform effort is as futile as trying to put out a serious fire with a glass of water. Training a teacher on how to use the glass of water more efficiently has certain limitations. To put out a fire you need a fire hose, not a glass of water used more efficiently.

What the Heuston Test thought experiment does is focus on the critical question: What traditional reform will solve the work shortfall problem the teacher faces with her needy students? And the answer is that none of them do because they cannot offer her the additional work she needs to accomplish her tasks, and neither will retraining her with some new wondrous method accomplish solving the work shortfall. Similarly, pick an ever popular reform such as teacher training. Then ask how would better teacher training help a teacher solve the approximation problem where the upper and lower third of the children are being either bored or terrorized by the teacher's inability to generate enough extra time and work to offer instruction to them at a level appropriate to their current knowledge and needs?

Or again, how would merit pay, team teaching, accountability, the Coalition of Essential Schools, Success for All, Accelerated Learning, Reading Recovery, or any other typical reform provide enough additional work to insure that the child receives enough instructional time to master the requisite skills required for educational success?

This is the Heuston Test, the recognition that if you test any standard reform against the needs of an actual classroom situation behind closed doors day after day, odds are that it will have only a minimal impact and will be unable to solve instructional problems because it cannot generate enough work to offer the necessary instruction to the diverse population in the class.

The implication of the Heuston Test is that parents or leaders who are interested in improving the education of young children in these settings must start with an analysis of where affordable extra work can be found to insure that the children can receive enough extra help to become successful. This is a new type of analysis which concentrates initially on estimating the quantity of potential work available to the system and not the quality. This is a difficult transition to make because any mature delivery system that has a fixed amount of work in it prospers by having its workers concentrate on improving the quality of their performance rather than dwelling on what improvements they might accomplish if they had additional resources.

Prior to adding powerful new technologies to a delivery system, the workers and managers generally think about only 2 variables:

(1) How many workers can they afford?

(2) How well can they organize and train them?

There is a third variable beginning to surface that analyzes the technologies being used by the delivery system because these technologies set the potential limits of what any delivery system can accomplish. This third variable asks:

(3) What are the technologies available to the system and how much additional work can they provide for the system?

This 3rd variable is where we begin to change our way of thinking about delivery system effectiveness. In other words we are beginning to start our analysis of any delivery system by determining the quantity of work available through the usual manual labor pools, and then adding the additional quantity of work provided by affordable technology to determine the final potential effectiveness of any delivery system.

Testing this new analytical approach on the educational delivery system, we can see that since the new chip technologies have been doubling in potential every 2 years for over 30 years at little or no additional cost—and will continue to do so for the foreseeable future—that the third variable (technology) is worth concentrating on and should be first in our thoughts about reform. Hence we must come to terms with this counterintuitive new rule that says that in order to improve quality, we must begin by first improving quantity if this is technically and financially possible.

Summary: The Heuston Test asks us to make a rough measurement of the available labor and contrast it with the needs of the students in the class. This test will quickly demonstrate the futility of most reform efforts because they ask the teacher to accomplish too much. Remember my description of the composition of the inner-city class described at the beginning of The Heuston Test; only technology can add enough work to support teachers and help them solve the problem.

Chapter Twenty: Ignition

The most important lesson that I have learned in my educational quest is that the potential effectiveness of any organized human endeavor is a function of the technologies used by that particular delivery system to help deliver its goods and services. Technologies such as transistors, microcomputers, lasers, and the Internet are in the process of changing the educational delivery system, and the purpose of this book is to sensitize the readers and help them understand how these new technologies will dramatically alter the potential of the educational delivery system.

Until leaders understand the potential of the new delivery systems, we will continue to waste precious economic resources as well as children's minds! We now know enough to understand the importance of education, but we need to understand that even though we crave and demand reforms, the current educational delivery system has matured, and once a delivery system has matured, pouring more resources into improving its standard components and technologies is a waste of capital.

The economic trajectory of nations has been changed dramatically whenever a new technology enables a delivery system to help humans generate exponentially more work delivering their goods and services. Those nations that can develop and utilize the new technologies will give their workers and their economies a significant advantage over others, much as England benefited from the technology of the steam engine which triggered their industrial revolution. The steam engine provided additional capacities (work) for workers as its uses evolved over a few decades from pumping water from mines, driving power looms for weaving fabrics, to developing steamships and then railroads, and agricultural machinery with all their attendant job opportunities. As we have learned in the earlier chapters, each new technological discovery adds to the capacity of human labor. Harnessing horses gave us the 10 miles per hour rate of the Pony Express, but harnessing the speed of light in the form of the telegraph introduced a much more efficient delivery system (67 million times faster) where the workers' task shifted from being an underweight and tough rider of horses with incredible stamina to a more knowledge-based worker who understood the Morse code and had the mental skills to transmit the code rapidly while sitting sedately in a chair tapping out the Morse code with the fingers of one hand, a long way from the exhausting effort of riding a horse all day at breakneck speed.

The primary worker in the educational delivery system (the teacher) had her job description change over 500 years ago with the introduction of the printing press. The printing press allowed schools and nations to store useful knowledge that could be scaled accurately and inexpensively in the form of a book to give children a portable and permanent access to knowledge supporting the teachers' efforts.

DELIVERY SYSTEMS AND OUR JOURNEY THROUGH LIFE:

Most of our lives are spent as part of delivery systems in which we live and work as we navigate our careers. We also negotiate our relationship with all of the delivery systems created to serve human needs. Initially our parents worked to provide for us, and then we entered the educational delivery system designed to educate us with its schools, teachers, and books. While being served by delivery systems involving the family, we live in homes that have been built by the construction industry and are maintained by plumbers, electricians, carpenters and their delivery systems as they provide their goods and services to us, and we are transported by a transportation delivery system whenever we leave our homes.

Even though humans both benefit from the services of delivery systems and frequently are part of delivery systems, they also are delivery systems themselves. Although it may be startling to view it this way, babies offer goods and services to their parents. One of the greatest of all human emotions is the love a parent has for a young child, and, conversely, the anguish some humans feel at being deprived of this experience is painful to observe. Husbands and wives provide goods and services for their partners. Teachers and children each offer services to one another, as do doctors and patients.

The value of humans is frequently established by their ability to deliver goods and services to others. And, as the message of this book implies, not only are delivery systems impacted by technologies, but so also are their basic components, i.e. humans. Thus we need to understand that since each individual is a microcosm of a larger delivery system, we must pay as much attention to organizing humans to implement technologies as we do their larger delivery systems. Such is the message of this chapter.

In fact, personal human delivery systems appear to be the ultimate method from which all other delivery systems are derived. If so, then it is worthwhile studying whether humans (as well as organized delivery systems) can benefit from using technologies to exponentiate the amount of energy they can bring to bear on their tasks and interests, assuming that they may be different during different epochs of their lives.

OUR PERSONAL DELIVERY SYSTEMS:

Most people understand that all individuals are born with a specific set of genes that can determine the limits of their intellectual and physical potential, but not everyone understands that there are 2 additional considerations that refine and define these nascent capabilities:

(1) The Education and Training of the Individual

(2) The Development of his or her Personal Delivery System

Phase I: Education: The first priority of parents is to teach their children their value systems and educate them. For the first few years of life, the family educates the child. Then for the next decade or 2 they transfer some of the educational training of their child to an external educational delivery system located outside the home. Usually these are schools staffed with teachers whose responsibilities are to teach the formal disciplines that society values. These educational years are important because they tend to define how their latent gene talents will be utilized. During the educational years the child will generally be molded and impacted by others.

Phase II: The Development of a Personal Delivery System: At some point children begin to develop their talents and become responsible workers in the available delivery systems. Many will ultimately stay in a specific delivery system all their lives, but, increasingly, individuals are discovering that they want to establish their own delivery systems or at least become independent delivery systems themselves while engaging intermittently with the standard delivery systems available to them wherever they choose to live. Here the software and new technologies will enhance personal delivery system capabilities because they will provide access to additional resources that normally would not be available in a traditional society.

Having access to the Internet and email while writing this book in my isolated summer home on a dirt road in the woods of Northern Vermont effectively connected me, in real time, to the databases run by Google. There I could collect my research while working with my assistant in Salt Lake City who stayed in contact with our testing expert in Pittsburgh who was analyzing data through our office in Romania that was monitoring and organizing the data for our support center in Salt Lake City that was tracking sites all over the world including Taiwan, Senegal, Rwanda, India, Columbus, Mississippi, La Quinta, California, and thousands of homes all over the United States. All of this is going on at the same time!

THE CURSE OF NEW SOFTWARE:

However, in order to use the new technologies, we need to learn exquisitely complicated sets of software packages so that we can harvest the work bonus inherent in the technology. The array of software available for a simple laptop is astonishing. Microsoft offers Word, Excel, PowerPoint, and Outlook just for starters, and Adobe has irresistible packages to help us in the graphic arts, photography, and PDF world. Then there are the worlds we must conquer in order to communicate with the emerging generations such as Facebook, YouTube, and a host of areas sponsored by Google which allow limitless access to information, including my ability to examine my home from above, search through streets, read scholarly books, and find catalogs of everything. Since I love photography, I have spent hundreds of hours trying to master Photoshop and Lightroom as well as Aperture and other photography programs. Apple has also contributed a brilliant series of technologies to add to my personal delivery system capabilities and given me access to great music in their iPod world.

Each of the technologies is also growing more sophisticated and complex as options are added with each new release. I now need 3 input devices just to use all the capabilities of my cable TV and Blu-ray players for my large LCD TV mounted on the wall. My powerful set of advanced digital cameras and printers from Canon with their assortment of lenses and accessories can pull me into a black hole where blocks of hours disappear as I utilize the many buttons and features. Then there are all the options on my BlackBerry such as the built-in camera and other wondrous features including voice input.

At night I am using another voice input program that is on its 11th version (Dragon Naturally Speaking), learning to handle my Kindle (an electronic device that can download a new book in a few seconds), and struggling with a new email program as well as an extraordinary array of new software from a limitless list of vendors that my friends and colleagues urge me to try.

While the struggle to keep up with software seems almost impossible, I believe that over time people will realize that the time and effort required to become proficient in the new hardware and software will be worthwhile because it will help them link their native talents to an ever increasing source of energy which is doubling without additional cost to the users every 2 years that can exponentiate the amount of work they can accomplish with their personal talents and delivery system.

The new software will add to the power of the old technologies that took centuries to develop (paper, pen, pencil, printing press, alphabets and books) and successfully educated most of the readers of this book. But there are a few societal changes that suggest that America needs the addition of the new technologies because we need to improve our educational delivery systems in order to compete in the new knowledge-based world where our democracy (1) carries a tax with it that hinders the efficiency of our traditional educational system in the elementary and secondary areas; and (2) is also handicapped by the disintegrating family units that are failing to provide the necessary preliteracy training for the children of many of our poorest families; and (3) that is raising a generation of children that assume prosperity and want to enjoy its fruits without contributing to the difficult and disciplined work required to sustain it.

The new hardware and software will insure that almost all children will be able to read and become independent learners. This will allow people not only to access information, but also to build a store of knowledge to make their decisions and activities more efficient. It will give them a way to connect with knowledge and important sources of new energy that can enhance their personal productivity.

Early in the evolution of a new technology, such as a steam engine, electrical plant, cotton mill, or automobile factory, the equipment is so expensive that workers must leave home and commute to use them. But the benefits are such that they are willing to do so even if the travel takes hours out of their days. As societies have transitioned from heavy industry to a knowledge-based society, the modern office has collected not only the machines necessary to conduct business such as telephones, faxes, copy machines, scanners, printers and computers, but also the personnel with expertise in different domains of knowledge such as accountants, technicians, salesmen, marketers, and secretaries to handle the work flow and facilitate communications in a cocoon of air-conditioned bliss.

However, the invention and distribution of the Internet is modifying the necessity for the modern office as the technologies continue to shrink in size while at the same time improving in function so that workers can work as well on the road as at home. I actually use all of these things at home more efficiently than I can at an office. I still work in an office, but not at the exclusion of other sites that allow my supporting technologies to help me almost anywhere. My cell phone has the same list of phone numbers in it as my assistant has on her computer. It also provides me with email, a daily schedule, photographs, and access to news media and markets. I also am using a speech dictation software package at home that allows me to dictate rapidly or input text verbally from any source I find useful. I also have a scanner that allows me to store and distribute photographs and articles throughout the organization. I also have a program that synchronizes my files on multiple computers at home and work so I do not have to email files to myself at other sites or carry the programs on a disk or portable memory stick.

A new cycle is now emerging: the expensive technologies and knowledge sources that forced us to leave our homes and commute to work are now becoming available to us at home or can be carried with us wherever we go. As Alvin and Heidi Toffler have noted in their wonderful books predicting the future of our cultures, we will find our homes revitalized as they morph into potential centers of learning and production as the price of new technologies continue to drop and their capabilities soar as they connect us to invaluable resources and to each other over the Internet.

The new task will be learning how to use the capabilities of these instruments that can enhance our personal productivity. Unfortunately there is a whole new world of exploration and mastery required for each new technological device, but the rewards of mastering them are extraordinary. In order to accomplish this we will have to adjust our daily habits to include a period when we consciously work to master the potential of all the emerging technological devices. We will not have the luxury of deciding we are too old to learn these irritating devices. If we do, then we will be bypassed by the productivity of others. At the Institute we are requiring that some of our most talented workers spend at least 30 minutes a day learning the new and advanced features of their technologies because the enjoyment and productivity gains possible are most impressive. Perhaps we can substitute the time required to learn the new technologies for the travel time that many of us can now avoid as we make fewer trips to the office.

PERSONAL IGNITION:

The new technologies, which are inherently interactive (computers, lasers, the Internet, wireless phones), in combination with the old trusted ones that we use passively (books, TV, movies) will increasingly help us to become formidably productive and continuously curious, interested, and excited citizens of the world we live in. I see this happening frequently in others as people gain access to information, talents and skills ignited by the new technologies available to them and fueled by the ideas that this access provides them. What is happening is they are experiencing a personal renaissance derived from mastering the energy and work potential of these new technologies to enhance their own personal delivery systems.

This personal mastery parallels societal mastery of the new technologies and exponentiates the available energy for each individual much as the mastery of the new technologies exponentiates productive work output of the larger delivery systems we all serve in some capacity during our working years. When this happens to someone I know, I call it ignition. I notice that they seem to ignite into an exciting proactive mode where they personally experience a renaissance of interest fueled by an exciting sense of curiosity and competence. There are 2 requirements for ignition:

(1) People have to understand the positive potential of the new technologies and grow beyond the personal lament phase where they damn them because teenagers (and even pre-teens) are misusing them. They may not want to join the world of "Facebook," but there is no excuse for ducking the world of Google, Kindle, Macs, PCs, the iPod and iPad, BlackBerry, email, Word, Excel, Amazon, Dragon Naturally Speaking, Lightroom, PowerPoint, and many other personal delivery system enhancers.

(2) Ignition also requires that people spend many hours becoming familiar with the new world of technology. Most people are too busy and do not understand they have to work hard, study books such as this one, and change their way of thinking about topics such as "education and technology" before the signs of ignition begin to appear.

Naturally they believe their lives are already full, and "Sufficient unto the day is the evil thereof." In other words, feeling exhausted from their daily labors, they do not have the energy or will to work late at night or early in the morning to understand new and difficult concepts and technologies.

I found it took years of ongoing efforts late at night or early in the morning for me to start to understand the new brain research on how children learn to read. I wince as I think about people struggling through this book who are tired and have a litany of extraordinary responsibilities and with people tugging at their sleeves for attention. I am sorry that in order to succeed in mastering the concepts of a delivery system and the potential of the new technologies, they will have to force themselves through my (at times) difficult prose if they want to understand how we can give Spence or Waterford to every child. But I can assure you that ignition is worth it, and there are few things as satisfying for us.

However when people pass these first 2 gates, I am stunned by their responses as they ignite. Many times the first symptom is a complaint or lament directed at me that they are getting too excited about the potential of the new delivery systems and are having trouble sleeping. The comment usually goes something like this: "I'm furious with you! Do you realize that I woke up at 3 or 4 this morning because of the implications of your ideas? Do you understand how hopeful this is for children? Why haven't you got your message out? Why haven't you done something? How can I get access to the materials for my children or grandchildren?"

When the symptoms persist I know I am watching ignition as people begin to hone their own personal delivery systems through their willingness to spend long hours mastering the software of the new technologies and learning new domains of knowledge by poring through books, articles, and the Internet in order to increase their understanding. There is nothing like ignition because above all else, it breeds a sense of hope and purpose which we need to sustain us through the constant struggle to successfully implement our own personal projects.

STUDENT IGNITION: SOME INHERENT ADVANTAGES OF TECHNOLOGY-BASED REFORMS:

Just as I hope all the readers of this book will accomplish some level of ignition in harnessing the new technologies and software to help their personal productivity and growth, I also hope that the students will ignite with the help of the astonishingly powerful and exciting software that is coming on stream. There are so many new advantages available from the emerging educational software that a whole book could be written about them, but I will offer a list of some of the more obvious ones to clarify my point.

- Any lesson can be scaled with total accuracy for little cost.

- The software can be distributed worldwide within seconds providing universal access any time or anywhere (wireless).

- The software, unlike teachers, can individualize the instruction for each child offering a different sequence for each student depending on the previous answer to each instructional item.

- The materials can be presented with stunning artistic beauty in 3D with animation and music.

- Enhanced software is highly motivating to the student users.

- Learner profiles will be developed by powerful new databases on each child so the materials can be presented in a manner that is most conducive to the wiring of the child's brain.

- Also testing will be conducted in real time by tracking the scoring of the items as the child learns and matching them to the child's learning decay rate. This will not only increase the accuracy of testing, but also provide the child with automatic refreshment of items that they are starting to forget (learning decay).

- Administrative programs will provide student tracking in real time. These will be graphed on large screens for administrators to track the progress of states, districts, schools, classrooms, and individuals.

- Careful privacy laws will be implemented to insure the confidentiality of student records.

- Each year by early October statistical programs tracking the student learning rate will be able to predict where each class and student will be at the end of the school year in June given their trajectory. This will allow additional resources to be scheduled before the students fail and the devastating sense of shame takes root in the children who are having difficulties.

- Special multisensory tutoring programs will be activated to remediate those with dyslexia and other learning difficulties.

- Programs will be developed to link to the homes so that additional instructional time and homework can be scheduled for all children.

- Technology and software supported by the state will also be available at home during the preschool years to provide priceless instruction to the children who need to (1) master a minimum speaking vocabulary and (2) start to achieve automaticity in decoding through developing phonemic awareness and phonics in order to enter school with an adequate skillset and vocabulary.

MY PERSONAL IGNITION: A SUMMARY OF WHAT I HAVE LEARNED ABOUT EDUCATION IN MY 56 YEAR QUEST SINCE COLLEGE:

(1) Comprehending that education is one of many delivery systems that offer goods and services to the public is critical to understanding how best to improve it. History has taught us that the real breakthroughs in delivery systems occur when a new technology is introduced and exponentiates the available work for the workers in the system. Education still uses teachers as its primary source of work although there is some support available from older technologies such as books, blackboards, chalk, pens, pencils, paper, etc. The new technologies are offering what will soon be limitless amounts of additional work support to help the teachers teach children much more efficiently both in school and home settings.

(2) The federal and state legislatures, state superintendents, superintendents of school districts, the Secretary of Education, the Department of Education, the National Science Foundation, and foundation leaders from all over the United States, need to take the time and effort to understand the rules of delivery systems and the importance of sponsoring technology and software as the primary reform for the educational delivery system. Lacking this knowledge, these leaders are unwittingly wasting billions of dollars on reforms that assume that by following new best practices identified by research, the schools can continue to become more efficient.

(3) They cannot continue to believe that their reforms can improve the efficiency of the educational delivery system! We have wrung out the efficiency algorithms and after tripling our investments in schools have flat-lined our improvement trajectory which refuses to go up no matter how much money is invested in the mature delivery system. Titanium horseshoes for the Pony Express horses and wind resistant capes for the riders, no matter how much money is invested, will not help them to compete with the telegraph.

(4) Although the words may seem a bit strong at first, I have learned that those leaders who refuse to take the time to understand the nature of delivery systems and the importance of introducing technology into them are guilty of a conflict of interest and are committing educational malpractice. The conflict of interest follows from their proclivity to fund the people they know and understand, the familiar, those who run the government agencies and schools who view the public funds as theirs to administer without doing the hard research to learn about the new delivery systems and technologies. Their habitual sponsoring of programs, people and processes they are familiar with instead of mastering the new frontiers of educational practices prevents them from expending funds on new technologies and leaves them open to a "conflict of interest" charge.

Instead of opening up the bids to technology and championing new delivery systems that can dramatically outperform the standard solutions, they are demanding allegiance to the old systems and their workers. Their standard solutions focus on using the workers more efficiently even though the current delivery system with its workers has reached maturity and a natural limit. When the delivery system becomes static (which the current one has) then the fallback position is to add a new reform that brings in many new workers. While adding work to the system by hiring more teachers, aides and staff can sometimes offer definable improvement, such an approach will render the reform too expensive to scale and further contributes to the deepening financial crisis in education.

The technologists cannot get a hearing and are therefore barred from competing at the federal level because both the leaders of the agencies running the projects and the reviewers they assign for "peer review" have failed to understand the potential of technology and dismiss the technology proposals as misguided or non-responsive. In their future competitive program offerings, they should begin to favor technology software grants. And the scoring in individual sections of the grants that allocate points must reflect major point assignments for those groups that can provide outstanding software development.

Their approach truly is a conflict of interest because the better solutions are denied a hearing and only the known and familiar are funded under pressure from their workers who are interested in seeing that all reform funds flow either directly to them in increased salaries and benefits or provide more salaries for hiring additional workers.

They are also committing malpractice because they are treating the students with solutions that will not work and failing to use new ones that can solve the problem. They have not taken the time to learn about technology, and what is worse, they have allowed flawed studies to debunk technology, studies that cannot stand up to scrutiny. Recall that a famous government study[1] disingenuously reported "no student gains" in a study on the impact of various software packages. Buried in the report was the confession that many of the sites used the materials

---

[1]See "The Effectiveness of Reading and Mathematical Software Products: Findings from the first student cohort," report to congress, March 2007, NCES 2007–4006, Washington, D.C.: U.S. Department of Education, P.O. Box 1398, Jessup, MD 20794-1398.

for less than 25% of the assigned time, but this devastating statistic was not included in the executive summary or the press releases because it would have revealed that the study was flawed.

No reputable medical study would report the failure of a drug when only a fraction of the patients took it during the evaluation. None of the leaders of the Agency commissioning the study or the organization hired to conduct the study understood that the most important metric in assessing the effectiveness of computer assisted instruction is the usage time and consistency. This is what brain research has revealed to us.

Schools tend to be very careless in ensuring that the materials are used daily for 15–30 minutes and tend to treat the scheduled computer time as a variable that can be cancelled for other activities such as play practice, honoring an ethnic group, working on bulletin boards, taking unscheduled trips, preparation time for test-taking, and celebrating special holidays or birthday parties.

Unfortunately this is damaging the education of many students and wasting billions of dollars in futile reforms that fail to take into account the concept of a delivery system and the impact technology can have on them. Our studies have demonstrated that poor usage can blunt the effectiveness of technology because there is little impact on learning for the first 1,100 minutes for the Waterford software, after which scores start rising dramatically. Most sites never used the materials enough to even reach the 1,100 minutes which would be about 3–4 months of usage at the rate of 15 minutes each day, or 2,700 minutes per school year.

(5) A new external support organization, a third source of education for children, will become commonplace that will monitor, motivate, and measure the effectiveness of usage both in the homes of the students and in their school classrooms in order to insure the technology is being used properly. The effectiveness of the technology must be understood and elevated to center stage rather than be treated as a supplementary aid that is used when there is nothing more important on the schedule. The process of regular monitoring with weekly reports on usage is highly motivating over time and insures adequate usage by the students.

(6) We need to find the strategy and metaphors to convince funding sources in the government, business community, and foundations that the reforms they have been sponsoring are usually not effective, scalable, or affordable. Recall the retiring head's speech mentioning that the reform I was going to offer at Spence 40 years ago had already been tried 3 times over the past few decades. The only thing new in this reform was the name given to it.

We have to be able to say (quietly but firmly) that if a reform is not using technology, then it is an efficiency reform that will fail because we have already developed a mature delivery system that cannot be changed with efficiency reforms unless enormous sums are spent to bring in many more manual workers (teachers and aides) which then renders the reform too expensive and non-scalable.

Recall that during Waterford's early research probes placing technology with the families that the cost is at most a third of a traditional preschool when distributed to modest numbers but is far more effective academically. But in high volumes in the decades ahead, the home-based technology reforms will drop to less than 5% of the cost of a good preschool. The cost savings of technology, as well as its superior effectiveness in training the cognitive skills will ultimately insure its acceptance.

(7) The number one priority for educational reform should be the funding of educational software so as to take advantage of the constantly improving technology that is coming on stream. Businesses are forced to improve their hardware in exciting competitive breakthroughs, which fuel rounds of attractive new hardware products, but this is not true of educational software which is extremely expensive to develop and support and has too limited a market to provide incentive for substantial future investment.

Furthermore, software developers are confronted by a problem of having too small a market for each product because every country may want the software modified to fit its language, customs, and even accents (e.g. American, British, Australian, or Native American English accents), not to mention their national commitment of allegiance to their own songs and stories which they expect to be interwoven throughout the reading instruction. Trying to modify software so that it teaches children to read in different languages, songs, and stories that fit the interests of a broad range of minorities and their traditions that are part of every nation is very demanding and expensive.

Notice that even in a culture like America, where we are proud of our democratic ideals, that there are major accent and cultural differences. A Native American on a reservation in Arizona will have difficulty communicating with a Boston Brahmin, as will a Spence girl from Park Avenue talking with an African American boy in a public school in Harlem a few blocks north of her school. Similarly, a southern Creole child in New Orleans will not be easily understood by a youngster from a small town in Utah.

Hardware vendors are able to distribute their products in high volumes. They may have to change a keyboard, but they can achieve high volumes of standardized equipment that is impossible for the software developers of instructional materials. Transistors and disk drives are blind to accents and politics. They know no international boundaries and can be used by every tribe and nation on the earth without modification.

(8) Schools will be unable to improve sufficiently until we can provide teachers with the ability to individualize the instruction through the use of technology. Right now most schools are limited to strategies that rarely address the precise needs of the students, and the teachers have to choose some approximate level when presenting the materials to the students that are midway between the slow and the bright students. This bores the bright and terrifies the slower students. More importantly it is a waste of time for both the slow and the bright students. The traditional way to go from approximation to precision is to utilize technology. Think of laser guided bombs versus those that were thrown over the side manually during the First World War. By utilizing the new technologies we will be able to individualize the instruction for all children.

Clayton Christensen has pointed out that the individualization will be especially important for students who are being raised in an era of plenty and lack the pressure to succeed because they take financial security for granted. If we lose the attention of too many of them and fail to excite them to the point of ignition, then they will be poorly educated as they enter a competitive international job market that will screen them out and deny our nation the benefits of their capabilities.

(9) We must concentrate our technological efforts, initially, on the preschool years in order to help weaker students acquire sufficient skillsets to keep them competitive. As Hart and Risley have noted, families with inadequate traditions of speaking frequently to their children are setting them up for failure by the end of their 3rd year. Also note that Heckman (a Nobel Laureate in economics) has shown that the greatest return on investment for school funds is in putting money into the early preschool years when children are ages 2 through 4. Unfortunately the funds for preschool activities are usually not part of the federal or state K-12 budgets or guidelines. Head Start is actually funded through Health and Human Services (HHS) and not the Department of Education. This restricts most of the state and federal agencies from providing serious reform funding for the preschool years. State legislatures may be the logical source of funds for preschool programs using technology and software for the homes that are capable of preparing the students to enter at grade level or above.

(10) We have demonstrated with our UPSTART program that it is possible to supply technology and the Internet in the homes of 3 and 4 year olds to prepare them to enter kindergarten at age 5 either reading or ready to read. Fortunately we found there was no difference in the learning rates of Caucasian suburban children, Native Americans on a reservation, African American children, or inner-city Hispanic children whose families spoke only Spanish. But even more importantly we discovered that through using an external support group (see point 4 above) and staying in touch with the families on a weekly basis, the children used the program beyond our expected minimums.

I believe this is one of the most important findings in educational history because it means we can eradicate most of the barriers that keep children from having democratic access to world class instruction and reach them in their homes and insure they have a healthy start in their literacy education.

The accelerating destruction of the family unit and its impact on the young children of single parents cries out for some sort of home intervention to minimize the educational damage to the child. Without technology this will be impossible to accomplish because sending people to millions of homes to train the parents and children is both too expensive and ineffectual. The brain research suggests that the core issue in educating the child at home is developing "an appropriate stimulation strategy for optimal daily enrichment." This will not be possible for a beleaguered mother to provide, nor of course can we afford to finance a daily visit by a reading expert.

(11) We must stop blaming schools for the mediocre performance of our students. The problem lies with the family which has much greater influence on the child's learning than most schools. Hart and Risley demonstrated that Great Society reforms failed because the families of the low SES students had provided inadequate vocabulary training for their children. The Coleman report in the 1960s unexpectedly proved that schools are quite equal in resources, and Alexander and Entwisle showed us in the 1980s that the schools do quite well during the school year when all students gain in their growth but begin to fall behind during the summer months.

- Waterford has also noted that our elementary schools suffer from a democracy tax that inhibits efficiency because we trust democracy over centralized control and believe that a melting pot approach incorporating diversity is best for the nation over time. Waterford also believes that standard reforms cannot make up the work shortfall from the democracy tax, and the only working solution is to incorporate technology to exponentiate the amount of individualized instruction available to students and provide it at home as well as school with guidance from a support center to enhance motivation and commitment.

- The greatest contribution from technology and its software will be to democratize education by providing access to it for all of our citizens so that an aristocracy of excellence is no longer restricted to those who have wealth or scholarships. The Mor-

rill land grant colleges and our community colleges helped remove the barriers of location by offering options to all students
throughout the United States. A positive consequence of the
Morrill policy was that in creating all of these new land grant
colleges, the act also initiated a subtle competition among these
institutions that has spread excellence through state funding
mechanisms. State leaders insure that their colleges and universities are not allowed to languish compared to other states. And
typically in Utah, Utah State competes with the University of
Utah, which is in turn competing with Southern Utah University, Dixie College, Utah Valley University, Weber State and a
number of private colleges and universities such as Westminster
and Brigham Young University. There are also some excellent
community colleges providing services and serving as bridges
for many students who will someday matriculate at the 4 year
institutions. Many loyal alumni appreciate the help that their
universities or private schools have given them, and their annual
giving and bequests have helped spread opportunity throughout our nation. As a result of our institutions of higher education, America has the strongest university system in the world.

But now noting the drag of the democracy tax on American
elementary and secondary schools, America must take the next
step and develop the finest educational software in the world to
help all of our younger citizens have both excellence and equity
available to them. We cannot depend on having only the most
talented students determine the output of our country. We need
to keep all of our citizens in the game, not just the privileged few.

• We must expand the aristocracy of excellence that has been
available only to the highly motivated whose knowledgeable
parents have helped them receive the finest education available
and insured that their salaries climb to rarefied heights.

While the lower and middle-classes have failed to make any
economic gains over the past few decades, those with wealth
have soared economically because their education has given
them a patent on how to make money. Rather than restrict

them we need to provide competition so that all can benefit from access to a world class education.

- Building the finest software in the world and making it available at reasonable prices will help check the runaway trajectory of the knowledgeable and wealthy. Through providing individualized, attractive, interactive instruction at home starting at 2 years old, we will be able to elevate all children to a level playing field rather than losing about a third of them before they graduate from high school because their homes are lean on love or vocabulary. This is where we must start!

- We need this for another reason also, because very large nations, such as India and China, have learned from our business prophets like Alvin and Heidi Toffler that education and technology will provide the route to success in a knowledge-based society. With their small families in China they are lavishing educational resources on their children to become mathematicians, scientists, economists and engineers preparing them to compete in a global market. At this time they have about twice as many students in their universities as America.

(12) Zero does not inflate even though educational costs continue to rise. The closer we keep our educational costs to zero the better our chance to fund education will be. If the costs are too high in quality elementary and secondary schools, the best schools will increasingly be restricted to the wealthy or the brightest students. The brightest are covered in honor public high schools such as Stuyvesant and the Bronx High School of Science in New York City, but this policy leaves out too many other students. The problem is even more poignant with colleges and universities in that their costs are soaring so far above zero that annual increases in costs are becoming quite substantial. In some cases their annual rise in costs is larger than the total cost for 4 years of tuition a few years earlier. For example when an Ivy League university costs $50,000 a year to attend, an 8% increase in costs now adds $4,000 to the bill that year. That $4,000 currently could cover the whole annual tuition at a number of other colleges, and could pay for 4 years of college a decade ago.

According to the New York Times in an article published in September 2010, the costs of a college education have risen from 250 to 300% over the last 30 years which is much higher than the inflation rate. The author of the article speculates that we may see the end of tenure in the universities because the costs are pricing many out of the market. He also notes 2 books have just been published called *Higher Education? How Colleges Are Wasting Our Money and Failing Our Kids—And What We Can Do About It*, and *Crisis on Campus: A Bold Plan for Reforming Our Colleges and Universities*.

At some point the costs become so high that students and their parents will turn to electronic software for their credentialing. The Western Governor's University headquartered in Salt Lake City sponsored by 19 states has accreditation and over 10,000 students working online electronically from their homes for a fraction of the cost of standard college tuitions.

Clayton Christensen of the Harvard Business School believes that only software will be inexpensive enough to provide the desired individual instruction for the future. He notes that schools and universities will be unable to keep raising their prices and will have to start cutting services. This will provide an opening for educational software vendors to offer instructional packages to replace those being cut, so the students who desire access to the subject matter such as foreign languages or advanced placement courses will at least have an option. He also wonders how even the Harvard Business School will be able to sustain constant cost hikes when students will have alternative inexpensive routes to obtaining their MBAs for a tiny fraction of the cost.

(13) Perhaps the most hopeful thought for the future of education is that presenting individualized software to a learner appears to be an ideal approach for the brain. As we learn more about the brain, we will be able to tailor the sequencing and daily chunks of instruction as students build their own brains into impressive learning machines. We have discovered, to our joy, that there is no need to require long hours of study from small children. We can produce spectacular results with just 15 minutes a day (1% of a day) of a child's time at home during the preschool years and throughout the early grades with the current

software. That we have been so successful in our earliest UPSTART trials suggests that as we improve the software and learn more about how to motivate parents and children from a distant support center, we may someday be able to start almost all children on a learning trajectory that will prepare them brilliantly for the evolving knowledge-based society they will face in the future.

(14) My real dream is that someday we will be able to continue the students' trajectories until these students ignite and become self-learners with an inherent and unstoppable love of life and the ability to affect eternity through their work and families as 2 of my heroes have: Benjamin Franklin who built his brain with great care and a scientific approach and James Parkinson who built his with a frontal assault on life with an impeccable taste for the authentic and the heart of a giant.

Chapter Twenty-One: The Future

The future of world education may have been accelerated by Muhammad Yunus whose pioneering work in Bangladesh has suggested a solution to what has seemed an almost unsolvable problem: How is it possible to offer a quality education to children in developing nations when the country is too poor to afford a robust public school system, and the parents are too poor to pay for private school? Even the geography of Bangladesh suggests the futility of pursuing workable policies. For example, this country that used to be part of India is the size of Florida and has a population of over 160,000,000 making it the 8th largest and most densely populated country in the world. Furthermore, during heavy rain seasons, a portion of the land goes underwater. America's view of Bangladesh was shaped during the Nixon years when Henry Kissinger characterized Bangladesh as "an international basket case." Many of us first heard about Bangladesh when rock bands sponsored benefit concerts for its worst disasters.

The genius of Yunus is that he devised a business model involving microcredit loans that enabled the poorest women in the villages to open businesses through accessing credit from the Grameen Bank that Yunus formed. A second contribution is his understanding of the importance of education for the children of the families involved with his bank. In their operating guidelines for their workers, the Grameen Bank has specified that their "Grameen Ladies" must guarantee that their children will attend school. This business tenet is significant because it provides a motivating force for parents to finance their children's education.

One of the Grameen companies is a cellular phone company that has provided a wireless network that extends out to the village level. Someday this network will be used to deliver educational software to tablets or computers where the users will lease the time just as they lease the time in minutes for talking on the cell phone. Other Grameen companies are leasing and selling portable solar devices to generate enough electricity to run cell phones, lights, and computers. These devices are marginally useful for providing electricity to computers, but over time the improvement to computer chips and the solar panels will provide an inexpensive solution to this problem. There is also the possibility that alternative sources of electricity will be developed over time.

We have never tried to use our software in Bangladesh, but given the extraordinary success of Yunus's efforts, I have studied the data and believe it will someday be possible to use our model there even though the poverty and infrastructure problems seem at first to appear unsolvable. As I conducted my analysis of a country I have never visited, I noted that 3 events have transpired that might help an effort be successful not only for Bangladesh, but for any country in the world.

THE THREE THINGS THAT HAVE HAPPENED ARE:

(1) The Nobel Laureate Muhammad Yunus developed a banking microcredit model (The Grameen Bank) that enabled the poorest citizens to become productive workers by opening their own businesses under the Grameen Bank's umbrella even in the impoverished areas of the country. Their stunning success is a hymn to modified capitalism which he calls the social business model. His bank now has over 8,000,000 borrowers and half a billion dollars in capital. What adds to his accomplishments is the knowledge that he started this enterprise with a personal loan in 1976 to 42 people totaling $27 with the sole intention of freeing them from local moneylenders who were crippling them with usurious rates.

He has taught us that even the poorest and illiterate citizens of his country who live on $2 a day or less, can be organized to start their own successful businesses with the help of a microcredit bank that makes collateral free loans to the women of the villages. His saga is very important because he has demonstrated through his development of the Grameen Bank and its subsidiary companies that given the proper microcredit banking policies, an impoverished nation can generate a powerful business climate by training and harnessing the talents of mothers who are fiercely committed to providing for their families. His policy is treat the poor as an asset, rather than a liability, by providing them with loans that will help them to start their own businesses. Since he started his efforts on behalf of the poor, Bangladesh has reduced its poverty rate from 74% to below 40%.

He believes the poor that have survived in their difficult environments have strong natural talents that can be put to use without attempting to train them for new sets of skills. If they can come up with a business model that can use any of their current talents, and they become part of a small group from his bank that meets weekly and are collectively responsible for any of the group's loans, then small loans will be advanced to them with the group's approval. His influence has helped many families survive through hard work, but he recognizes that his model is not a financial panacea that will generally produce great individual wealth. His workers gain dignity and stability but rarely acquire significant wealth through their efforts. By 2007 the bank had lent money to over 80,000 villages.

He recognizes that the children of those who are building their modest businesses may be much more successful financially if they acquire a good education, so his workers must pledge to see that their children are educated. For those that appear to have academic talent and a good record, the bank will loan money for higher education. The program was started in 1997 and within 10 years had distributed about 21,000 loans for 234 medical degrees, 292 agricultural degrees, 50 MBAs, 960 masters' degrees, and almost 19,000 Bachelor degrees. In 2007 there were over 7,200 student loans made.

By requiring that they educate their children, Yunus also unleashes a second generation family that is equipped with enough education to prosper in a knowledge-based world at a much higher level than their parents.

(2) The speed of light has unexpectedly entered the picture in the form of wireless signals reaching out to the humblest villages as cell phone networks were constructed beginning in 1996. At some point these wireless networks will provide access to powerful inexpensive computer-based instruction for children over the Internet. Recall that only 15 minutes a day is required to teach reading. The cell phone ladies have developed a tradition of selling inexpensive minutes to villagers which could become a model for selling instructional minutes where public education is either poor or non-existent. This is significant because anytime we can devise a means of harnessing the speed of light, we find that the delivery system where it appears can scale almost overnight and provide services equivalent to those of the most advanced societies. For example, there is no difference between a phone call initiated in a poor village in Bangladesh by an illiterate farmer and a call initiated on the floor of the Chicago Mercantile Exchange. Both use the speed of light to carry the voice signal. In fact, Yunus notes wryly, and with some pride, that some of the illiterate Bangladesh farmers call the Chicago Exchange daily with rented cell phone minutes to track the future market for their goods.

(3) To insure that children can develop literacy and numeracy skills no matter what their financial condition or location, the Waterford Institute has developed both the necessary educational software in English and the means to support it as part of a 34 year quest to start off young children with the fundamentals of a good education at home or in school. In order to accomplish this, the Institute has invested over $135 million in software for young children ages 3–8 in reading, math, and science; and has also developed a distance learning support model to insure successful usage of the materials called "the third source." The name signifies that in addition to the 2 traditional sources of education for young children, the home and the school, there is now a third source: the use of technology supported by a Waterford distance learning team. This third source uses a support

center connecting computers over the Internet as well as telephones with the users to provide guiding intelligence on their performance. The service personnel monitor, motivate, and measure the usage for the parents or teachers of the children using the materials.

While such a service with all of the sophisticated networks and hardware behind it sounds prohibitively expensive, the volumes inherent in its design can reduce the costs to pennies per transaction. Notice the volumes of usage that Yunus generated in Bangladesh with his mobile phone company serving the poorest of the poor in 1996 as he organized his work-force of women into distributors of a cell phone network. He provided loans to a phone lady to buy a cell phone and pay for it by selling access to it on a minute by minute basis to the villagers who suddenly were provided a portal to the outside world. Within 13 years (2009) there were 25 million subscribers supported by as many as 400,000 Grameen phone ladies in Bangladesh alone. The number of Grameen phone ladies has started to decline as more villagers are beginning to purchase their own phones, but the increased volume of usage is strengthening the wireless phone networks.

The inadvertent byproduct of his successful cell phone company is that the nucleus for an educational renaissance is now in position because this network will soon be capable of carrying enhanced instructional content that will be affordable in the most humble settings using the newest inexpensive computer technologies. Yunus's Grameen Bank has even opened a portable solar panel business to provide power for the cell phones and lights so that the students can study after dark.

The enhanced educational software that is coming on stream will be identical to the instructional materials being used by the most advanced societies, including our own research school in Salt Lake City, Utah. While it is true that, in some settings illiterate sales ladies will be selling and supporting the materials for illiterate mothers, their children will have an opportunity to experience a world class education even if they are not enrolled in a village school. Using the third source model and its powerful educational software package, Waterford has demonstrated that a child can be taught to learn to read in only 15 minutes a day in any setting. This means that the technology can be shared with many students at a modest cost.

This new cell phone network is coming on stream all over the earth with the support of microcredit policies that will allow at least modest usage of this network for most of the world's population. This will provide them with a portal not only to communicate to the outside world, but also a means of educating their children. Some microcredit banks will undoubtedly imitate the follies of the larger banks during the current worldwide recession by extending credit beyond rationality to burnish next quarter's numbers, but this will self correct over time and will not stop the healthy growth and survival of the microcredit industry and the expansion of priceless wireless networks throughout the world.

Thus instead of having to wait for a generation or 2 while schools are constructed and a mature teacher corps is trained, mothers will be able to take matters into their own hands and insure that the children have a start during the critical learning years from age 3 through 8 when the "learning trajectory" is set for most children.

THE NEED FOR ENLIGHTENED TECHNOLOGY LEADERSHIP IN AMERICA:

My goal as an author is to help the reader understand that we need to begin to transfer our educational decision making to the new metaphors and convince our leaders to do the same. This will be much more difficult than we might think. Consider for example the stranglehold the old educational metaphors have on the current scene. This is not a criticism, but a statement of fact and a recognition of the power of old metaphors. But of course there is also a tinge of frustration considering the damage we are doing to our children when there is an affordable answer waiting in the wings that is being ignored. Notice the breadth of leadership that has to be convinced of the significance of the new metaphors:

- **Business Leaders and Their Corporate Giving:** Not a single business leader who has made his or her money in technology hardware, software, or communications has embraced and funded high quality core curriculum software required to activate the potential of the new technologies. Having made money in their businesses and displayed considerable talent in understanding the potential of hardware and software to produce new businesses, they have failed to transfer this skill when thinking about education.

Instead they revert to the old and familiar metaphors they were raised with during their own schooling. Usually they back one of the traditional reforms or start to introduce a new set of metaphors that they have grown comfortable with in their competitive business culture. For example, they might stress productivity, accountability, competition, merit pay, capitalism, team building, choice, vouchers, or charter schools. Sometimes they fund dormitories, science buildings, or other classroom buildings, and sometimes they identify an area to help such as scholarships, "reading," dyslexia, or autism; but they still think traditionally and not of developing scalable software. The core problem is not that they are necessarily wrong in their insights, but that they are missing the larger issue that made them successful: Their success came from their ability to harness the potential of new technologies and fashion businesses using this new power. The Pony Express had plenty of accountability, productivity, competition, merit pay, capitalism, etc. What it did not have was a new technology that could harness the speed of light. Once a group showed up with this capability, they destroyed the Pony Express business model in 2 days.

This lack of funding has restricted the core contribution of educational technology because ironically not a familiar business leader or foundation he or she left behind has contributed serious capital to harnessing the new technologies for educational purposes. They have given many hundreds of millions to school systems or universities in support of the traditional metaphors, but they have failed to transfer their entrepreneurial brilliance to education and opted instead for the familiar components of the current manual delivery system that they grew up with.

A curriculum problem needs a curriculum solution. A few of them have dabbled at the fringes, but none have the vision to understand how their investment could be scaled worldwide to help billions of children, not just the few who benefit from the new classroom building or science labs they have built.

I call it a manual delivery system because most of the labor is supplied by the teacher whom we know is available less than half the days in the year and can at best offer about a minute a day of individual instruction in the 6–6½ hours the school is open. In other words, there are severe delivery system restrictions in the traditional educational delivery system that these entrepreneurs overlook, even though they have the intelligence and grit to blow open new technology and software delivery systems in their respective arenas by harnessing the power of the new technologies in an original manner that provided goods and services for their customers that would have otherwise been impossible prior to their vision.

Given that the best and the brightest business leaders and their foundations are dealing with yesteryears' educational metaphors, one would expect that other leaders outside the field of technology would be even less sensitive to the potential of the new technologies. And that is precisely the case.

- **Government Agencies and Leadership:** Government agencies such as the National Science Foundation (NSF), the Department of Education, and the National Institutes of Health (NIH) have excellent rosters of first rate scholars helping them in peer review of grants which should on the surface appear to be an ideal source of funds for the development of educational software. But unfortunately they too have the same metaphorical problem because they tend to be represented by the peers of yesteryear rather than the peers of tomorrow. Their real job should be to help fund the development of brilliant, scalable, inexpensive, interactive, individualizable, artistically stunning curriculum, and this means the leadership of these agencies will have to train and develop a new generation of program officers who are infused with the new metaphors and have developed policies to support them. Of course this also means the leaders will have to learn the new metaphors themselves in order to lead and guide their agencies properly.

- **Peer review:** which helps the agencies to decide whom to fund is valid if the reviewers are up to date in their technology metaphors. Most of them are not because when we apply for grants as a nonprofit research organization we are almost always turned down because the reviewing scholars know little about the field. The height of folly from my perspective was the review of one of my proposals where 3 of the 4 reviewers simply wrote that "It is not possible to teach science using technology."

  This is an example of the metaphor problem where only the familiar is valid. Furthermore it misses the key point that technology has the capability to build virtual experiments in 3D imitating the original apparatus that scientists developed while making their discoveries. Someday students will be able to change the variables of the actual experiments and relive the experience of the original inventors. With adequate funding, not only will the virtual apparatus be available, but narrative stories with exciting plots will be able to replicate the characters, setting, and actual experiences that ensued as they made their original discoveries. The drama of the conflicting opinions and missteps of the teams that made the discovery will make the core issues live for the students and allow them access to running the virtual equipment as if they were actually there.

  A secondary problem is that these agencies are staffed with rotating scholars who make decisions based on the scholarly credentials of the applicant and not on the organization's capabilities. The production of software materials requires a huge team effort to develop quality curriculum that is even more complicated than filming a Hollywood movie. Our materials combine the cost of filming a movie, writing many books, writing original music scores, and also very expensive and complex computer programs to direct the instructional sequencing. The staffing of our teams is very counterintuitive to a Washington project officer who is used to backing specific credentialed scientists in an experiment. We hire many outstanding scientists as advisors, but the real work for us is to produce an artistically and academically successful product that the students, parents, and teachers want to use and which will educate the students effectively. Both the investment and the awards are given to Hollywood productions, not to PhDs who provide technical advice. They are given to the director and his crews that produce the products.

At one time earlier in my career I had 36 PhDs on my staff, a number of whom were distinguished mathematicians, but I learned that this emphasis on PhDs was a prescription for disaster. They were more interested in experimenting with their personal approaches than in producing a product. Their goal also differed from mine. Unknown to me, they were using the development resources and time to work out new approaches to teaching standard math topics because they were looking forward to developing textbooks using their unique approach, forgetting our goal was to produce a product for computers (another example of the familiar metaphor problem). Most of them moved on and later published some more textbooks which further enhanced their reputations and careers. But unfortunately I never was able to produce the desired software because I ran out of money after spending millions of dollars on the effort waiting for the teams to produce the products. Since then I have learned to use unheralded developers whose resume does not include academic honors but who are geniuses at running development teams. Unfortunately the peer reviewers always discard their proposals because they fail to fit their scholarly model.

They still believe a better manual approach using some scholar's theory is the best way to improve instruction. Lacking the metaphors, they fail to understand that magnificent instruction artistically presented can be made available anytime or any place individualized to each child's needs at a fraction of the cost of any alternative. If designed as part of a project, the curriculum can also be supported at a distance by experts monitoring, motivating, and measuring the student's progress. And instead of offering a tiny gain by stressing a new approach which is the norm, the state of the art educational software can be used at home as well as school to produce a significant life changing instructional competence for many children.

The peer review problem is further compounded by the "assignment of points" problem. Each reviewer is told what he or she must look for in the proposal, and each of the goals is assigned a possible maximum point spread that directs how the reviewer may assign points in evaluating the proposal. This is a fatal shortcoming that must be addressed because it allows prejudice to be codified and warps the judging of the proposals' quality. This is done by having the government (in the name of fairness) assign point awards for different issues the proposal must address in order to produce a desired outcome. The entire proposal totals 100 points, so different sections typically are assigned 5 to 25 points which add up to a100 point total.

This arbitrary assignment of points by the government is frequently biased against imaginative and truly original ideas because there are no points assigned for this even when the competition is described as one stressing innovation. For example there may be 20 points assigned for meeting federal fairness policies or an obscure workplace proviso, or for being a good collaborator, and/or 30 points for meeting some other government policy being pushed such as the National Clean Air Act.

One proposal we had an interest in was drafted by state personnel guided by new legislation from the state legislature to insure that the software package being bid upon had reading, math, and science software as well as a computer adaptive test and a multisensory tutoring program for 4 year olds that could be delivered in their homes and monitored at a distance. When we bid on the project we found that those in charge of the bid process had decided there would be no points assigned in the proposal for any of these software requirements even though they were the purpose for the bid. In other words someone could have won all 100 points and the bid without having to deliver any software at all. Fortunately the legislature sent the Request for Proposal (RFP) back to be rewritten when they discovered that their legislative intent was being ignored.

- **Foundation Giving:** We have discussed how difficult it is to make good educational decisions when the wrong metaphors guide the decisions. We have noted this in the educational giving patterns of national technology business leaders who nurture the old metaphors and not the new, and how the government does the same. Unfortunately, the foundations have shown the same proclivities as they have provided billions of dollars in grants to education for the same traditional elements of the current mature delivery system.

  The danger of this approach is that although the grants may help a few, the projects will never be scalable and effective enough at the delivery system level to have a national impact. This is not true of those areas described by the new metaphors which are designed to impact the delivery system capacity and hence provide a national audience with affordable interactive individualized artistically pleasing instruction. The advantage of adopting such an approach is that it will provide both excellence and equity to many children that are currently failing in their academic pursuits for reasons documented in this book. The business, government, and foundation problem of committing to yesteryear's metaphors is deeply rooted and will be extremely difficult to change.

  The educational workers (the teachers, parents, and students) need this software to accomplish their educational goals just as much as the consumers and businesses need Microsoft's spectacular Office software packages to enable them to solve a host of business or consumer requirements with programs such as "Word" or "Excel," and to roam through the Internet with "Internet Explorer," or make slides with "PowerPoint," or play music or videos with "Windows Media Player." At a considerable investment of capital, Waterford has been able to build outstanding enhanced educational software for young children from preschool up through the 2nd or 3rd grade, but now another significant task needs to be funded which is to extend this enhanced software up through the elementary, secondary, and, ultimately, college years.

THE FIRST STIRRINGS OF UNDERSTANDING?

After noting above that not a single business leader, national government leader, or substantial foundation has articulated and funded programs using the new technologies to develop the core instructional software needed to activate the potential carried by the emerging hardware, I am pleased to report that I have recently come across scattered data that suggest we may (Fall/Winter of 2010/2011) be experiencing the first stirrings of hope, and that our leadership is beginning to think more seriously about technology's potential.

- Arne Duncan, the U.S. Secretary of Education, has been working on the third draft of a 5 point National Educational Technology Plan. The 5 goals include (1) using technology to individualize instruction and make it more engaging, (2) developing a new generation of assessments, (3) connecting teachers with peers and experts to keep them up to date on available resources available to help them, (4) building infrastructure that lets schools support access to technology in and out of the classroom, and (5) harnessing the power of educational technology to increase district productivity and student achievement.

  So far there has been funding only for the student assessment modules. This is a problem because educators tend to believe if they can find out the status of all their learners that they will be able to address them with more efficiency. But since they are limited to at best a minute a day of individual instruction, the information is interesting but not sufficient. A new generation of enhanced software will first have to be built to provide the necessary interactive individualized instruction for the advanced elementary and secondary grades to help eradicate the students' learning problems that have been revealed through assessments.

- The Gates Foundation has announced a new program for Higher Education which focuses on the use of technology. This is a thoughtful first step. But once again the metaphors that define it have some shortcomings because they are a carry-over from a series of foundation funded efforts over the past few decades that have tried to encourage the distribution of college courses on technology through consortiums that maintain the instructional products and offer them with a free license as part of a free software movement.

SOME PROBLEMS WITH THE GATES APPROACH:

(1) Although it saves money to develop and support courses with head and shoulder shots of faculty teaching their courses in institutional settings, these courses are limited in appeal and impact. They use only a small portion of the potential of instructional technology as contrasted with the fully enhanced courses that use the full gamut of instructional possibilities.

The free software groups have been ignoring the development of expensive software that provides the ability to individualize the instruction for each child in real time. Using artificial intelligence techniques with a built-in sequencer, such a program can constantly change the instruction to fit the needs of each student as he or she progresses through the instructional materials in the most efficient manner. No time is wasted on group presentations that may or may not be appropriate to the student's needs at that moment.

They are also ignoring the costs of maintaining quality software. As I explain in the book's chapter on maintaining software, the costs to maintain what I call "enhanced software" with all of its expensive code is so high that it is impossible to support it without a strong revenue stream. Courses that cost only a few hundred thousand dollars to write end up costing millions of dollars a year to maintain. Free software means that the provider will not receive the necessary revenue required to maintain and improve the product.

(2) A second problem is that the research findings that have been collected for the past few decades suggest that the real battlefield for educational success will be fought in the preschool and early elementary years. The students who start to drop out in high school are slowly playing out a devastating academic death spiral in the spirit of a Greek tragedy that starts when they are 3 and 4 years old. My 34+ years of working with technology and schools has been an extensive lesson in learning to work with younger and younger children with our software. In our home-based program called UPSTART in Utah we have discovered that we can identify learning problems within a few weeks when teaching reading, math, and science to 4 year old students using technology in their homes. Once we discover this we can place them almost instantly on a new multisensory tutoring program that uses the latest remediation research and individualizes the instruction for the child having difficulties.

The most devastating data I have been confronted with in the decades I have worked with technology and schools was the discovery, in 1990 during a large New York City project, that if children fall behind by the end of the 1st grade in their reading, and it is not immediately corrected, that they will as a group never catch up. As I documented and graphed this phenomenon earlier in the book, I noted that the problem is a mathematical one because the only way for them to catch up with the class is to learn the materials 4 times faster than their peers. What are the chances that the weakest students in a class will be able to learn 4 times faster?

Instead, when we find 4 and 5 year old children having difficulty learning, we can use the third source paradigm to track student usage and progress from our Waterford Learning Center and place them in a multisensory remediation package that meets many of their needs 4 to 5 years sooner than most schools are able to identify and remediate the problem. The delayed identification of the problems until the 3rd or 4th grade has devastating psychological consequences causing the children to suffer from "print flight" and a paralyzing sense of "shame" that blocks any further learning efforts. These are terms used by the National Institutes of Health in their outstanding research efforts over a couple of decades and were summarized earlier in the book as I discussed Reid Lyon's work.

As I review the research in the previous chapters of this book, I believe the reader will come to the same conclusion I have, which is that although there is a tendency to think the really important subject matter or core curriculum (math, science, foreign languages, grammar, punctuation, history, writing, and serious logical analysis) cannot be introduced fruitfully until the children are about to enter their teens, in reality there are a series of academic skills that have to receive serious attention and daily exposure as early as preschool in order for many children to succeed academically.

Opposing my view, the new Gates Foundation effort seems to be driven by the metaphor that "later is better." As the New York Times technology reporter Steve Lohr wrote in an October 2010 article, Gates believes, "The potential benefits of technology are greater as students become older, more independent learners. Making that point, Mr. Gates said in an interview that from kindergarten to about 5th grade 'the idea that you stick them in front of a computer is ludicrous.'"

Unfortunately, as I argue and document in the earlier chapters of this book, our 34 years of research at the Waterford Institute suggest precisely the opposite, as does the research of scholars such as the Nobel Laureate James Heckman. He has published some brilliant analysis demonstrating that the return on investment for preschool and early elementary children is far greater than on older students with their expensive remediation requirements. His work has been a major influence on the universal preschool movement. Without a healthy early start in their education, the children with academic difficulties overwhelm a school system and become fodder for the dropout stampede that can take out half the students in the system in some of our major cities.

Our data at our own research school show that it costs more and is less productive to work with older students who are failing than young ones. For example, we discovered in our research school that when we tested for learning difficulties in the preschool and intervened with a tutoring program immediately, that instead of having to tutor 12 students after their kindergarten year, we only had 2 students that needed tutoring.

Without the early intervention, the students rapidly develop a negative view of schooling, with its attendant psychological baggage, that is destructive to them and their peers. We have discovered that when we start them out properly both in home and school with the new enriched software when they are younger and malleable, we can keep them abreast of their peers and wean them from a dependency on special remediation classes with their inevitable psychological consequences.

Notice also that as their basic learning trajectory fails to ignite, the children are thrashing uncomfortably and are not progressing productively while their peers are. Even if we work hard and salvage some students part way through high school, their peers may have a decade's worth of learning that they do not and never will have. Ten years of potential learning is a terrible thing to waste!

I am sure that, over time, as the Gates Foundation tracks its program impact on higher education, just as it did in its earlier high school program, the leadership will also initiate programs for younger children. But, for now, it is a great comfort for the field that the Foundation is starting to invest in the use of technology, and its powerful new metaphors, instead of just trying to improve the standard components of the traditional educational delivery system. In this way they will honor their extraordinary heritage of developing exquisitely useful Office software to connect us to the potential of the hardware that is doubling in capacity every 2 years without additional cost. This formula, of course, is precisely what education needs to accelerate the effectiveness of its student learning trajectories.

- In addition to Duncan and Gates beginning to address the use of technologies for education, an excellent thinker, Frederick M. Hess from the American Enterprise Institute has published a book clarifying how we need to move beyond retrying the same old reform chestnuts onto something new. His title and subtitle leave little doubt about his message: *The Same Thing Over and Over: How School Reformers Get Stuck in Yesterday's Ideas.*[1]

Hess recognizes how the constant thrashing in our quest for more efficiency in the school systems of America has reached a dead end, and in 4 different sections of his book he addresses the potential for the technological tools to be applied fruitfully to educational practice. In his own words:

> The potential of new tools and technologies to upend teaching and learning has not escaped notice. New technologies create unprecedented opportunities for curricular customization; for schools to escape geographic constraints; for students to interact with teachers and each other in new ways; for parents to be looped into school-student communications; for teachers to escape the confines of their classroom; and for data systems that permit granular monitoring and intervention on a previously impossible scale (25).

He also points out that it is a mistake to just add the new technologies to the standard delivery system. "Thus, our preference for using technology has typically amounted to pouring new computers and software into the same old classrooms, rather than using them to rethink the shape of schooling" (68). Our experience in the Utah UPSTART project which is discussed in great detail in the text of my book confirms his intuitions.

He is particularly sensitive that technology offers the ability to circumvent geographical limitations. "Many tasks central to teaching and learning, such as lecturing, tutoring, and assessment, might be pursued more powerfully (and certainly more cost-effectively, more

---

[1]Frederick M. Hess, *The same thing over and over: How School Reformers get stuck in Yesterday's Ideas*, (Cambridge: Harvard University Press, 2010).

conveniently, and in a more customized fashion) through web-based technologies" (219).

And in his concluding section on The Technology Challenge he expresses concisely my core theme, which I have not seen in other writers: "quantum leaps in productivity are always about using new advances in technology and management to render skilled employees more productive." He also notices how the Elementary and Secondary Education Act of 1965 decrees the technology shall "supplement, not supplant" classroom teaching which restricts it to a subordinate role that may or may not be used properly. He wants this changed and admonishes us to recognize that "Harnessing the power of web-based instruction and other new tools is only possible if they begin to displace, and not merely augment, traditional routines" (225–226).

On December 22, 2010 Hess wrote a column (Rick Hess Straight Up) that was critical of simply sprinkling technologies throughout schools. He notes that the Durham North Carolina public schools spent $3.5 million in Race to the Top funds to outfit 2 low-performing schools with Apple iPads because in the words of the Superintendent "This is how we learn. This is what we want." But when Hess observed the classroom usage, he noted that most of the time the equipment was "used in 1 of 2 ways. Neither impresses me. The first involves students working graphics, clip art, PowerPoints, or adding sound and visual effect to video shorts. The second is students Googling their way to Wikipedia for material to cut-and-paste into PowerPoints or word files." He then continues:

> This was all brought home to me again, just the other week, when I had a chance to spend a couple days visiting acclaimed "technology-infused" high schools. Yet, most of what I saw the technology being used for was either content-lite or amounted to students using Google-cum-Wikipedia as a latter-day *World Book Encyclopedia*. Making PowerPoints and video shorts is nice, but it's only us "digital tourists" who think it reflects impressive learning.
>
> Twenty years ago, even rudimentary video editing was technically challenging and required real skill. Today, technology makes most of this stuff a snap. It's the same reason videogames like *Halo* or *Madden '11* can seem enormously

challenging or complex to an adult but instinctive to a kid. It's not a question of deep knowledge so much as a learned set of routines. Unfortunately, it's easy for adults to get so distracted by the visuals, stylings, and sound that we fail to note that the content is vapid or mostly consists of Wikipedia-supplied factoids.

Hess's work shows some excellent thinking and will help create support for the innovative support of software development for the new technologies.

- A fourth positive argument on behalf of technology comes from the Foundation for Excellence in Education located in Florida and chaired by Jeb Bush who is a former Governor of Florida. Digital learning is just one of the foundation's educational interests, and on December 1, 2010 the foundation published its report (Digital Learning Now!) which published a 10 point manifesto cosigned by Bob Wise who is a former Governor of West Virginia. The points described in the paper are sound, but, as in the case of the Gates' first initiative, the audience they have in mind is the high school student.

Clearly, technology is suddenly in the air. This is very meaningful because America desperately needs some sort of a successful educational reform that is effective and affordable. We have many reforms that are affordable but not effective, and a few that are effective but not affordable. We know this because, over the past few decades, every conceivable reform has been tried and found wanting except a few that are prohibitively expensive and therefore are not scalable.

We have not discovered any magic bullets even though we continually try. Unfortunately the failure of any one reform never has impacted the collective consciousness because by the time the data is clearly negative, the reformers have moved on to other interests, and there is another new crop of enthusiasts slaying the old and bringing on the new. As I note in chapter three, I have lived too long to believe in the tooth fairy, but long enough to see that many in the educational community still do.

I have also grown to understand that true change can only come from core systemic reform of the delivery system. This means that any standard delivery system can only be fundamentally changed by introducing new technologies which can increase the amount of work that an individual worker can accomplish. We forget that teachers are manual workers whose job is to personally use their physical energy to instruct children aided by older technologies such as pens, pencils, chalkboards, books, etc.

Thus, we have a dream situation emerging where the source of the energy that is fueling the delivery system is doubling exponentially at no cost every 2 years. This offers a basis of hope that, sooner or later, we will be able to offer a quality education to all children that is now only available to a few. Having learned this potential and been part of the movement at Waterford, where we have struggled to implement our insights, has made my life rich and full, and I invite the reader to enjoy a sense of hope, at least, and to join, if possible, in this path-breaking saga to give all of our children the finest education imaginable.

AFTERWORD

As I have thought about the devastating and accelerating "education premium" that favors the educated economically and is compounding against poorly educated children who are then penalized in their lifetime earnings, I want to note one more time that the only hope we have of providing equity and excellence for all children is to start them young with outstanding software. David Brooks has clarified the issue in his book *The Social Animal* where he has collected data that highlight the emerging crisis. Here he notes that 40 or 50 years ago there was little or modest economic advantage for college graduates compared to non-college graduates, but times have changed and the advantage of education can be measured with frightening clarity.

The Education Salary Premium for Families with Degrees and Diplomas:

• The graduate degree mean annual salary is $93,000.

• The undergraduate degree mean annual salary is $75,000.

• The high school diploma mean annual salary is $42,000.

• The high school dropout mean annual salary is $28,000.

The Impact of Family Salary on Children's College Graduation Rate before age 24:

• $90,000 income has ½ of their children graduate from college.

• $70,000 income has ¼ of their children graduate from college.

• $45,000 income has 1/10 of their children graduate from college.

• $30,000 income has 1/17 of their children graduate from college.

319

The Impact of Family Income on attendance at one of the top 146 Colleges & Universities:

• Only 3 percent of the children in the lowest economic quartile attend one of the top 146 colleges and universities.

NAEP Results:
The results of our most trusted national reading test (NAEP) for 4th grade performance at grade level show:

• African Americans 14 percent at grade level.

• Hispanics 17 percent at grade level.

• Whites 43 percent at grade level.

We have to stop this accelerating inequality by individualizing instruction for our youngest children with stunning artistic quality that provides them with optimal daily instruction and sets them on a learning trajectory that will place and keep them on what Clayton Christensen calls the "promising path" through high school and college. As Marilyn Adams writes, "Their lives depend on it." Education is no longer a luxury; it is the new necessity. We know enough now to understand that we cannot succeed in restructuring manual reforms. Notice the economic trend is getting worse every year. We need to halt this trend and reverse it lest our society be torn apart with dissension. Clearly we need to build the software (real software, not games) that can harness the limitless power of the emerging technologies on behalf of our most precious resources: our children.

BIBLIOGRAPHY

Adams, H. (1995) *The Education of Henry Adams.* New York: Penguin Classics, pp. 360–362, 463, 467, 469.

Adams, M.J. (1990). *Beginning to read: Thinking and learning about print.* Cambridge, MA: MIT Press.

Adams, M.J. (2006). The promise of automatic speech recognition for fostering literacy growth in children and adults. In M. McKenna, L. Labbo, R. Kieffer, R., & D. Reinking (Eds.), *Handbook of literacy and technology, Volume 2,* pp. 109–128. Hillsdale, NJ: Lawrence Erlbaum Associates.

Adams, M.J. (2008). Decodable text: Why, when, and how? In Elfrieda H. Hiebert and Misty Sailors (Eds.), *Finding the right texts for beginning and struggling readers: Research-based solutions,* pp. 23–46. New York: Guilford Publications.

Adams, M.J. (2008). The limits of the self-teaching hypotheses (and how technology might help). In Susan Neuman (Ed.), *Educating the other America: Top experts tackle poverty, literacy, and achievement in our schools,* pp. 277–300. Baltimore, MD: Paul H. Brookes.

Adams, M.J. (2009). The challenge of advanced texts: The interdependence of reading and learning. In Elfrieda H. Hiebert (Ed.), *Reading more, reading better: Solving Problems in the Teaching of Literacy,* pp. 163–189. New York: Guilford Publications.

Alexander, Karl L., Entwisle, Doris R., & Olson, Linda Steffel (2007). Lasting consequences of the summer learning gap. *American Sociological Review, 72,* 167–180.

Allington, R.L. & Woodside-Jiron, H. (1998). The politics of literacy teaching: How "research" shaped educational policy. *Educational Researcher, 28(8),* 4–12.

Anglin, J.M. (19930. Vocabulary development: A morphological analysis. *Monographs of the Society for Research in Child Development, 58(10,* Serial No. 238).

Beals, D. (1997). Sources of support for learning words in conversation: Evidence from mealtimes. *Child Language, 24,* 673–694.

Beck, I.L. & McKeown, M. (1990). Conditions of vocabulary acquisition. In R. Barr, M.L. Kamil, P.B. Mosenthal, & P.D. Pearson (Eds.), *Handbook of reading research,* (Vol. 2, pp. 789–814). New York: Longman.

Beck, I.L. & McKeown, M.G. (2004, May). *Promoting vocabulary development in the early grades.* Paper presented at the annual conference of the International Reading Association, Orlando, FL.

Beck, I.L. & McKeown, M.G. & Kucan, L. (2002). *Bringing words to life: Robust vocabulary instruction.* New York: Guilford Press.

Beck, I.L., Perfetti, C.A. & McKeown, M.G. (1982). Effects of long-term vocabulary instruction on lexical access and reading comprehension. *Journal of Educational Psychology, 74,* 506–521.

Becker, W.C. (1977). Teaching reading and language to the disadvantaged—What we have learned from field research. *Harvard Educational Review, 47,* 518–543.

Biemiller, A. (2005). Size and sequence in vocabulary development: Implications for choosing words for primary grade vocabulary instruction. In A. Hiebert & M. Kamil (Eds.), *Teaching and learning vocabulary: Bringing research to practice* (pp. 223–242). Mahwah, NJ: Erlbaum.

Biemiller, A. (1993, December). Lake Wobegon revisited: On diversity and education. *Educational Researcher, 22,* 7–12.

Biemiller, A. (1998, April). *Oral vocabulary, word identification, and reading comprehension in English second language and English first language elementary school children.* Paper presented at the annual meeting of the Society for the Scientific Study of Reading, San Diego, CA.

Biemiller, A. (1999a, April). *Estimating vocabulary growth for ESL children with and without listening comprehension instruction.* Paper presented at the annual conference of the American Educational Research Association, Montreal, Quebec, Canada.

Biemiller, A. (1999b). *Language and reading success.* Cambridge, MA: Brookline Books.

Biemiller, A., & Slonim, N. (2001). Estimating root word vocabulary growth in normative and advantaged populations: Evidence for a common sequence of vocabulary acquisition. *Journal of Educational Psychology, 93,* 498–520.

Biemiller, A. (2002) A personal conversation July, 2002.

Bjork, R. Bjork Learning & Forgetting Lab at UCLA.

Boulton, D. *Children of the Code* at *www.childrenofthecode.org.*

Brabham, E.G. & Lynch-Brown, C. (2002). Effects of teachers' reading-aloud styles on vocabulary acquisition and comprehension of students in the early elementary grades. *Journal of Educational Psychology, 94,* 465–473.

Brady, S., Scarborough, H.S., & Shankweiler, D. (1996). A perspective on two recent research reports by Merzenich et al (1996) and Tallal et al. (1996). *Perspectives, 22(3),* 5–8.

Brett, A., Rothlein, L., & Hurley, M. (1996). Vocabulary acquisition from listening to stories and explanations of target words. *The Elementary School Journal, 96,* 415–422.

Brooks, David. (2011). *The Social Animal: The Hidden Sources of Love, Character, and Achievement* (p. 327). Random House.

Cantalini, M. (1987). *The effects of age and gender on school readiness and school success.* Unpublished doctoral dissertation, Ontario Institute for Studies in Education, Toronto, Ontario, Canada.

Carney, J.J., Anderson, D., Blackburn, C., & Blessing, D. (1984). Pre-teaching vocabulary and the comprehension of social studies materials by elementary children. *Social Education, 48,* 195–196.

Carroll, J.B., Davies, P., & Richmond, B. (1971). *The American Heritage word frequency book.* Boston: Houghton Mifflin.

Case, R. (1985). *Intellectual development: Birth to adulthood.* New York: Academic Press.

Case, R. (1992). *The mind's staircase: Exploring the conceptual under-pinnings of children's thought and knowledge.* Hillsdale, NJ: Erlbaum.

Catts, H.W., Fey, M.E., Zhang, X., & Tomblin, J.B. (1999). Language basis of reading and reading disabilities: Evidence from a longitudinal investigation. *Scientific Studies of Reading, 3,* 331–361.

Chall, J.S. (1996). *Stages of reading development.* (2nd ed.). New York: Harcourt Brace.

Chall, J.S., & Conard, S. S. (1991). *Should textbooks challenge students?* New York: Teachers College Press.

Chall, J.S., Jacobs, V.A., & Baldwin, L.E. (1990). *The reading crisis: Why poor children fall behind.* Cambridge, MA: Harvard University Press.

Charity, A.H., Scarborough, H.S., & Griffin, D. (2004). Familiarity with "School English" in African American children and its relationship to early reading achievement. *Child Development, 75(5),* 1340–1356.

Comer, J. (2004) Interview on Public Agenda Online, (accessed 14 May 2004) http:www. Publicagenda.org/specials/learning/experts 1.htm.

Contemporary Sociology. (1980). "Schooling Does Make a Difference", *Contemporary Sociology* Vol. 9, No. 6 (Nov., 1980), pp. 799–802.

Coyle, D. (2009) *The Talent Code,* (New York: Bantam, 2009), pp. 52–53.

Cunningham, A.E., & Stanovich, K.E. (1997). Early reading acquisition and its relation to reading experience and ability 10 years later. *Developmental Psychology, 33,* 934–945.

Curtis, M.E. (1980). Development of components of reading skill. *Journal of Educational Psychology, 72,* 656–669.

Curtis, M.E., & Longo, A.M. (1999). *When adolescents can't read: Methods and materials that work.* Cambridge, MA: Brookline Books.

Curtis, M.E. (1987). Vocabulary testing and vocabulary instruction. In M.G. McKeown & M.E. Curtis (Eds.). *The Nature of vocabulary acquisition* (pp. 37–52). Hillsdale, NJ: Erlbaum.

Cutting, L.E., & Scarborough, H.S. (2006). Prediction of reading comprehension: Relative contributions of word recognition, language proficiency, and other cognitive skills can depend on how comprehension is measured. *Scientific Studies of Reading, 10(3),* 277–299.

Dale, E., & O'Rourke, J. (1979). *The living word vocabulary: The words we know.* Boston: Houghton Mifflin.

Dale, E., & O'Rourke, J. (1981). *The living word vocabulary.* Chicago: World Book/Childcraft International.

Dehaene, S. (2009) *Reading in the Brain* (New York: Penguin, 2009).

Dickinson, D.K., & Smith, M.W. (1994). Long-term effects of preschool teachers' book readings on low-income children's vocabulary and story comprehension. *Reading Research Quarterly, 29,* 104–122.

Duncan, G., Brooks-Gunn, J., & Klebanov, P. (1994). Economic Deprivation and early childhood development. *Child Development, 65,* 296–318.

Elley, W.B. (1989). Vocabulary acquisition from listening to stories. *Reading Research Quarterly, 24,* 174–186.

Feitelson, D., Goldstein, Z., Iraqi, J., & Share, D.I. (1991). Effects of listening to story reading on aspects of literacy acquisition in a diglossic situation. *Reading Research Quarterly, 28,* 70–79.

Feitelson, D., Kita, B., & Goldstein, Z. (1986). Effects of listening to series stories on first graders comprehension and use of language. *Research in the Teaching of English, 20,* 339–356.

Flavell, J.H. (1992). Cognitive development: Past, present, and future. *Developmental Psychology, 28,* 998–1005.

Fowle, W. Edward E. Ford Foundation, Doris McGowan and David Thomas of the Charles E. Merrill Trust, and James E. Koerner of the Alfred P. Sloan Foundation.

Gough, P.B., & Tunmer, W.E. (1986). Decoding, reading and reading disability. *Remedial and Special Education, 7,* 6–10.

Graves, M.F., Juel, C., & Graves, B.B. (1998). *Teaching reading in the 21st century.* Boston: Allyn & Bacon.

Gregory, D., Earl, L., & O'Donoghue, B. (1993). *A study of reading recovery in Scarborough: 1990–1992* (Publication No. 92/93-15). Scarborough, Ontario, Canada: Scarborough Board of Education.

Hargrave, A.C., & Senechal, M. (2000). Book reading intervention with language-delayed preschool children: The benefits of regular reading and dialogic reading. *Journal of Child Language, 15,* 765–790.

Hart, B., & Risley, T.R. (1995). *Meaningful differences in the everyday experience of young American children.* Baltimore: Brookes.

Hazenberg, S., & Hulstijn, J.H. (1996). Defining a minimal receptive second-language vocabulary for non-native university students: An empirical investigation. *Applied Linguistics, 17,* 145–163.

Hess, F. (2010) *The same thing over and over: How School Reformers get Stuck in Yesterday's Ideas*, (Cambridge: Harvard University Press, 2010).

Heuston, E.B.H. (2010). *Effects of computer-based early-reading academic learning time on early-reading achievement: A dose-response approach.* Unpublished Doctoral Dissertation, Brigham Young University, Provo, UT.

Heyns, Barbara, (1987). Schooling and Cognitive Development: Is there a season for learning? *Child Development, 1987,* 1151–1160.

Huttenlocher, J., Levine, S., & Vevea, Jr. (1998). Environmental input and cognitive growth: A study using time-period comparisons. *Child Development, 69,* 1012–1029.

IES National Center for Educational Evaluation. (2009) *Effectiveness of Reading and Mathematics Software Product,* NCEE 2009–4041 by the Department of Education entitled (February, 2009).

Madden, N.A., Slavin, R.E., Karweit, J. L., Dolan, L.J., & Wasik, B.A. (1993). Success for all: Longitudinal effects of a restructuring program for inner-city schools. *American Educational Research Journal, 30,* 123–148.

McKeown, M.G., Beck, L., Omanson, R.C., & Perfetti, C.A. (1983). The effects of long-term vocabulary instruction on reading comprehension: A replication. *Journal of Reading Behavior, 15,* 3–18.

McKeown, M.G., & Curtis, M.E. (Eds.). (1987). *The nature of vocabulary acquisition.* Hillsdale, NJ: Erlbaum.

McLloyd, V.C. (1998). Socioeconomic disadvantage and child development. *American Psychologist, 53,* 185–204.

Morrison, F.J., Williams, M.A., & Massetti, G.M. (1998, April). *The contributions of IQ and schooling to academic achievement.* Paper presented at the Annual Meeting of the Society for the Scientific Study of Reading, San Diego, CA.

Nagy, W.E., & Herman, P.A. (1987). Breadth and depth of vocabulary knowledge: Implications for acquisition and instruction. In M.G. McKeown & M. E. Curtis (Eds.), *The nature of vocabulary acquisition* (pp. 19–36). Hillsdale, NJ: Erlbaum.

Nagy, W.E., & Herman, P.A., & Anderson, R. C. (1985). Learning words from context. *Reading Research Quarterly, 20,* 233–253.

Nicholson, T., & Whyte, B. (1992). Matthew effects in learning new words while listening to stories. In C.K. Kinzer & D.J. Leu (Eds.), *Literacy research, theory, and practice. Views from many perspectives. Forty-first Yearbook of the National Reading Conference* (pp. 499–503). Chicago: National Reading Conference.

Office of Planning and Research, United States Department of Labor. (1965) "The Negro Family: The Case for National Action," (March 1965), www.dol.gov/asp/programs/history/webidmeynihan.htm.

Penno, J.F., Wilkinson, A.G., & Moore, D.W. (2002). Vocabulary acquisition from teacher explanation and repeated listening to stories: Do they overcome the Matthew effect? *Journal of Educational Psychology, 94,* 23–33.

Piaget, J. (1971). Piaget's theory. In P. H. Mussen (Ed.), *Carmichael's manual of child psychology* (3rd ed., pp. 703–732). New York: Wiley.

Pinnell, G.S., Lyons, C. A., Deford, D. E., Bryk, A.S., & Seltzer, M. (1994). Comparing instructional models for the literacy education of high-risk first graders. *Reading Research Quarterly, 29,* 9–38.

Ravitch, D., et al. "A Tribute to Jeanne Chall," *American Educator* 25 (1): 16–23.

Robbins, C., & Ehri, L.C. (1994). Reading storybooks to kindergartners helps them learn new vocabulary words. *Journal of Educational Psychology, 86,* 139–153.

Sampson, Robert J., Sharkey, Patrick, & Raudenbush, Stephen W. (2007). Durable effects of concentrated disadvantage on verbal ability among African American children. *PNAIS, 105,* 845–852.

Scarborough, H.S. (2009). Connecting early language and literacy to later reading (dis) abilities: Evidence, theory, and practice. In F. Fletcher-Campbell, J. Soler, & G. Reid (Eds.), *Approaches to difficulties in literacy development: Assessment, pedagogy and programmes* (pp. 26–39). London: Sage.

Scarborough, H.S. (2005). Developmental relationships between language and reading: Reconciling a beautiful hypothesis with some ugly facts. In H. W. Catts & A. G. Kamhi (Eds.), *The connections between language and reading disabilities* (pp. 3–24). Mahwah, NJ: Erlbaum.

Scarborough, H.S., & Dickman, G. (2004). Identifying and helping preschoolers at risk for dyslexia: The role of parents. *Perspectives, 24 (2), 7–10.*

Scarborough, H.S., Ehri, L.C., Olson, R.K., & Fowler, A.E. (1998). The fate of phonemic awareness beyond the elementary school years. *Scientific Studies of Reading, 2,* 115–142.

Scarborough, H.S. (1998). Early identification of children at risk for reading disabilities: Phonological awareness and some other promising predictors. In B.K. Shapiro, P.J., Accardo, & A.J. Capute (Eds.), *Specific reading disability: A view of the spectrum* (pp. 75–119). Timonium, MD: York Press.

Scarborough, H.S., & Dobrich, W. (1994). On the efficacy of reading to preschoolers. *Developmental Review, 14,* 245–302.

Scarborough, H.S. (1991). Antecedents to reading disability: Preschool language development and literacy experiences of children from dyslexic families. *Reading and Writing, 3,* 219–233.

Scarborough, H.S., Dobrich, W., & Hager, M. (1991). Literacy experience and reading disability: Reading habits and abilities of parents and young children. *Journal of Learning Disabilities, 24,* 508–511.

Scarborough, H., & Dobrich, W. (1985). Illusory recovery from early language delay. *Proceedings of the Research Symposium on Child Language Disorders, 6,* 90–99.

Schulte, Brigid, (2009). Putting the brakes on "summer slide". *Harvard Education Letter, 25,* 1–3.

Senechal, M. (1997). The differential effect of storybook reading on preschoolers' acquisition of expressive and receptive vocabulary. *Child Language, 24,* 123–138.

Senechal, M., & Cornell, E.H. (1993). Vocabulary acquisition through shared reading experiences. *Reading Research Quarterly, 28,* 360–374.

Senechal, M., Thomas, E., & Monker, J.-A. (1995). Individual differences in 4 year old children's acquisition of vocabulary during storybook reading. *Journal of Educational Psychology, 87,* 218–229.

Slavin, R. E. (1989) "PET and the Pendulum: Faddism in Education and How to Stop It," *Phi Delta Kappan,* June 1989, 752–758.

Stahl, S.A. (1999). *Vocabulary development.* Cambridge, MA: Brookline Books.

Stahl, S.A., & Fairbanks, M.M. (1986). The effects of vocabulary instruction: A model-based meta-analysis. *Review of Educational Research, 56,* 72–110.

Stahl, S.A., Richek, M.A., & Vandevier, R.J. (1991). Learning meaning vocabulary through listening: A sixth grade replication. In J. Zutell & S. McCormick (Eds.), *Learner factors/teacher factors: Issues in literacy research and instruction. Fortieth Yearbook of the National Reading Conference* (pp. 185–192). Chicago: National Reading Conference.

Stanovich, K. (1986) "Matthew Effects in Reading: Some consequences of individual differences in the acquisition of literacy," *Reading Research Quarterly,* Fall 1986 XX14 pp. 360–406.

Sticht, T.G., & James, J.H. (1984). Listening and reading. In D. Pearson (Ed.), *Handbook of research on reading* (Vol. 1, pp. 293–317). New York: Longman.

Storch, S.A., & Whitehurst, G.J. (2002). Oral language and code-related precursors to reading: Evidence from a longitudinal structural model. *Developmental Psychology, 38,* 934–947.

Webster's third new international dictionary of the English language. (1981). Springfield, MA: Merriam.

White, T.G., Graves, M.F., & Slater, W.H. (1990), Growth of reading vocabulary in diverse elementary schools: Decoding and word meaning. *Journal of Educational Psychology, 82,* 281–290.

Wixson, K.K. (1986). Vocabulary instruction and children's comprehension of basal stories. *Reading Research Quarter, 21,* 317–329.

INDEX